FENWAY PARK

The CENTENNIAL

To my Royal Rooters—
Michelle, Jason, and Rachel

FENWAY PARK
The CENTENNIAL

100 Years of Red Sox Baseball

WITH COMMENTARY BY
THREE GENERATIONS OF BOSTON RED SOX

SAUL WISNIA

CARLTON FISK
DVD SHOW HOST

St. Martin's Press/New York

Saul Wisnia was born a Tony C home run from Fenway Park as the Red Sox were about to launch their 1967 "Impossible Dream" season, and he has been closely linked to Boston baseball ever since. A former sports and feature correspondent for *The Washington Post* and a feature writer for the *Boston Herald,* his work has also appeared in such publications as *Sports Illustrated, Boston Red Sox Magazine, Boston Magazine,* and *The Boston Globe.* He is the author of numerous books on baseball and other subjects, including *For the Love of the Boston Red Sox, Chicago Cubs: Yesterday & Today, Spinal Cord Injury and the Family* (with Michelle Alpert, MD), and *The Jimmy Fund of Dana-Farber Cancer Institute.* A member of the Boston chapter of the Society of American Baseball Research and the Boston Braves Historical Association, he proudly chronicles the Red Sox-Jimmy Fund relationship as publications editor at Dana-Farber Cancer Institute. Wisnia lives six miles from Fenway with his wife, two kids, and Wally the cat (not the monster).

Picture Credits

Front cover: **Getty Images**
Back cover: **AP Images**
Back flap bottom: **AP Images**

AP Images: 63, 72, 74, 75 top, 76, 77 left, 90, 91, 93, 97 right, 98 bottom right, 101, 107, 110, 113 top, 116 bottom, 119 bottom, 121 left, 123, 126, 129 left, 130 left, 131 bottom, 138 bottom, 141 bottom, 143, 144, 145, 146, 147 left, 148, 149 left & right, 150, 151, 152, 153 left & right, 154, 155, 156 bottom, 161, 165, 166, 168, 169 left and bottom, 171, 172, 173. **Boston Public Library:** 11, 12, 13, 15, 16, 17 left & right, 18 left & right, 22 right, 24 top & bottom, 25 left, 28, 29 right, 32 bottom, 35 left, 38, 40 right, 41 top & bottom, 42 right, 45, 46, 47 left, 48, 49, 51, 52 top, 54 left & right, 55, 57 left, 57 right, 59 top & bottom, 60, 64, 65 left, 68, 79, 81 left, 83, 84, 85 left, 86-87, 88, 92 right, 96 bottom, 97 bottom, 98 bottom left, 104, 105, 108, 109 left, 115 right, 116 top, 119 top. **Courtesy of the D'Angelo Family:** 102, 106 top. **Christian Elias:** 163. **Facts That Matter Collection:** 10, 14, 19, 22 left, 26 right, 27 bottom, 29 left, 33, 36, 39, 42 left, 43 left & right, 44, 47 right, 50 left, 52 bottom, 56, 69, 70, 71, 73, 77 right, 80 left & right, 81 right, 82, 85 right, 89, 97 left, 99, 106 bottom, 109 right, 112, 114, 115 left, 121 right, 124 left, 129 right, 133, 135, 138 top, 140 left, 142, 147 right, 158, 162. **Getty Images:** end sheets, 21, 30, 37, 67, 95, 96 top, 98 top, 103, 111, 113 bottom, 118 bottom, 120, 124 right, 125, 127 left, 128, 130 right, 132, 134, 136, 137, 140 right, 141 top, 156 right, 157, 159, 167, 169 top. **Heritage Auctions (www.HA.com):** 20, 25 right, 26 left, 27 top, 30 top, 31, 32 left, 34, 35 right, 40 left, 53, 62, 65 right, 66, 75 bottom, 78, 86 left, 92 left, 94, 100, 113 right, 118 top, 122, 131 top. **Courtesy of The Jimmy Fund of Dana-Farber Cancer Institute:** 127 right. **Mark Rucker Collection:** 50 right. **JM Sahr:** 160. **Saul Wisnia:** 9, 156 left, 164, 170.

 Printed in Malaysia. For information, address St. Martin's Press, 175 Fifth Avenue, New York, N.Y. 10010.

www.stmartins.com

Library of Congress Cataloging-in-Publication Data Available Upon Request

ISBN 978-0-312-64274-7

First Edition: September 2011

10 9 8 7 6 5 4 3 2 1

Acknowledgments

A lifetime of attending games at Fenway Park was the primary resource for this book, but of course there are many people to thank as well.

Dick Bresciani and Debbie Matson from the Red Sox were gracious with their time and historical resources, and Susan Goodenow was helpful in granting access to current players and the nooks and crannies of the ballpark.

Many Red Sox players, coaches, opponents, fans, sportswriters, historians, and other Citizens of Fenway have shared their stories and help over more than 20 years; special thanks to: George Altison, Mike Andrews, Rob Barry, Uri Berenguer, Tim Bogar, The BoSox Club, Bob Brady, Tom Brewer, Steve Buckley, Brian Cashman, Ken Coleman, Billy Conigliaro, Joe Castiglione, Arthur and Bobby D'Angelo, Bobby Doerr, Lib Dooley, Christian Elias, Jack Fabiano, Boo Ferriss, Suzanne Fountain, Rich Gedman, Joe Girardi, Pumpsie Green, Joanne Hulbert, Nick Jacobs, Sam Jethroe, Dick Johnson, Mabray "Doc" Kountz, John Lackey, Jordan and Shelley Leandre, Bill Lee, Len Levin, Jim Lonborg, Fred Lynn, Frank Malzone, Kevin McCarthy, Tim McCarver, Bill Monbouquette, Walpole Joe Morgan, Peter Nash, Daniel Nava, Bill Nowlin, David Ortiz, Scott Paisner, Marvin Pave, David and Johnny Pesky, Rico Petrocelli, Ken Powtak, JM Sahr, Dave Shulman, Sibby Sisti, Bob Stanley, Glenn Stout, Frank Sullivan, Sharon Sullivan-Constatin, Tim Wakefield, Bill Werber, Ken Wright, and Kevin Youkilis.

I've been collaborating on books with David Aretha for close to 20 years and it never gets old. He's a fantastic editor and sounding board. I thank Marc Resnick and George Witte of St. Martin's Press, as well as co-publisher Les Krantz, for giving me the opportunity to take on this project. It's a big plus having an agent like Jake Elwell of Harold Ober Associates who both believes in you and understands the significance of Bob Bailey in Red Sox lore. Paul Adomites delivered excellent ninth-inning assistance, and Jim Slate did an outstanding job with the design. The folks in the microtext room at the Boston Public Library were helpful as always, and Michael Buller and Steve Singer at Dana-Farber Cancer Institute were supportive, understanding bosses. The Boston chapter of SABR and the Boston Braves Historical Association provided inspiration and friendship.

The thing about writing a book on Fenway Park is that everyone has great stories to share—and five more folks they suggest you call. There was not room for every tale here, and by the time you read this I will hopefully have a "Fenway Memories" blog or Website up where I can share more and other people can add memories of their times on Jersey Street/Yawkey Way. Please look for it and join in the reflections.

Finally, my deepest thanks to my family, especially the folks at home who put up with the late nights and other sacrifices required to write books as a second job—Royal Rooters Jason and Rachel, Wally the lap-warming cat, and Michelle, the reluctant (but always supportive) fan.

Sources

Several books detailing Red Sox and Fenway Park history were consulted in the preparation of this manuscript, most notably *Red Sox Century* by Glenn Stout and Richard Johnson (Houghton Mifflin, 2005), *Boston's Royal Rooters* by Peter Nash (Arcadia, 2005), *Diamonds* by Michael Gershman (Mariner Books, 1995), *Shut Out: A Story of Race and Baseball in Boston* by Howard Bryant (Routledge, 2002), *The Glory of their Times* by Lawrence Ritter (Vintage Books, 1985), and *Pumpsie and Progress* by Bill Nowlin (Rounder Books, 2010). Websites frequented were *baseballreference.com,* and *redsox.com,* as well as the online resources of the *The Boston Globe, The New York Times, Boston Herald, Sporting News, The Christian Science Monitor, The Washington Post,* and *The Los Angeles Times.* All quotes are from author interviews conducted over the past two decades, or from primary sources.

Contents

1946 WORLD SERIES
FENWAY PARK
American League vs. National League
GAME 5
RAIN CHECK
1946 WORLD SERIES
FENWAY PARK
GRANDSTAND SEAT
Est. Price $5.00
Fed. Tax $1.00
TOTAL $6.00
SEC. 26
ROW 10
SEAT 25
ENTER JERSEY ST.
GATE A

Red Sox
50c
1960

75th
FENWAY PARK
ANNIVERSARY
1912
1987
BOSTON
RED SOX

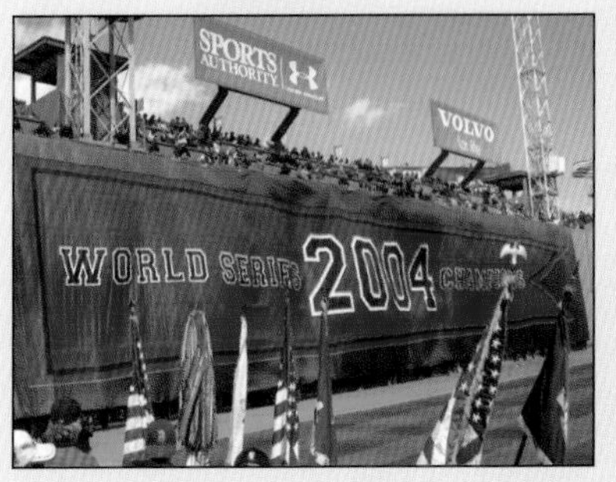

SPORTS AUTHORITY
VOLVO
WORLD SERIES 2004

Preface

When Rob Barry walks the hallways of prisons in his job with the Massachusetts Department of Corrections, he typically doesn't get the catcalls or insults you might expect. From the cells of desperate men comes a more unique refrain: "HEY, PEEEEEEANUTS!"

Even though he's not carrying the tools of his trade, inmates recognize Barry from his second job—selling peanuts at Fenway Park. Stuck inside steel cages most of the day, they see Barry and are immediately taken back to someplace familiar and comforting. That's the way I imagine a lot of people feel about Fenway; it's a safe haven from sins real and imagined, a meeting place for the masses.

For generations of New Englanders, and for baseball fans from all parts, Fenway has been a symbol of continuity in an ever-changing world. The ballpark has certainly been altered and updated through the years—never more so than in the past decade—but it is still easily recognizable to a fan who went to his or her first game a half-century or longer ago. The field that Crawford and Pedroia play on was once the workplace of Ruth and Foxx. The left-field scoreboard still has the Morse code initials of Tom and Jean Yawkey. Much of the brick and mortar and steel forged together a century ago remain intact. The capstone high above Gate A, the one reading "1912," still looks down on all who enter as a subtle, silent beacon to the past. Many of the old ticket booths have been turned into miniature shrines filled with artifacts from championships past, but you can still explain what they were to a wide-eyed little boy.

Fenway's history has been shaped by those who have performed here. This is where Harry Agganis, New England's most celebrated athlete, excelled on both the gridiron and diamond. It's where FDR gave his last campaign speech. Where Jackie Robinson got a raw deal and Jim Rice persevered. Where Pele dazzled on a summer night. Where Dent and Morgan dashed hopes and Fisk and Papi forged them. Where Tony C went down—and where he got back up to the plate. Where Orr dropped the puck at center ice. Where Ted tipped his hat as a young man and an old man. And where seven-year-old Jordan Leandre found the courage and joy to run in front of 35,000 people when he wasn't sure he could run at all.

My own life has been closely connected to this place. I was born just a few blocks from Fenway, and for most of my life I have lived less than 10 miles away. On the summer night in 2004 that my daughter Rachel was born, I could see Fenway's lights from the hospital windows. I still know that she was the lucky charm that prompted the Sox to win 22 out of 25 and then the big ones in October. For the past decade, I've worked right across the street from Yawkey Way. The flashing Citgo sign greets me each night as I cross the parking lot.

Today I can sit in the stands at Fenway and still taste Cokes from the 1970s, the ones that spilled in your lap when you pulled the cellophane off and tasted increasingly like paper as your cup slowly dissolved. I can still smell the cigars the old men in the upper grandstands used to smoke, and I can smell the sweat of fellow college kids as we stood atop railings at the back of Section 26 watching "Morgan Magic" unfold. I can still hear organist John Kiley and ballpark announcer Sherm Feller, and I still remember the look on my son Jason's face when he was tossed his first game-used ball by an accommodating batboy.

I've been lucky enough to see many great games at Fenway. I saw Fisk hit his homer and Yaz take his farewell lap; saw Bruno make his sliding grab and Papi poke his 14th-inning single. I even saw Ted Williams make a great running catch in an old-timer's game. But I was never more struck by the ballpark's magic than at a seemingly meaningless contest on the final day of the 2010 season.

The fans knew going into that game that the Red Sox were not going to the postseason, but they had a ball anyway—singing "Happy Birthday" to Johnny Pesky, holding up signs to salute Mike Lowell in his final game, cheering for Jason Varitek in what many thought would be his last game with the Sox, and delighting in a win over the Yankees that denied them the American League East title. After it was all done, as a thank-you from management, fans got to run the Fenway bases before heading home. As they filed out, everybody was smiling.

The season was over, but they knew they'd be back.

Rachel and Jason Alpert-Wisnia with "Big League Brian" on Yawkey Way

Saul Wisnia

PROLOGUE

Before Fenway

1871–1911

Prior to Fenway Park's construction in 1912, professional baseball flourished in Boston for 40 years. Boston's American League club even won the first-ever World Series—at Huntington Avenue Grounds—with the "Royal Rooters" cheering them on.

Rooter's Souvenir
BOSTON - PITTSBURG
Oct., 1903. M. T. McGreevy

TESSIE,
You Are The Only, Only, Only.

Chorus.
Tessie, you make me feel so badly;
Why don't you turn around.
Tessie, you know I love you madly;
Babe, my heart weighs about a pound.
Don't blame me if I ever doubt you,
You know, I wouldn't live without you;
Tessie, you are the only, only, only, -ly.

3d Base. Nuf Ced.
Who Kidnapped the Pittsburg Band
Nuf Ced—McGreevy.

If the Royal Rooters had only sung *these* lyrics during the 1903 World Series instead of harassing Pittsburgh star Honus Wagner, the outcome might have been different. Instead, Boston defeated the flustered Pirates five games to three.

Although he was the proprietor of a popular local saloon, Mike McGreevy was not pouring drinks on the afternoon of October 13, 1903. Along with throngs of other baseball fans—then commonly referred to as "cranks"—he was at a ballpark a few blocks away, cheering on his beloved Boston Americans (who would become the Red Sox) in what he hoped would be the deciding game of the World Series.

McGreevy, a 5′4″ gent in a bowtie and walrus mustache, greeted patrons as he stood on the outfield grass watching the Americans warm up. Known as "Nuf-Ced" for the impassioned way he ended all saloon arguments with those two words and a bang of his fist upon the bar, he led a group known as the "Royal Rooters." This fan club brought a large bass drum and other noisemakers to the park to serenade their heroes and rattle the enemy. Now, as Game 8 of Boston's best-of-nine series with the National League's vaunted Pittsburgh Pirates got underway, this 200-man contingent let rip with cheers and jeers that seemed to shake the ground beneath them.

Occupying a special roped-off section behind home plate, and backed by the 35-piece Boston Letter Carriers Band, the Rooters spent much of the contest belting out their trademark tune of "Tessie"—which served as both an ode to their favorite ballclub and a thorn in the sides of Pittsburgh players. McGreevy often revised the original words and shouted them out through a megaphone to poke fun at legendary shortstop Honus Wagner and his Pirate teammates. "Tessie, you make me feel so badly" thus became "Honus, why do you hit so badly?" From the well-heeled patrons of the box seats to the cranks who spent the entire game perched atop 12-foot walls surrounding the ballpark, thousands joined in the anthem.

The Royal Rooters were no ragtag bunch of *a capella* crooners. Here they are in their special section during the 1903 World Series. (Are they wailing another chorus of "Honus"?) A brass band complete with uniforms and cool hats keeps them on key.

This 1879 aerial view shows the first South End Grounds park (*left of dead center*), which hosted games from 1871 to 1887 before being demolished.

When Boston pitching hero "Big Bill" Dinneen struck out Wagner to finish off a 3–0 shutout and clinch the series, cranks stormed the field and then paraded around it, accompanied by the band. McGreevy was front and center as always, and victorious players who caught a glimpse of this character undoubtedly smiled. Pittsburgh third baseman Tommy Leach would later credit Boston fans for playing a large part in the surprising outcome, admitting that the constant barbs and strains of "Tessie" unnerved the Pirates. Dinneen and his teammates, meanwhile, could toast their championship with McGreevy at his bar, which was named 3rd Base because, as the owner proudly proclaimed, it was "the last stop before you go home."

It's easy to imagine this scene unfolding at Fenway Park, where the atmosphere is always electric and fans sing "Tessie" after each Red Sox victory, but it actually took place at a site long since reduced to rubble and memory: the Huntington Avenue Grounds. In the decades before Fenway was built outside Kenmore Square, cranks like McGreevy cheered on Boston ballclubs a few miles away at this and other wooden predecessors. In fact, the reverence with which people hold the Red Sox and their home today is a natural outgrowth of this earlier period, when baseball was exploding in popularity nationwide and the city known as "the cradle of liberty" played an important role in the growth of America's pastime.

Early Glory

Boston's baseball roots can be traced back to the early nineteenth century, when British-born colonists raised on ball-and-bat games such as cricket and rounders developed new versions for their new homeland. There were no formal ballparks then, but by the 1850s organized matches were being held before large gatherings on the Boston Common and at local colleges. The game quickly grew in popularity across the country, and in 1869 the first acknowledged professional club was formed—the Cincinnati Red Stockings. Traveling from coast to coast and taking on all challengers, the Cincinnati squad drew some of its biggest crowds during visits to Massachusetts. This made an impact on Red Stockings outfielder Harry Wright, who captained the club and handled its business affairs. When the team's popularity in Ohio fizzled, he found a financial backer to transfer it to Boston.

This lavish and dramatic park, dubbed South End Grounds II, sat in the same spot as its considerably less glorious predecessor. Despite its grand appearance, it seated fewer than 7,000 fans. It burned down in 1894, just six years after it opened.

There they played in a small ballpark set beside the tracks of the New York, New Haven, and Hartford Railroad, within the city's South End neighborhood (hence the park's adopted name, the South End Grounds). It was a modestly built venue, with only the best seats covered, but there was nothing humble about its tenants. Joining the first pro league—the National Association of Professional Base Ball Players—for its maiden 1871 season, the newly dubbed "Bostons" won championships for four straight years (1872–75) behind Harry Wright, his brother George at shortstop, and pitching ace Albert Goodwill Spaulding. Fans packed the South End Grounds beyond its capacity for big games, leaving others to watch from nearby rooftops. Entrepreneurs saw that profits could be made, and soon hand-drawn refreshment signs began appearing in the stands.

The National Association was a rowdy circuit that featured widespread cheating, brawling, and drinking by ballplayers (as

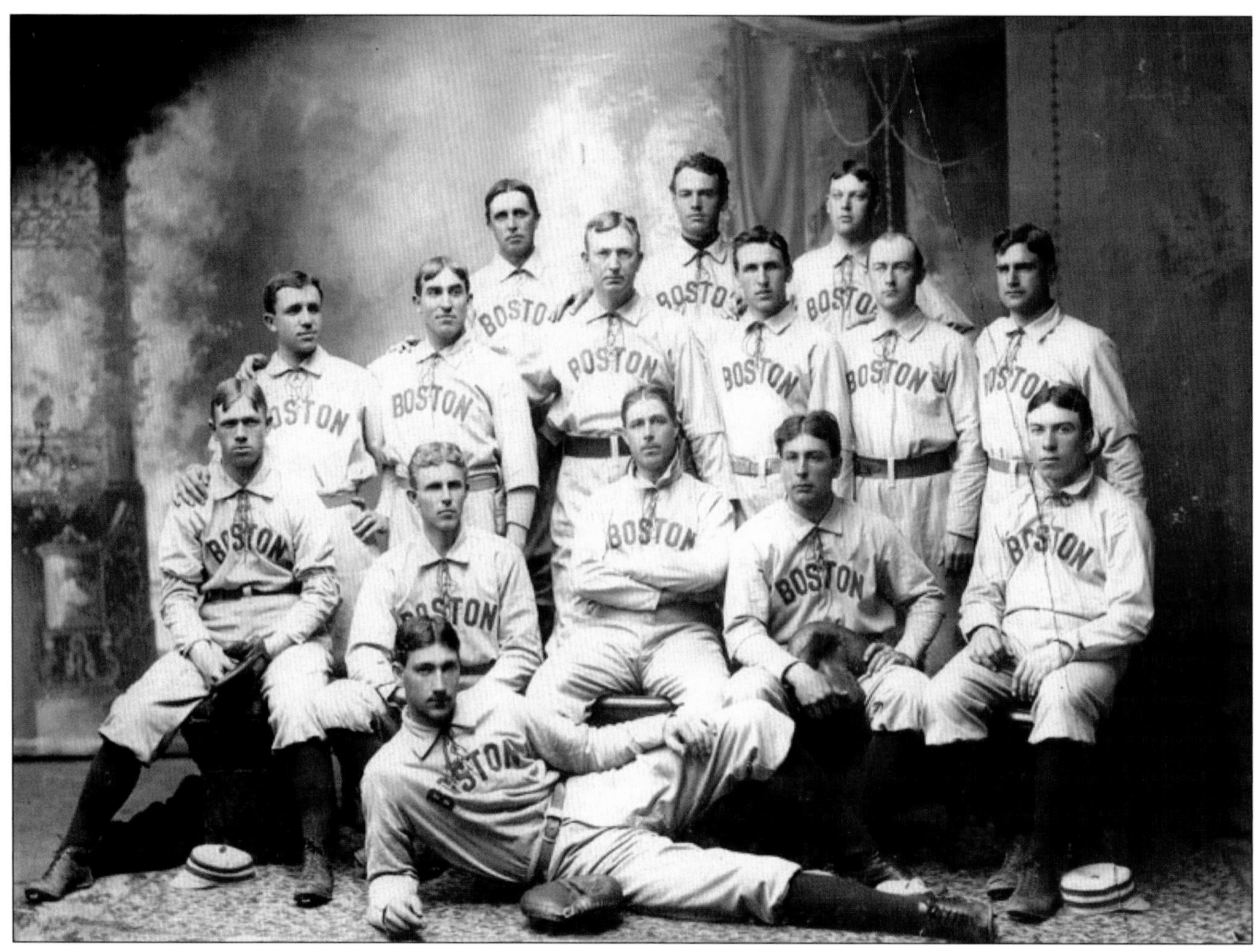

They hadn't yet adopted the name Red Sox, but this is the first Boston American League team, from 1901. Officially known as the Americans, they were also variously tagged the Somersets, Puritans, and Pilgrims. First baseman Buck Freeman (*top row, center*) led the 1901 team in batting, homers, and RBI (.339–12–114).

well as some fans). When it folded and the more tightly run National League (NL) was formed the next year, the Bostons signed on as one of its eight original entrants. The South End Grounds played host to its first NL game on Saturday, April 29, 1876, and a chain of unprecedented continuity began. People have often confused both this Boston team and the original Red Stockings as the forefathers of today's Red Sox, but such is not the case. The Red Sox were not "born" until 1901. The Opening Day victors of '76 are now playing in Georgia as the Atlanta Braves—the only franchise that can trace its lineage directly back to the maiden season of baseball's first true "major league."

In addition to being a charter member, this was also the new circuit's top club. The Bostons captured eight NL pennants by the end of the century, and more heroes emerged: Michael "King" Kelly thrilled fans with his daring base running, Charles "Kid" Nichols won 25 or more games for nine straight years, and Rhode

Island native Hugh Duffy batted .440 in 1894—still a big-league record. During the 1890s alone, there were six future Hall of Famers on the roster.

Such a grand team deserved a grand home, and in 1887 ownership tore down their simple ballpark and replaced it with one of the most beautiful sports facilities of this or any era. Still known as the South End Grounds, the new park was distinguished by a 2,000-seat, double-decked section that curved around behind home plate and was known as the Grand Pavilion. Featuring ornate carved columns, its roof was topped with six tall, conical spires known as "witches' caps" made of hand-stamped tin and festooned with pennants. The pavilion, designed by architect John J. Deery, gave this venue a castle-like feel befitting its regal occupants. Its semicircular shape also maximized the number of fans who would be close to the action—forward thinking for the time. Writer Michael Gershman referred to it as "a setting where Sir Lancelot would have felt right at home," and it symbolized how Bostonians felt about their team.

There was only one problem with this diamond palace: It was made almost entirely of wood. On May 15, 1894, during the third inning of a game with the visiting Baltimore Orioles, some boys set fire to a pile of rubbish in the far right-field bleachers, igniting a blaze that quickly engulfed the entire structure. It took just 45 minutes for the ballpark to burn to the ground, and an estimated 170 other buildings in the vicinity were destroyed as well. Although all 3,500 fans escaped, there was approximately $1 million in damage to area homes and businesses. And to make matters worse, because the park was underinsured at just 60 percent of its value, the third (and final) South End Grounds had to be constructed on a far tighter budget that made no provision for a second deck or Grand Pavilion.

Crossing the Tracks

Competitive fire rather than the combustible kind was at the center of the city's next major ballpark project. In 1901, the American League emerged as a rival to the National League by placing teams in eight cities including Boston. AL President Ban Johnson was well aware that the South End Grounds was home to baseball's most passionate fans, and he decided to challenge the establishment head-on.

With the financial backing of Charles Somers, a coal and shipping magnate,

The winningest pitcher of all time had his own personal catcher. Lou Criger (*left*) was the guy Cy Young (*right*) wanted to handle his pitches. Cy was burly and Lou was slight, but the catcher had a terrific throwing arm and a feisty attitude.

> "I think those Boston fans won the Series. . . . We beat them three out of the first four games, and then they started singing that damn 'Tessie' song. . . . Sort of got on your nerves after a while."
> **—Pirates third baseman Tommy Leach**

the Huntington Avenue Grounds was constructed for this new club—to be known as the "Boston Americans"—directly across the railroad tracks from the city's existing NL venue. It clearly outshined its postfire neighbor, featuring three cement grandstands with room for nearly 800 fans each and a covered lobby where as many as 300 could wait out rain delays. Total capacity was more than 10,000. As a former sportswriter who knew the power of positive press, Johnson even made sure the new facility included a separate room with lockers for newspapermen.

Johnson had no trouble finding athletes to call the Huntington Avenue Grounds home. National League salaries had been capped at $2,500 by tight-fisted owners, but by offering more money Johnson enticed more than 100 players to make the NL–AL switch. Boston star third baseman and captain Jimmy Collins was an early jumper for $4,000. After being installed as manager of the city's newest club, Collins convinced several of his NL teammates (whose club was now being called the "Nationals") to cross the tracks as well. There they were joined by another prize recruit pillaged from the NL's St. Louis Cardinals: ace right-handed pitcher Denton True "Cy" Young.

Already sympathetic to the plight of the players, Royal Rooters watching this shift in power unfold were hooked for good when they heard about the 25-cent grandstand tickets that would be available at the AL ballpark—half the price of similar seats at the South End Grounds. In a pregame ceremony on May 8, 1901, heroes from Boston's proud baseball past rode in from center field to home plate in carriages as fans waved American flags. A standing-room-only crowd of some 11,500 watched Young and the Americans inaugurate the Huntington Avenue Grounds with a 12–4 victory. Less than half that number (including 3,500 school kids let in for free) trekked to the South End Grounds for the National League opener that same afternoon, making the

They said that 18,801 fans attended this game in Boston, the third in the 1903 World Series. Thanks to a four-hitter by Deacon Phillippe (*FIL-uh-pee*), the Pirates took a two-games-to-one lead, but they could manage only one more win.

message clear: Boston was now an American League city.

Within two years it was also a champion, as Collins and Young led the Americans to their first World Series in 1903. By this point, the National League had accepted that its rival was here to stay, and owners from each circuit agreed to hold a nine-game postseason playoff between their champions and split the gate receipts. The first three games of the ensuing "World Series" between Boston and the Pittsburgh Pirates drew overflow crowds in excess of 15,000 to the Huntington Avenue Grounds, with thousands of fans happy to stand for nine innings in roped-off portions of the outfield. Rowdy patrons were kept at bay by police officers armed with bats and rubber hoses, and nearby roofs and telephone poles were popular viewing points for those who couldn't get in.

Mike McGreevy and his crew watched the action from their field-level seats, and after four games in Pittsburgh they were back again for the aforementioned clincher. McGreevy even snuck into the official photo of the two teams taken before the game. After Wagner's final swing and miss ended the series, several of the champions were carried around on the shoulders of celebrating cranks. A band started in on "The Star-Spangled Banner," and although this tune was years away from being a pregame staple, it was recognizable enough to prompt singing from many of the fans and players on hand.

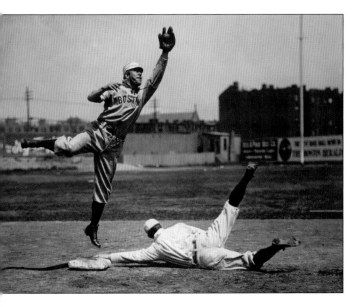

Taylor Made

Soon after Jimmy Collins raised the first "world's champions" banner at the Huntington Avenue Grounds on Opening Day of 1904, his club found itself in the thick of a wild five-team race for the pennant. By August, two clubs emerged from the pack—the Americans and New York Highlanders (who would become the Yankees a few years later). In the earliest days of what would become baseball's greatest rivalry, they played three straight doubleheaders at Boston from September 14 to 16 before an estimated crowd of 48,000—including 25,000 for the single-admission twinbill on the 16th.

This may have been the largest paid crowd to ever watch major-league action in Boston prior to the construction of Fenway Park, as fire laws that limited the number of patrons one could cram into a venue were still far in the future.

Not all fans paid to see the 1903 World Series. A few merely climbed a pole to get a bird's-eye view.

With spectacular speed and daring, Jimmy Collins revolutionized the third base position. As Boston's first manager, his team won two pennants (1903 and '04) in his first four years at the helm.

Another favorite perch at the Huntington Avenue Grounds was the 14-foot-high right-field wall, which was plastered with ads for rye, shoes, and beer.

Sixty extra subway cars were procured to handle the mass of humanity headed for Huntington Avenue. Once there, fans far outnumbering available seats battled for the best vantage points. Scores stood on barrels in front of the right-field bleachers to see over the bowler hats of patrons in front of them, while still others filled up every free inch of space atop the outfield walls. Enterprising peanut vendors even sold their empty boxes to short men, who flipped them over to use as makeshift stepladders.

Each team took two games of the series, with two contests declared ties due to darkness. Boston wound up edging New York for the pennant, but there would be no opportunity for the victors to defend their World Series title. Owner John T. Bush of the NL champion New York Giants, who didn't want to chance losing to the cross-town rival Highlanders or any team from the American League, refused to play Boston. *The Sporting News,* the nation's leading baseball publication, declared the Americans "World's Champions by default," but this gesture could not replace the roughly $1,500 in World Series bonus money that Boston players lost out on. For most on the roster, this was more than half a year's salary.

The next several years would offer little for fans at the Huntington Avenue Grounds to cheer about. Although the Americans became the Red Sox in 1907, their on-field performance was discouraging by any name. They slid to fourth place in 1905, dipped to a frightening 49–105 record a year later—losing 19

As ballclub president, John I. Taylor was an uninformed tightwad. As real estate developer, he was brilliant. He was responsible for the location of Fenway Park. He and his father happened to own the land.

straight games on one home stand!—and through 1911 had finished no closer than third since their '04 pennant run. They inexplicably stayed among the American League team leaders in attendance, perhaps because the alternative for baseball-starved Bostonians was watching the city's even more hapless National League club (by now known as the Braves).

Those hoping for a turnaround could not gain much solace in looking to ownership. *Boston Globe* newspaper publisher and Civil War veteran Charles "General" Taylor had bought the soon-to-be Red Sox in 1904 and had placed his playboy son, John I. Taylor, at the helm as president. The champions quickly became also-rans under his watch, as John I. traded promising ballplayers, sold off legendary pitcher Young for $12,500 and two useless hurlers, and feuded with manager Collins.

In reality, the Taylors were more interested in real estate than baseball. Although they owned the Huntington Avenue Grounds, they knew that the lease on the land on which the ballpark stood was expiring after the 1911 season. That September, the General sold half of the Red Sox to Washington Senators manager James McAleer and Ban Johnson's secretary, Robert McRoy, for a reported $150,000. As part of the deal, John. I. went from president to vice president in charge of developing a steel and concrete ballpark for the team. This was the new trend underway in the majors, and he knew just where to build one. With money earned from the sale of the club, the General and his partners purchased 330,000 square feet of land from the Fenway Realty Company (of which he was a major shareholder) for $300,000. A mortgage securing $275,000 in 5 percent nontaxable land bonds was obtained, and construction began on the new site in late September. Father and son would both come out winners.

Word of the sale and the Taylors' intentions broke in late September, and the words "Fenway Park" first began appearing in newspapers. On a cold, windy day a few weeks later, the Red Sox closed out the '11 season with an 8–1 victory over the Washington Senators at the Huntington Avenue Grounds.

Barely a decade old, this venue was about to become obsolete.

A fleet centerfielder who played extremely shallow, Tris Speaker still holds MLB career records for outfield assists (449) and two-base hits (792). He starred with Boston from 1907 to '15.

How the Red Sox Got Their Name

After stealing away its best players and its fans, it only seemed fitting that Boston's American League franchise should find a way to make off with the socks of its National League rival as well.

Actually, the Americans had their much-maligned president, John I. Taylor, to thank for a new look and a new nickname. The Boston Nationals stopped wearing red stockings with their uniforms in 1907, the legend goes, because their owner, George B. Dovey, feared red dye would cause spike wounds to become infected. Taylor, having no such concerns, had his players adopt the practice of wearing red socks for home games the following season—and renamed the club accordingly.

While the stockings worn by the Nationals had been a deep, dark crimson, Taylor went with a bright fire-engine red. He did take some precautions. As the *Boston Journal* reported, "the officers of the club decided that it would be better to try them [red socks] on the home populace and among friends at first. If they do not interfere with the fans' vision of the game or do not incite the crowds to riot they may be worn on the road another year."

No unrest ensued, and the name stuck: Boston Red Sox. A little while later, John I. took to briefly calling his club the "Speed Boys," but thankfully this moniker failed to take hold. Although the Sox were leading the league in steals at the time, they would become the most lead-footed team in baseball as the century wore on.

CHAPTER 1

The Grand Opening

1912–1919

Three rainouts delayed the very first Opening Day at the new ballpark, and the sinking of the Titanic *initially dimmed enthusiasm. But the Red Sox took the opener on a Tris Speaker walk-off hit, igniting a year—and a century—of excitement and glory at Fenway Park.*

The rain had finally let up, and Peter Davis was busy. Standing beside his green pushcart in front of brand-new Fenway Park, he was handing bags of peanuts to fans as fast as they could slap coins into his hand. His powerful arms, which had already been taxed by pushing the cart several miles to Jersey Street from its downtown holding pen, were starting to ache. He didn't mind a bit.

Davis had never seen this many people in one place. It reminded him of the lines he had encountered at the docks after coming over from Greece years before. When the Red Sox played at the smaller Huntington Avenue Grounds in previous seasons, the most fans they ever drew to a game was approximately 10,000. This crowd had to be at least double that, and it seemed like all of them were walking right by his cart.

This clever pennant not only announces the Elks Athletic Carnival's date and place, but also the starting time. (The Sox were in Detroit that day.)

It was nice to see folks smiling as they looked up at the beautiful red-brick façade of Boston's first steel and concrete ballpark. But with three straight rainouts and the distressing news about the RMS *Titanic* unfolding over the previous several days, the excitement leading up to Opening Day of 1912 had been largely subdued—even with the added factor of Fenway's grand unveiling. People were more concerned with scanning the lists of survivors that appeared in each day's newspapers, hoping they would find their relatives and friends among them, than reading how Tris Speaker and Joe Wood had fared during the season's first five games at New York and Philadelphia. For a week, baseball wasn't much discussed. But now, with the shock of the disaster having set in and the Red Sox and New York Highlanders set to play under sunny skies, Bostonians could fully focus on Fenway.

Fenway Park hosted its first major-league game on April 20, 1912. The outfield expanse was huge for its time. The distance to the deepest center-field niche was 550 feet. Left-center was 379, and the right-field power alley was a full 405.

It wasn't uncommon for Michael "Nuf Ced" McGreevy (*fourth from left*) to pop up in team photos. The saloon owner and leader of the Royal Rooters may be the most legendary baseball fan in Boston history.

As Davis kept up his work outside the ballpark, John Fitzgerald took a good look around the inside. As mayor of Boston, he had been asked to throw out the first ball before that afternoon's game. Unlike many politicians who have performed this task before and since, the charming, flamboyant "Honey Fitz" was a true fan who was genuinely interested in watching the on-field action rather than just courting votes in the stands (although he enjoyed that, too). Born in Boston during the Civil War and the son of Irish immigrants, he had been devoted to his city's baseball teams for most of his 49 years.

As a rising young congressman in the 1890s, Fitzgerald had joined up with the "Royal Rooters" fan club headed by his equally ebullient friend, saloon owner Michael "Nuf Ced" McGreevy. A top-hatted Honey Fitz had led the Rooters in their march down 165th Street to New York's Polo Grounds during the final days of the 1904 pennant race, and his Irish brogue could often be heard singing "Tessie" and other favorites during home games. He had been denied an opportunity to purchase the Red Sox in their early years—done in by shrewd maneuvering on the part of a political rival—but he never stopped being a fan.

Fitzgerald felt immense pride watching the new park fill up. Boston was a city known for cultural and educational achievements, and here was a sports venue it could hold up alongside its renowned universities, public library, opera house, and art museums as a symbol of that status. It was a place that generations of families would enjoy, and in future years he would delight in taking his own grandsons—Joe, Robert, Ted, and John Fitzgerald Kennedy—to see games there.

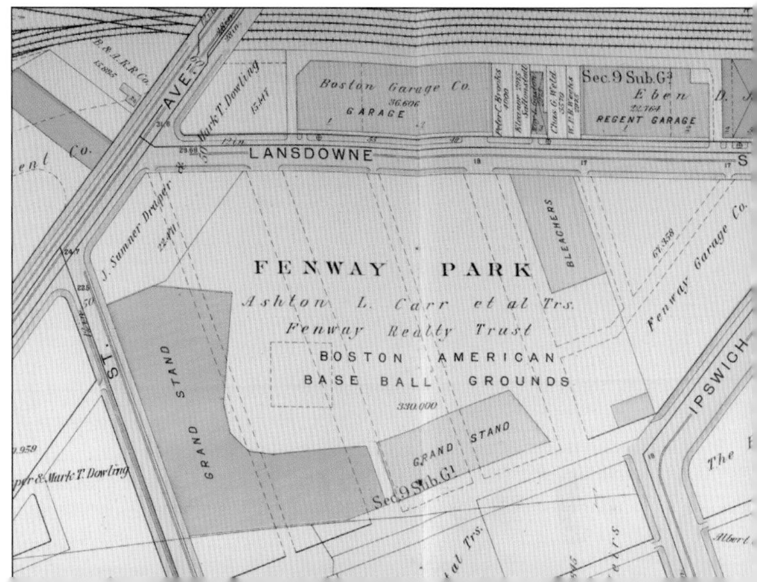

To be certain the setting sun wouldn't blind Fenway batters, the field was laid out with home plate at the southwest corner of the 365,308 square-foot plot. Only the rightfielder would be bothered.

"It's in the Fenway, isn't it? We'll call it Fenway Park."
—Red Sox Vice President John I. Taylor

A "Mammoth Plant"

When it hosted its first major-league game on April 20, 1912—the same afternoon that Navin Field (later Tiger Stadium) opened in Detroit and just two days after *Titanic* survivors reached New York—Fenway Park represented the latest in ballpark design and safety. Fires had destroyed numerous wooden ballparks in the years just before and after the turn of the century, including the majestic, double-decked South End Grounds that was home to Boston's National League club. Fenway and Navin Field were part of a new wave of steel and concrete parks built from 1909 to 1915, including Comiskey Park, Ebbets Field, and Wrigley Field. Each venue had its own distinctive appearance and character, and each was made to last.

Considering its longevity, it is interesting to note how quickly Fenway went up. Almost immediately after Red Sox owner Charles Taylor sold half the club to James McAleer and Robert McRoy in September 1911, his son John I. Taylor (former team president and now vice president under the new arrangement) began overseeing construction of the new ballpark on a parcel of land purchased in the Fenway. A largely underdeveloped part of town, "the Fens" were located just a few blocks from the intersecting point of two major thoroughfares—Commonwealth Avenue and Beacon Street—in growing Kenmore Square. Though they no longer held the majority interest in the team, the Taylor family would own the new park and call the shots on how it went up.

Because of the odd shape of the 365,308 square feet on which it was built and how that space fit into the surrounding neighborhood, architect James McLaughlin's already-completed design had to be altered. In fact, the quirks that are such a big part of Fenway's appeal today were more the result of happenstance than anything else.

As explained by Dick Johnson and Glenn Stout in their seminal history of the

Sewage and Swamp Water

Fenway Park is nestled into the streets surrounding it like an odd-shaped jigsaw puzzle piece. But the spot where Red Sox owner Charles Taylor decided to build his team's new venue was once anything but an easy fit.

Just a few decades before, the Fenway section of Boston had been comprised of what one historical account describes as a "noxious tidal swamp and creek left over from the times when the whole Back Bay was a shallow body of salt water," where "sewage and swamp water that infiltrated the area created a serious health problem as well as a foul stench." It was not an ideal place for a ballpark, but by the time Taylor came along things were looking up. In the 1880s, famed landscape architect Frederick Law Olmsted developed a seven-mile stretch of walkways and parkland in Boston known as the "Emerald Necklace," and Fenway had been part of his clean-up project.

A few blocks away from the site was Kenmore Square, which was representative of the exciting changes going on in the nation's fifth largest city during the early 20th century. The streets of the square were not yet paved, but they were already filled with signs of progress. Boston was home to the first major subway system in the United States, and streetcars regularly shared space around Fenway with gas-powered automobiles and horse-driven buggies. Electric streetlamps shined down on the activity, and billboard advertisements hyped auto shows and new tires. With plenty of hotels and restaurants to choose from, it was an ideal spot to go before or after a game.

The 1912 Red Sox loved their home cooking. They were 48–27 on the road but a sensational 57–20 at their new ballpark.

Fans pack the left-field stands, along with the temporary seats erected on "Duffy's Cliff" (*far right, below ads*), for the 1912 World Series.

team, *Red Sox Century:* "He [McLaughlin] could have easily created a more symmetrical park on only a portion of the parcel, but the Taylors were dumping the entire plot. McLaughlin was ordered to design a park that completely enclosed the site, resulting in the field of play being much larger than required by the way the game was played at the time. He was further ordered to retain the orientation of the Huntington Avenue Grounds in relation to the sun, with the third-base line pointing almost due north. This placed the left-field fence hard against Lansdowne Street, barely 300 feet from home plate.

"But that distance was of no concern, for at the time no one hit the ball that far. Had it been an issue, the street could easily have been acquired. This is the only reason Fenway Park is so misshapen today."

Distance was no concern because this was the Dead Ball Era, roughly a decade before Babe Ruth and subsequent sluggers redefined the home run and made it a far more common part of the game. Frank Baker had led the American League with just 11 homers in 1911, a season in which *entire teams* hit fewer than 20. Much of the reason was the baseballs they were hitting, which were scuffed, muddied, and otherwise beaten up by pitchers and general wear-and-tear but were seldom replaced during a game. As a result, they were rarely struck great distances. Yet nobody really minded. Line drives and hit-and-run plays were the preferred style carried out by pre-1920 clubs, and short outfield fences were not considered a major deterrent in a ballpark's design.

Besides, Fenway really wasn't *that* small. It was still well over 380 feet to the right-field fence, and the deepest center-field corner fence was nearly 550 feet from home plate. The wall running from left field to center was considerably closer, but it was also 25 feet high. The wall served as a long, wooden smorgasbord of ads that pitched everything from whiskey to biscuits. This was the predecessor of today's Green Monster, which would replace it in 1934.

Fenway's cozy image stems in large part from its lack of a second deck, and this was due to circumstance rather than planning. Perhaps thinking about both the majesty of the

A World Series pin, meant to look like a red baseball, rests on an actual Red Sox sock from the era.

Red Sox mascot Jerry McCarthy employs a megaphone to fire up the Royal Rooters in their special roped-off corner of the left-field stands. (Don't you love the "Red Sox" hat bands?)

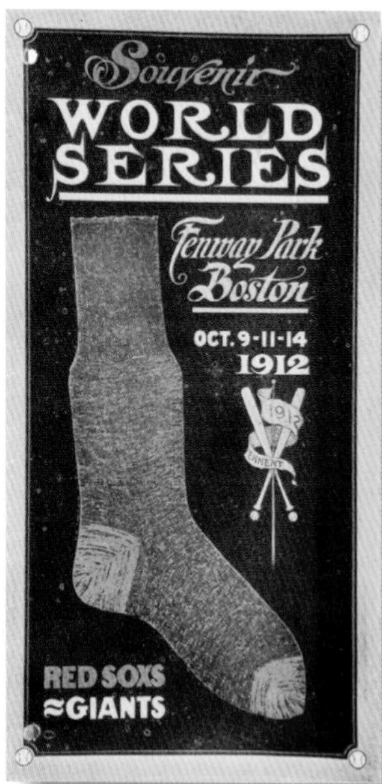

The 1912 World Series was a nonstop adventure. The teams alternated between Boston and New York for each game, and there was only one off day scheduled. There were brainy plays and boners, clutch hits and mega-muffs. Even the Royal Rooters had a direct impact on one game.

old South End Grounds and the potential for bigger paydays, Taylor initially envisioned building a double-deck ballpark like Navin Field and many of the other new venues. But since he wanted to be ready by the home opener—just six months away—such plans had to be put on hold.

For the time being a single, uncovered grandstand would surround the infield, while a roofed pavilion would run down the right-field line. There would also be a naked bleacher section in deepest right field, and the design left provisions for a second deck to be added later. Original capacity was about 29,000, nearly three times what the Huntington Avenue Grounds could "officially" hold but less than most other parks built during the period. To meet a growing demand for reserved tickets, management offered a "special price" of four box seats to all 77 home games for $250.

One sign of the times noted by author Michael Gersham in *Diamonds,* his excellent anthology of ballparks, was the decision to add a parking lot behind the outfield. The automobile had exploded in popularity in recent years. Car ads dominated the Boston newspapers, and dealerships were popping up all around the city—including in Kenmore Square. *The Boston Post* even ran a daily feature, "Gossip for Motorists," which let drivers know which streets had the worst potholes and how to avoid accidents.

With these and other revised plans in place, ground was broken for the new

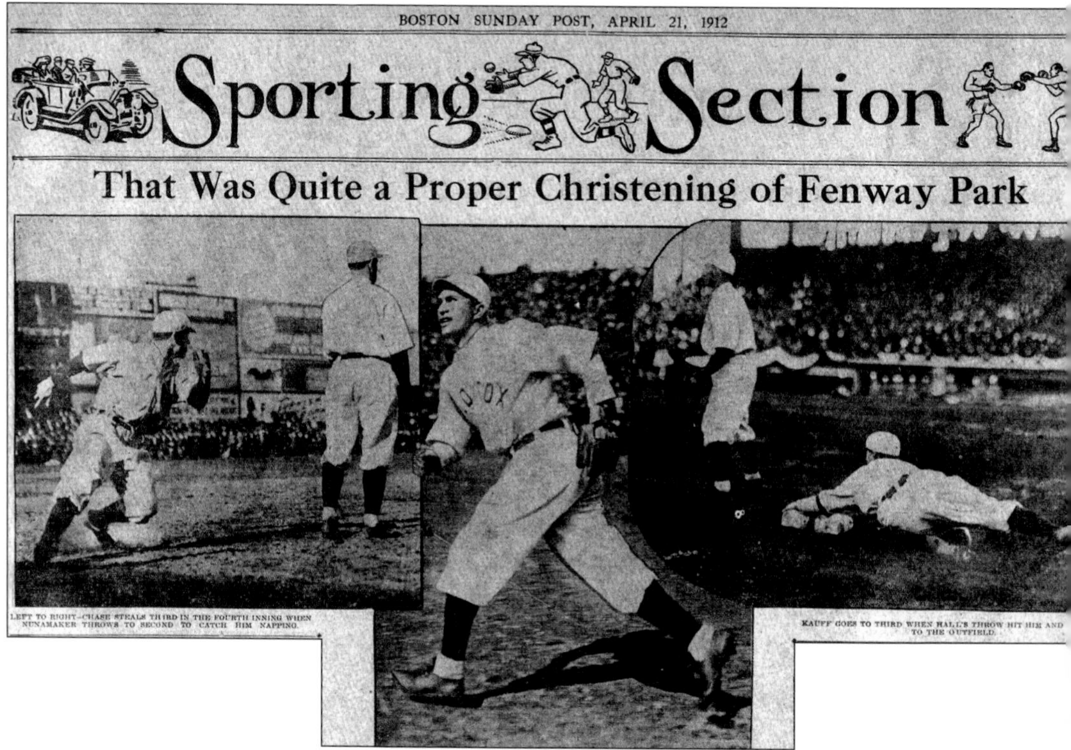

BOSTON SUNDAY POST, APRIL 21, 1912

Sporting Section

That Was Quite a Proper Christening of Fenway Park

LEFT TO RIGHT—CHASE STEALS THIRD IN THE FOURTH INNING WHEN NUNAMAKER THROWS TO SECOND TO CATCH HIM NAPPING.

KAUFF GOES TO THIRD WHEN HALL'S THROW HIT HIM AND TO THE OUTFIELD.

On Opening Day, 1912, fans entered through one of 18 turnstiles and enjoyed an 11-inning, 7–6 Red Sox win, duly noted on the first-ever electric scoreboard in left-center field.

facility on September 25, 1911, a week before the Red Sox finished their last season on Huntington Avenue. Major design and civil engineering work was undertaken by Osborn Engineering of Cleveland, a large firm that was simultaneously designing Navin Field and a few years later would aid in the construction of Boston's other modern major-league ballpark: Braves Field. (Ironically, Osborn in the early 1920s would also help design Yankee Stadium—so long a house of pain for Red Sox teams and fans.)

As a way of honoring the team's former home, sod from the Huntington Avenue Grounds was removed and replanted in Fenway as construction continued through the winter of 1911–12. By the time the Red Sox completed their long train ride up from spring training in Hot Springs, Arkansas, the new facility was ready for action. The first game played at Fenway was an exhibition match on April 9 between the Sox and Harvard University, which the big-leaguers won 2–0 amid a cold wind, snow flurries, and 3,000 shivering fans.

The park's regular-season opener with New York was slated for April 17, but warmer climes merely turned the snow to rain and forced its cancellation. Three more games, including the traditional Patriots' Day morning-afternoon doubleheader held in concurrence with the Boston Marathon, were also wiped out. At least one of these contests could have been played were the field properly covered, but a new tarp ordered from Detroit had not yet arrived. This resulted in more than 10,000 frustrated fans heading home in the bright sunshine after the water-slogged field was declared unplayable.

When the inaugural contest finally came off on April 20, it didn't disappoint. Although the Red Sox looked flat in falling behind the Highlanders 5–1 in the early going—as noted on the park's newfangled electric scoreboard—they rallied to tie and then win 7–6 on a single by Tris Speaker in the 11th inning. The outcome delighted the mayor and most of the 24,000 fans on hand, who had passed through 18 turnstiles—which, noted *The Boston Globe*, were "more than at any ball

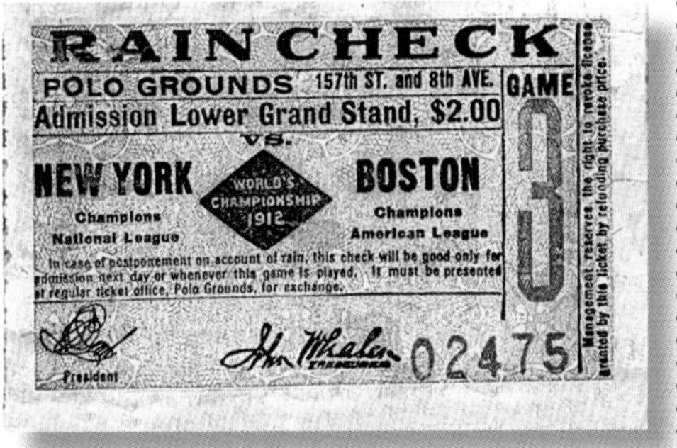

Yes, the rain check says Game 3, Polo Grounds. But Game 3 was played in Boston. Why? Game 2 had ended in a 6–6 tie after darkness had shut down further play. So the teams had to replay the game, in Boston, the next day. The Giants won 2–1.

The outside of Fenway was similar to another contemporary field, Shibe Park in Philadelphia. Both featured red brick and Colonial-style architecture. Of course, Shibe closed more than 40 years ago; Fenway marches on.

"The Boston Braves borrowed Fenway Park from the Red Sox that day, because the Braves' own park was too small to hold the crowd. They put ropes up in the outfield and thousands of people were sitting and standing behind the ropes, right on the playing field. They were standing right behind my back in center field."

—Fred Snodgrass of the New York Giants, recalling a game vs. the Braves at Fenway during the 1914 pennant race

The Boston Braves host the Philadelphia A's in the 1914 World Series at Fenway Park. Several things in this photo are interesting: the handful of motor cars; the line of fans waiting to get in (where are they going to sit?); the ad for Turkish baths; and the construction workers who get a "sky box" view of the game.

The Royal Rooters had no trouble switching their allegiance to the NL Braves for the 1914 World Series. A pennant is always enough reason for a party. Only two games were played at Fenway, and the Braves took both to sweep the Series.

park in the country, with the exception of the Polo Grounds in New York." The bad views that had hampered standing-room-only fans at the Huntington Avenue Grounds were less of a factor here, thanks to a sloping hill that ran up to the base of the tall outfield wall and allowed those watching in back a better glimpse of the action. The 10-foot knoll created a defensive challenge. Because it was expertly guarded most often in its early years by Red Sox leftfielder Duffy Lewis, it was quickly dubbed "Duffy's Cliff."

"The mammoth plant, with its commodious fittings, met with distinct approval," Paul Shannon reported in *The Boston Post* the next day. However, not all early reviews were positive. Although Fenway is praised for its intimacy today, fans in 1912 were not yet used to having seats so far from the playing field as those in the new center-field bleachers. One *Boston Globe* cartoon showed two patrons using telescopes to take in the action, and a front-page story in *The Sporting News,* the weekly national publication known as the "baseball bible," was entitled "Boston's Odd Ways—Reasons for Patronage at New Fenway Park: It's Too Big for Fans to Exchange Pleasantries About Weather and They're Used to Going in Another Direction."

"The fact that the park is not as handy to reach and get away from as the old park has hurt some and will until people get accustomed to journeying in the new direction," T. H. Murnane reported in the article. He asserted that "the kings of the bleachers . . . resent the idea of being pushed back to make room for the big grand stand." Because the new park featured two separate entrances on its opposite

An early-day photograph of Fenway was colorized for this treasured postcard.

This patch of leather features photos of the 1915 Red Sox. Going 55–20 at home and leading the league in attendance, the Red Sox finished 101–50 and won the pennant by 2.5 games over Detroit. They defeated the Phillies in five games to win the World Series.

ends, rather than one long passageway like at the Huntington Avenue Grounds, Murnane worried that there was less opportunity for fans to run into friends. Even the length of the games was seen as a culprit; more drawn-out contests were causing patrons to miss their trains.

Still, Murnane saw hope: "I am sure . . . with improved weather and everything else connected with the running of the establishment, the old crowds will come back, and the fans will grow warmer to the new park." He also anticipated that Fenway's formal dedication ceremonies on May 17 would draw "25,000 or 30,000 red blooded fans, from the finest base ball fan army in the country." The crowd wasn't quite that big in the end, but it was a great event nonetheless, with the grandstands draped in tri-color bunting, potted plants lining the walkways, and a band that played throughout the afternoon. Before the contest, Red Sox and White Sox players marched to the flagpole and raised Old Glory as the fans sang "The Star-Spangled Banner." The only thing keeping it from being a perfect day was a ninth-

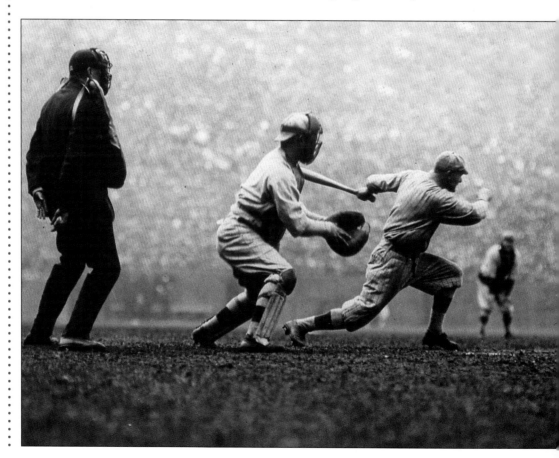

In 1916, the Red Sox battled the Brooklyn Robins in the World Series. Here, Brooklyn's Hy Myers belts an inside-the-park homer off Babe Ruth in Game 2. The homer was the last World Series run Babe would allow for almost 30 innings.

Just 25 cents got you into Fenway Park in 1916, a season in which the Red Sox went 91–63 and beat out Chicago by two games for the AL flag. Babe Ruth led the staff with a 23–12 record, but he hit just .272 with three homers in 136 at-bats.

inning comeback win by Chicago, but such outcomes would be a rarity during Fenway's maiden summer.

Home of Champions

At least until 2004, Fenway's greatest year may have been its first. Led by Speaker's .383 average and league-leading 10 home runs, and Wood's 34–5 record on the mound, the Red Sox went 105–47 and earned a World Series berth. There they faced the New York Giants and John McGraw—the same manager and team that had refused to play them in the 1904 postseason—and the battle that ensued was a true fall classic. Four games were decided by one run, another ended in a darkness-induced tie, and the final contest went down to the bottom of the 10th inning before a champion could be decided.

As they had in 1903, fans played a major role in the World Series on and off the field. The Royal Rooters were out in full force, both in Boston and in New York, where Mayor Fitzgerald used his political pull to garner some 300 seats for those who followed the team to the Polo Grounds. Fenway's capacity was pushed past the breaking point for the first three home games, with crowds of 30,000 or more jamming the stands—including temporary bleachers placed in front of the left-field wall on Duffy's Cliff. Many waved pennants and wore pins on their lapels, which were emblazoned with the team's official motto: "Oh, You Red Sox." The Royal Rooters sang not just "Tessie" but another popular song that Chief Rooter Mike McGreevy had written himself to honor the team's ace pitcher: "Knock Wood."

The Red Sox took a three games to two lead and were poised to clinch at Fenway

A Pair of Aces

Of the many great pitching performances turned in at Fenway Park during its first decade, two stand out—one as a spectacle and one as an oddity.

On September 6, 1912, Joe Wood faced Washington ace Walter Johnson in a match-up hyped in newspapers like a prizefight between a legend and an up-and-comer. Veteran Johnson had won an American League-record 16 consecutive games earlier that season, while the 22-year-old Wood was at 13 straight and counting. Historian Glenn Stout estimated that as many as 40,000 fans crammed into 27,000-seat Fenway Park that afternoon, including roped-off patrons in the outfield and (for the first and only time) along the perimeter of the infield, just inches from the foul lines. Both teams had to abandon their dugouts due to the crowds.

The tighter field conditions wound up helping the home club. A two-out, sixth-inning hit by Tris Speaker down the third-base line landed in the standing-room section for a ground-rule double, and Duffy Lewis followed with a double to right—plating Speaker with the game's only run. Wood went on to tie Johnson's mark of 16 straight victories, and a few weeks later he won the World Series clincher.

Washington was also the opponent when ace Babe Ruth took to the hill on June 23, 1917, but the big left-hander wasn't there long. Ruth walked leadoff man Ray Morgan. He then was thrown out of the game for punching umpire Brick Owens after the two argued over Owens's calls. Ernie Shore quickly came on to relieve Ruth, and catcher Sam Agnew promptly nabbed Morgan trying to steal second. Shore retired the next 26 men in order, and since he had been on the mound for all 27 outs, he was credited with a perfect game. However, it was later changed by a statistical analysis committee to a combined no-hitter.

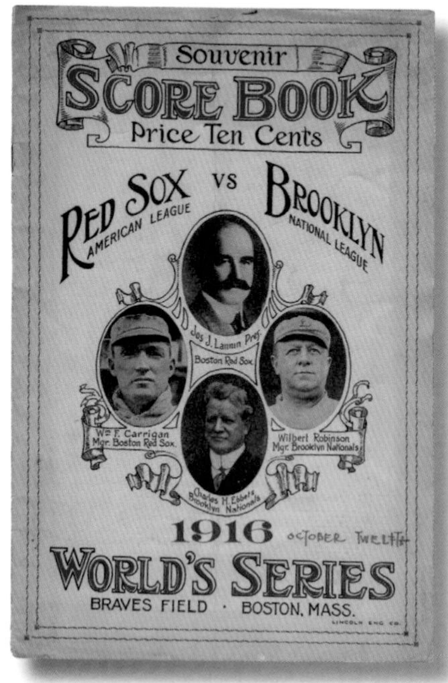

Two of Boston's three home games in the 1916 World Series were attended by more than 40,000 fans. Those who laid out a dime for this scorebook couldn't have imagined that it would be worth several thousand dollars someday.

with Wood pitching in Game 7 (Game 2 had been a tie). As had become their custom, the Royal Rooters marched around the perimeter of the field singing and waving their pennants before the contest, only this time a shock awaited them. When they arrived at the bleacher seats in left field, from which they had watched each of the other home games, they found them occupied by other fans. An innocent mix-up had occurred. But fueled no doubt by pregame toasts at the 3rd Base saloon, the Rooters were not in an understanding mood. As police on horseback tried to maintain order, McGreevy and his mates rushed up Duffy's Cliff; to fans, it must have looked like a reenactment of Teddy Roosevelt's charge up San Juan Hill.

Eventually space was found for the Rooters elsewhere in the park, and the game was allowed to start. Wood took the mound, but the long delay seemed to unnerve him. The Giants batted around in the first inning, raking the young right-hander for seven hits and taking a 6–0 lead from which Boston never recovered. The 11–4 final score set up a winner-take-all finale at Fenway the next day, and a far smaller crowd would be on hand to see it.

While Mayor Fitzgerald convinced Red Sox President Jimmy McAleer to personally apologize to the Royal Rooters, they were so miffed by their seating slight that they organized a boycott of Game 8. Their influence was clear; just 17,034 fans were on hand the next day to

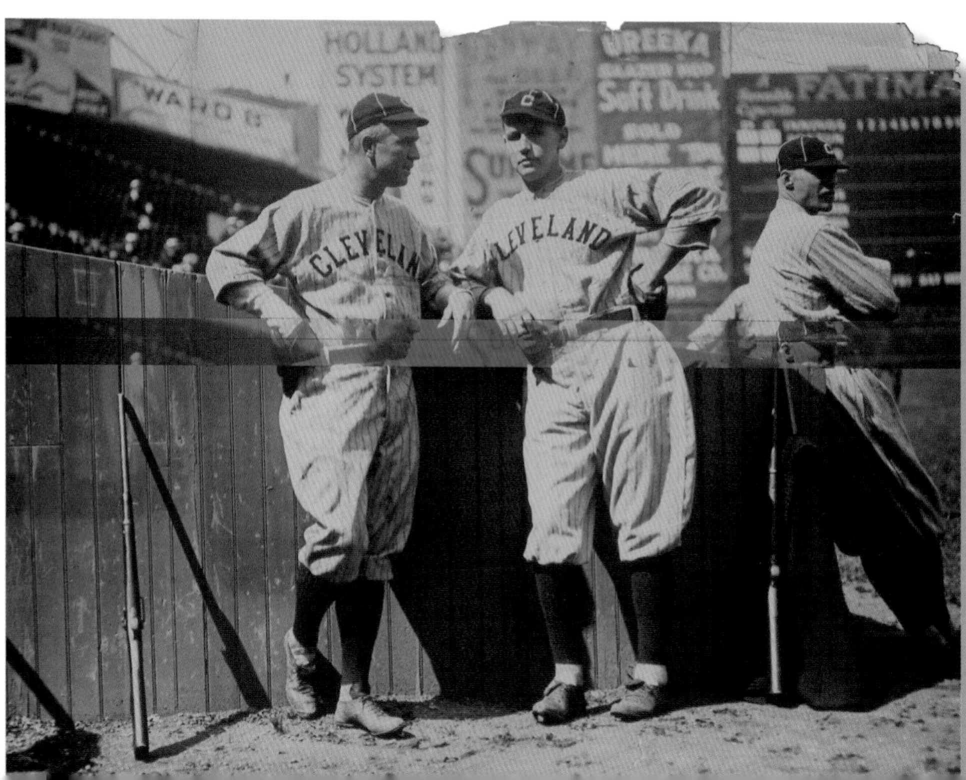

Two Sox stalwarts, Tris Speaker (*left*) and Joe Wood, reminisce at Fenway in Cleveland uniforms in 1917. Speaker had been traded to the Indians after a salary dispute following the 1915 season. Boston management had wanted to cut his salary after his average dropped to 322.

"I'd go out to the ballpark [during the] mornings and have somebody hit the ball again and again out to the wall. I experimented with every angle of approach up the cliff until I learned to play the slope correctly. Sometimes it would be tougher coming back down the slope than coming up. With runners on base, you had to come off the cliff throwing."

—Duffy Lewis, on playing Fenway's challenging left field

This is one of the few photos in existence that shows the expanse of Fenway's playing field during the 1910s. This image dates from 1917, when the Sox finished in second place, nine games behind Chicago.

see the season end just as it had begun—with the Red Sox rallying in the late innings. With Boston trailing 2–1 in the 10th against the great Christy Mathewson, the Red Sox tied it on an RBI single by Speaker and won the game and the championship on a sacrifice fly by Larry Gardner.

The Rooters got over their slight, and during the next several years they were rewarded for their loyalty with the second dynasty in Boston baseball history. Just as the city's National League club had dominated the 1890s by finishing first five times, the Sox took control of the teens with American League pennants in 1915, 1916, and 1918 to go with their '12 title. Each time they won the ensuing World Series as well, providing their "Junior Circuit" with bragging rights over the vaunted National League.

Fans at Fenway had numerous stars to cheer for during this period. The outfield trio of Speaker in center, Lewis in left, and Harry Hooper in right, which was broken up with Speaker's shocking trade to the Indians in 1916, might have been the greatest defensive unit in history. Speaker shined the brightest. Stories abounded of his playing so shallow that he could sneak in behind runners to pick them off at second base. Yet he could also run down balls hit over his head. Any pitcher with this group at his back would have an advantage, and Boston had one of baseball's best staffs in Ernie Shore, Rube Foster, Carl Mays, and Dutch Leonard. Injuries severely limited Wood's output after 1912, but he was brilliant when able to perform.

The most intriguing personality on the team, however, and the best left-handed pitcher in the American League, was a young man who would soon become baseball's premier slugger: George Herman "Babe" Ruth. Winner of 23 and 24 games in 1916 and '17, Ruth began playing the outfield or first base on days he didn't pitch so that the team could keep his productive bat in the lineup. This thrilled Fenway fans, who had taken to the colorful Babe's larger-than-life stature. He was a barrel-chested 6′2″, huge

Home of the Braves (Briefly)

Although the Red Sox and Braves competed for city bragging rights and fans during most of their 52 seasons together, they shared something special for a few years: ballparks.

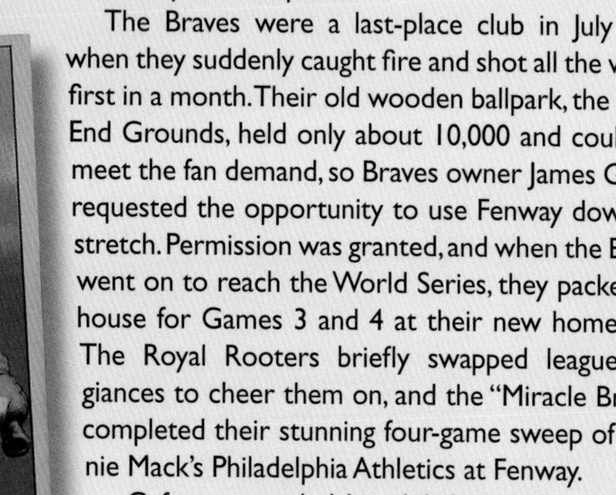

The Braves were a last-place club in July 1914 when they suddenly caught fire and shot all the way to first in a month. Their old wooden ballpark, the South End Grounds, held only about 10,000 and could not meet the fan demand, so Braves owner James Gafney requested the opportunity to use Fenway down the stretch. Permission was granted, and when the Braves went on to reach the World Series, they packed the house for Games 3 and 4 at their new home park. The Royal Rooters briefly swapped league allegiances to cheer them on, and the "Miracle Braves" completed their stunning four-game sweep of Connie Mack's Philadelphia Athletics at Fenway.

Braves outfielder Johnny Bates

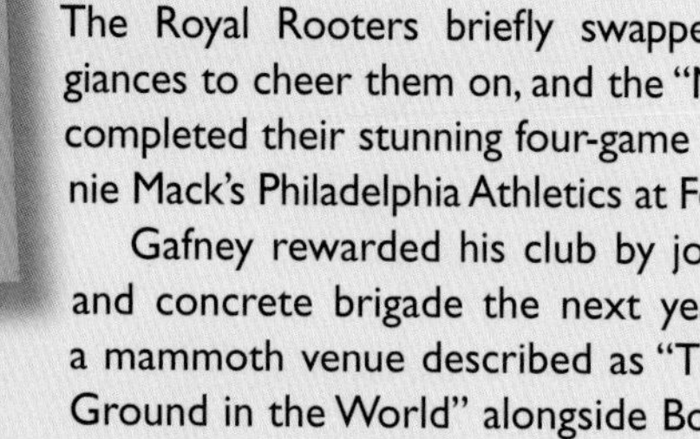

Gafney rewarded his club by joining the steel and concrete brigade the next year. He created a mammoth venue described as "The Biggest Ball Ground in the World" alongside Boston's Charles River. Braves Field opened in August 1915, and since it sat approximately 42,000 (more than 10,000 more than an overstuffed Fenway), the Red Sox were allowed to play there when *they* went to the postseason in both 1915 and '16. World Series bonuses were based on ticket revenue, so these arrangements meant several thousand dollars more for each Boston player each year—back when the average player's salary was considerably below $10,000.

for the era. In 1918, Ruth simultaneously led the league in home runs (with 11) and still went 13–7 on the hill.

That fall, Ruth completed an MLB-record $29\frac{2}{3}$ straight scoreless innings pitched in World Series play. The 1918 World Series was noteworthy because it was held a month early due to World War I and because the start of Game 5 at Fenway was delayed more than an hour as players negotiated for a higher share of the gate receipts. Owners had cut their percentage to aid war charities and to account for a dip in Series attendance. Harry Hooper helped facilitate a last-minute settlement, but fans jeered the players when they finally took the field.

Ruth was negotiating as well—for a chance to play every day—and in 1919 manager Ed Barrow let him man the outfield on an almost regular basis while pitching part-time. The result was astounding: a major-league record 29 home runs, which represented more than several *teams* in the AL could muster and was 88 percent of the Red Sox's total. The defending World Series champs fell to sixth, however, and Sox owner Harry Frazee grew tired of Ruth's demands to double his $10,000 annual salary.

Boston fans were looking forward to seeing the Babe slam balls out of Fenway throughout the 1920s. They would get their wish, but it wouldn't be quite how they expected.

Pitching ace Babe Ruth emerged as a power hitter in 1918, leading the league with 11 home runs. Teammate Harry Hooper suggested that Babe play the field when he wasn't pitching. In 1919, he slugged 29 homers, nearly three times as many as anyone else. The revolution was on.

In 1919, Red Sox owner Harry Frazee (*second from right*) was growing unhappy with malcontent Babe Ruth. To Frazee, the idea of selling his prized commodity seemed more and more appealing.

CHAPTER 2

After the Babe

1920–1932

With owner Harry Frazee dealing Ruth and other talented players, the Red Sox fell into a perennial funk, finishing in last place nine times in 11 years. Ironically, Fenway seemingly drew big crowds only when Babe and the Yankees came to town.

Yankees Buy Ruth and Home Run Bat for Over $100,000

Great Hitter Sure to Be a Big Drawing Card for the New York Club.

Home Run Star

Likely to Play Right Field and Is Sure to Add Strength to the Team.

(Continued From First Page.)

"BABE" RUTH

Cost of Baseball Goes Up.

The sad, sad news in big, big type. This icy act of commerce put nearly half a million dollars in Harry Frazee's pocket and changed the face of American sports (and America!) forever.

John Dooley was on his feet cheering, like the rest of the crowd inside a very cramped Fenway Park. Yankees superstar Babe Ruth had just hit his second home run of the day—his 46th of the 1920 season. A massive crowd that overflowed the stands, ran down the first- and third-base lines, and surrounded the edges of the outfield grass in a semicircle was letting the pitcher-turned-slugger know how much he meant to them. Ruth tipped his cap while rounding third, and the roars grew louder.

Dooley was nearing the halfway point of a remarkable stretch of Boston fan longevity, attending major-league games in the city—including every Red Sox or Braves opener—from 1882 to 1971. He was credited, in fact, for helping the fledging American League gain its footing in his hometown. Dooley's close relationship with a prominent local businessman enabled AL President Ban Johnson to lease the Huntington Avenue Grounds site for the Sox in 1901. Dooley counted many former and current big-leaguers among his friends, and Johnson affectionately called him "my little Irishman from Boston."

Now, as daredevil fans perched high atop nearby billboards overlooking the park joined in the ovation, Ruth crossed the plate and headed to the dugout. In years past, this would have required no more than a slight turn to his left, but now he had to make a hard, exaggerated cut in the opposite direction toward the third-base on-deck circle. That's where the visiting team's dugout was situated at Fenway, and that's where the Babe belonged: with his new Yankee teammates.

Under the circumstances, cheering for the enemy was an easy task for Dooley and his fellow patrons. The Yankees were battling for first place in the American League, while the Red Sox were under .500 and going nowhere.

New York Yankee Babe Ruth takes a hack at Fenway Park. In their first 17 years, the New Yorkers had zero pennants while the Sox had five. In just nine seasons after the Ruth sale, the Bronx Bombers surpassed Boston's total.

Governor Frank G. Allen held that job only two years (1929–31), but he helped Bostonians get to Fenway when he founded the Massachusetts Transit Authority. Here he throws out a ceremonial first ball.

That day's sun-splashed doubleheader even included "Babe Ruth Day" festivities between games, when the man who had led Boston to three World Series titles from 1915 to '18 was given a pair of cufflinks by a local Knights of Columbus chapter. Newsboys would soon be gathering outside Fenway with evening editions that trumpeted his heroics.

A few miles away in Medford, Massachusetts, 10-year-old Mabray Kountze smiled when he saw the headlines. The son of a former slave whose family had migrated to the Boston area along with thousands of other newly freed men and women after the Civil War, Kountze loved following baseball at every level. Besides the all-white Red Sox, he cheered on the all-black West Medford Independents of the Greater Boston Colored League, a top semipro club on which his brothers Hillard and Al both starred. Like others in his racially mixed neighborhood, Kountze heard the rumors that Ruth himself might have some African blood flowing through his powerful body. Players throughout baseball heard them as well, and the boy figured that the Babe's former Sox teammates had spent the weekend good-naturedly peppering Ruth with vulgar nicknames such as "Niggerlips."

Later, Kountze would recall that he knew many black baseball fans who would not attend games at Fenway Park because of the unspoken but obvious color line that existed in the major leagues. Until Jackie Robinson and Larry Doby came along to break this racial barrier, black fans often stayed

> **"After the 1920 season I held out for $15,000, and Frazee did me a favor by selling me to the White Sox. I was glad to get away from that graveyard."**
> **—Outfielder Harry Hooper, on leaving Fenway and the Red Sox**

away from Fenway, not because of the occasional insult that would get hurled their way—they could handle that—but rather out of principle. If their brethren were not allowed on the diamond, they wouldn't be in the stands.

Kountze could not have foreseen that he would one day help break the color line in Boston (in the role of journalist), but for now he was content imagining that at least one player, the Babe, was already doing so. And during this period, as the Red Sox struggled through their worst stretch of play ever, the chance to see Ruth and other members of the visiting Yankees up close was a major incentive for fans to come to the park. Everybody loved a winner.

Ruth Still Rules

At the time he sold Ruth to the Yankees for $100,000 cash and a $300,000 loan in January 1920, Red Sox owner Harry Frazee passionately believed that he was doing what was best for his ballclub. The Sox had finished 66–71 in 1919 despite Ruth's record-breaking 29 homers. Frazee felt the team would be better off without the distractions that came with a player who feuded with management, broke rules, and refused to pitch more than he desired. It was long believed, and later debunked, that Frazee was in dire financial straits when he made the deal and was more interested in funding his true passion as a Broadway theatrical producer. Whatever his intentions, the results are irrefutable.

Sending Ruth and other talented young players (such as Waite Hoyt, Sam Jones, Joe Dugan, and Everett Scott) to the Yankees over the next several years, and getting mostly players who failed to pan out in return, Frazee almost singlehandedly shifted the American League's base of power from Fenway Park to the Polo Grounds (and, starting in 1923, Yankee Stadium). By the time Frazee sold out to a syndicate ownership headed by Bob Quinn in the summer of '23, the Red Sox were a shell of the proud club

Harry Hooper, glorified on a Perez Steele postcard, was a sensational outfielder and an excellent leadoff hitter. After Boston sold him to the White Sox, he hit even better.

Fenway in Flames

Babe Ruth's Yankees weren't the only thing heating up at Fenway during a mostly dreary period for the home team. On the evening of May 8, 1926, a small fire broke out in a pile of trash strewn underneath the wooden bleachers running down the left-field side of the empty ballpark. Although a night watchman and multitasking Red Sox manager Lee Fohl tried to put it out with fire extinguishers, strong winds enabled the flames to spread and grow into a three-alarm blaze. The fire department had to bust through a fence beyond the bleachers to get water in, and they had to cut holes in the grandstand roof to let trapped heat out.

Quinn was already struggling to make ends meet with his cellar-dwelling club, and although he was able to repair the roof and fence after a $25,000 insurance settlement, he used much of the money to make payroll and didn't replace the charred bleachers. With so few fans coming to games, he probably figured that the bleachers would not be missed. This logic bourn of desperation left an unsightly cinder-laden hole on the left-field side of the ballpark. In addition to adding a tremendous amount of extra foul territory to Fenway's configuration, it served as a daily reminder of how far the team had fallen.

Old Glory is raised before a full house at Fenway. While the flagpole has always been located in left-center field, it was removed from the field of play in 1970.

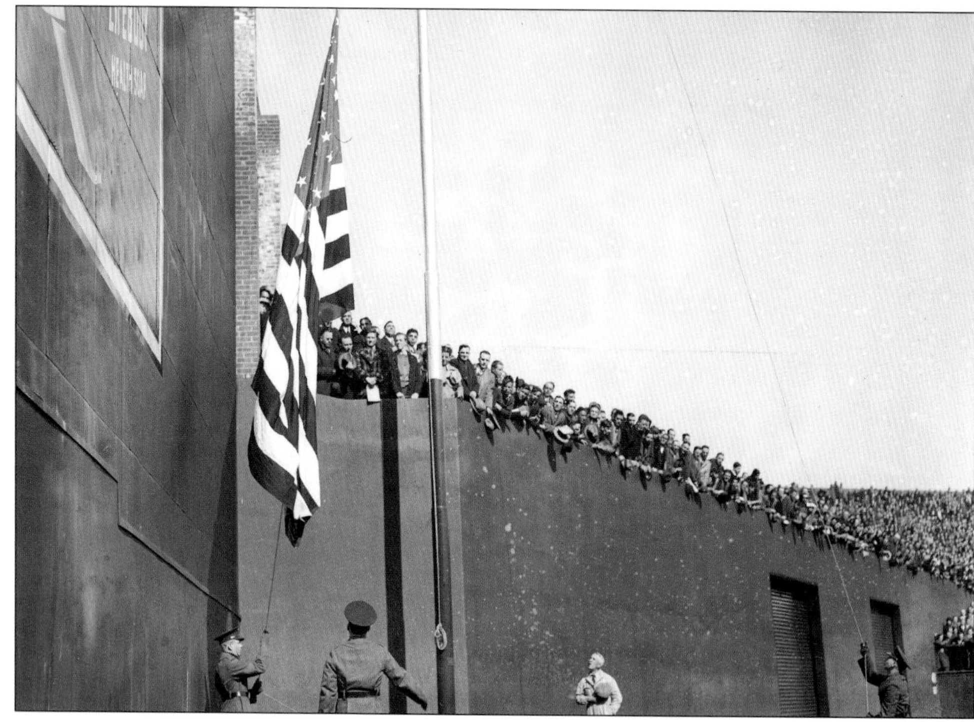

The rich royal blue of the original oaken Fenway seats still looks elegant and Bostonian. When the ballpark was originally built, Fenway could seat just 27,000 fans. Expansions and improvements raised that to 36,974 for day games and 37,402 for night contests through 2010.

that had dominated the 1910s. That fall, when the Yankees won their first World Series, it was with a lineup and pitching staff filled with former Boston players.

Even without postseason baseball, Fenway was busy. Football was rising in popularity nationwide, and the ballpark was routinely a venue for gridiron match-ups during the '20s. Boston College, Dartmouth, and other New England colleges played there on a regular basis, and many area high schools used it as a neutral site throughout their fall seasons. On Thanksgiving morning, 1927, 20,000 fans watched English High top Public Latin and Dorchester High run roughshod over the High School of Commerce in a football doubleheader at the Fens. Religious revivals and annual memorial masses to honor servicemen lost in World War I were also held at the ballpark, as were collegiate and high school baseball games.

The Red Sox were still technically the "stars" of Fenway, but when they took the field the big crowds usually disappeared. Given the team's performance, it was understandable. After clinching their fourth World Series title in seven years in 1918, the Sox quickly went from dynasty to doormat—finishing fifth or sixth in the eight-team American League from 1919 through '21 and then dead last for nine of the next 11 seasons. Five times in the stretch they lost at least 100 games, and the aging Royal Root-

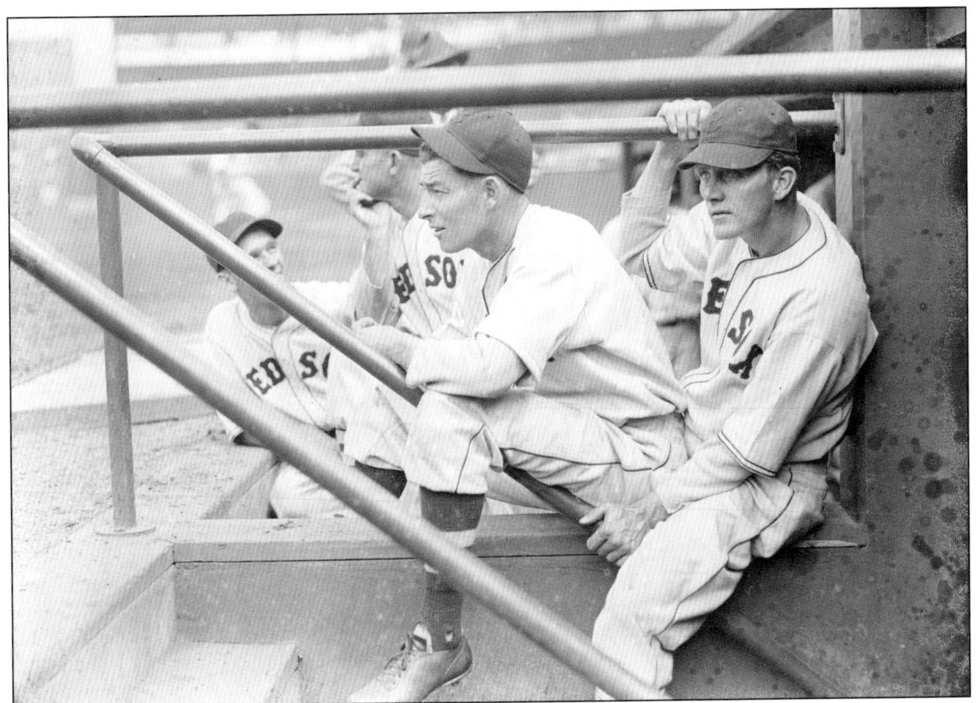

The year is 1930, and the Babe has been gone 10 years. No one seems to be having much fun. That season, in the "Year of the Hitter," the Yankees outscored the Red Sox by 450 runs.

This packed house in 1930 must mean one thing: the Yankees are in town. Overall that year, the Red Sox averaged just 5,767 fans per game.

It was long believed that Harry Frazee sold Babe Ruth to finance this play, but that assertion has been debunked. *No, No, Nanette* did not reach Broadway until 1925, five years after Frazee sold Ruth and two years after he had sold the Red Sox.

ers (and most everybody else) took to staying home. The Sox became one of the majors' worst-drawing teams, routinely playing to just a few thousand fans. On many days, they were outdrawn by semipro "Twilight League" games in Lynn, Cambridge, and other nearby communities. At Fenway, it was easy to spot the pockets of gamblers who huddled together near the right-field foul pole, betting on the outcome of virtually every pitch.

Only during the 11 games a year that the Yankees came to town was Fenway consistently filled to a respectable capacity. This was never more the case than in 1927, when Ruth and teammate Lou Gehrig were both threatening the Babe's vaunted record of 59 home runs set six years before. This dynamic duo came to Boston in early September, and nearly 34,000 people packed the ballpark well past capacity for a meaningless doubleheader. Ruth gave them what they wanted—slugging three homers during the twin bill—and for a moment fans could forget that the Red Sox trailed the Yankees by nearly 50 games.

A handful of Red Sox players shined during these lean years. Ira "Pete" Flagstead mastered the deep expanse of Fenway's center field and was a .290 hitter through most of the 1920s. Bespectacled Danny MacFayden, a native of nearby Somerville, Massachusetts, anchored the slim pitching staff of the late 1920s and early '30s. Earl Webb set a major-league record that still stands with 67 doubles in 1931. However, perceptive Fenway fans (and sportswriters) noticed him holding up at second base on sure triples

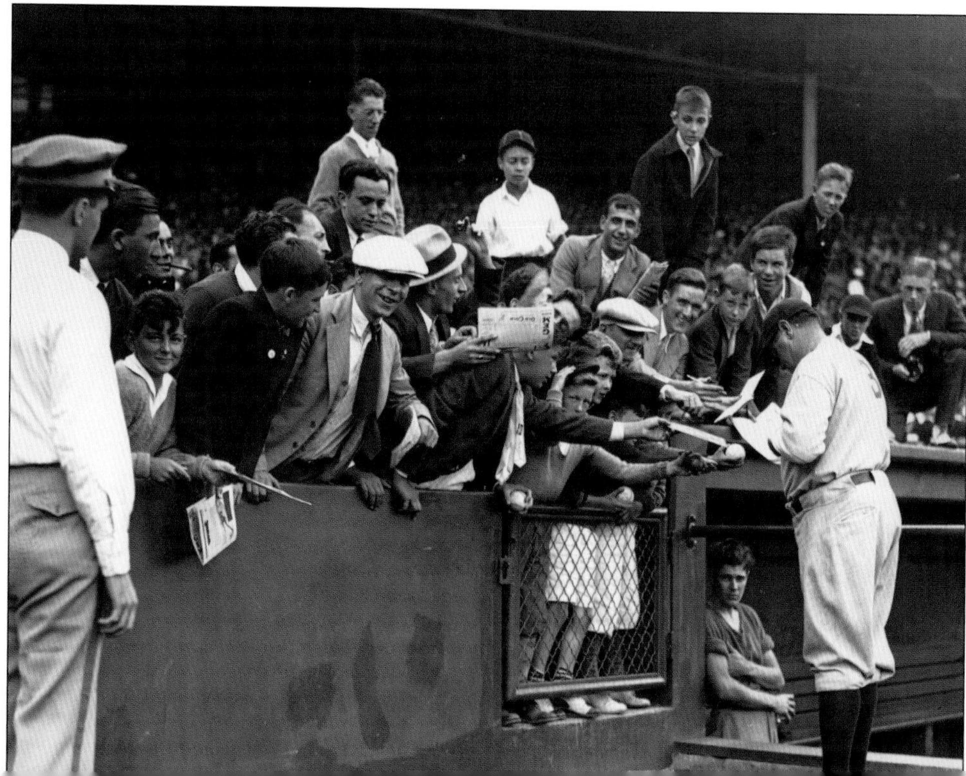

Ten years after he was shipped off to New York, these Red Sox fans still loved the Babe. At the time, Bostonians simply considered the Ruth deal to be simply a bad move—not a "curse."

late in the season—the type of me-first attitude that made him the perfect star for a 62–90 club.

That finish was actually good enough for sixth place in '31, the highest spot the Red Sox had reached in 10 years. Perhaps the "success" went to their heads, because things completely bottomed out the next season when the Sox dropped back to last with the worst record (43–111) in franchise history. In finishing a whopping 64 games behind the first-place Yankees, Boston drew just 182,150 fans to Fenway—an average of under 2,400 per game. If not for the crowds brought in by Ruth, Gehrig, and their pinstriped pals, the numbers would have been considerably lower.

If any player symbolized the 1932 Red Sox, it was leftfielder Smead Jolly. An excellent hitter whose 18 homers and 99 RBI easily led the moribund club, he was a disaster at manning Duffy's Cliff, routinely stumbling down the sloping outfield knoll that its namesake had so deftly tended. Fans watching Jolly's foibles could not help but reflect on the glory days of the recent past, and the path back to respectability seemed steeper than ever.

The economic Depression gripping the country had impacted all big-league teams, and with little money in the till for upkeep, 30-year-old Fenway was showing signs of age. Beleaguered and nearly broke, Red Sox President Bob Quinn was looking for a savior. He would soon find one, and when he did, the team and ballpark would undergo the greatest makeover imaginable.

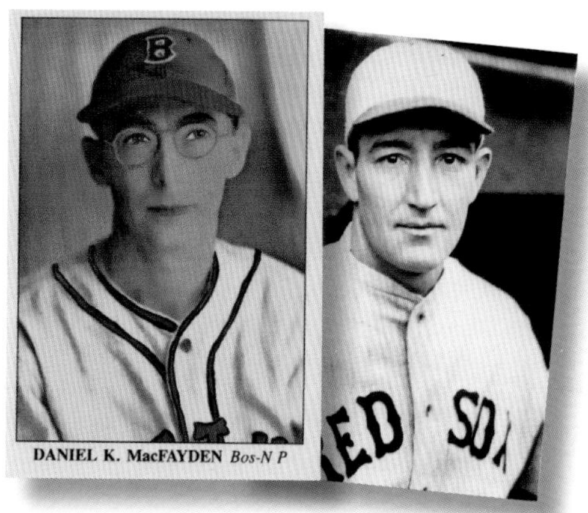

Local boy Danny MacFayden (*left*) was a pretty good pitcher for some genuinely crummy Red Sox teams. Earl Webb (*right*) was the closest thing to a hero the Sox of that era had. His 67 doubles in 1931 remain a big-league record.

Never on a Sunday

While the hapless Red Sox compiled some awful losing streaks at Fenway Park during the 1920s, they had a perfect record in the ballpark on Sundays—when no games were played there.

Although Sunday baseball was allowed in many major-league cities during the first decades of the 20th century, powerful church groups and politicians in puritan Boston kept the Christian Sabbath holy and hardball-free into the late 1920s. What frustrated Red Sox and Braves fans about the ban was that this was the only day that many workers had off, and in other cities teams were drawing their biggest crowds on Sundays. Over time, proponents started swinging public opinion by making a case that Sunday should be seen as a day of leisure rather than a day of rest. If folks could see a movie or vaudeville show on the Sabbath, they argued, why not a baseball game?

This logic prevailed in a 1928 ballot referendum, as Massachusetts voters overwhelmingly supported the "Sunday Sports Question." The Boston City Council approved the measure in time for the '29 season, but the new law stipulated that Sunday games could not be played within 1,000 feet of a church—and there was a Unitarian parish just a short way down Jersey Street from Fenway Park. As a result, the Red Sox *could* play on Sundays, but they had to do so at Braves Field until the law was amended three years later.

On July 3, 1932, Fenway finally hosted its first Sunday ballgame, a 13–2 loss to New York. God, apparently, was a Yankees fan.

CHAPTER 3

Yawkey's Palace

1933–1940

With a fortune at his disposal, Red Sox owner Tom Yawkey spared no expense in renovating his ballpark. New Fenway Park opened in 1934, after which Yawkey continued to spend. He acquired such superstars as Jimmie Foxx, who would take a young Ted Williams under his wing in 1939.

Ken Coleman never tired of the ritual. Each summer Sunday that the Red Sox were home during the late 1930s, he and his father would go to nine o'clock mass, eat a big breakfast, and then take the short trip in from Quincy to Kenmore Square with bag lunches packed by Mom. Arriving at Fenway Park when its gates opened at 11:00 A.M., they would watch batting and infield practice and then settle into their 55-cent seats for the afternoon. Since Sundays always meant doubleheaders throughout the majors, they got two games for the price of one. And as they munched on their sandwiches, they could track how the other American League clubs were doing on the huge scoreboard that fronted Fenway's mammoth left-field wall.

Back in the day, pins like this were a handy way to strut your colors for your favorite team.

From their vantage point in the center-field bleachers on August 13, 1939, the Wall looked about a mile high as it stretched toward Coleman. The 13-year-old knew from reading the sports pages that it was actually 37 feet from top to bottom, not counting the big net that Red Sox owner Tom Yawkey had added to save windows and windshields on Lansdowne Street from being smashed by Jimmie Foxx's long home runs. The sloping hill that previously had extended to the base of the old wooden wall was pretty much gone, and the bleachers had been extended all the way to the new cement wall when Mr. Yawkey renovated the ballpark five years earlier. It seemed to Coleman that he could almost reach out and touch the Wall, which had a tin surface covered with pockmarks where Foxx, Joe Cronin, and other Sox sluggers had slammed balls off of it.

When the first game of the doubleheader against the Washington Senators began, Coleman turned his attention to right field, where rookie Ted

With a youthfully joyful grin, rookie Ted Williams scores another run in 1939. "The Kid" wowed the Fenway faithful that season with 31 homers, 131 runs, and a league-high 145 RBI.

A giddy crop of young fans surrounds two of Tom Yawkey's more significant acquisitions: Joe Cronin (*right*), the manager and shortstop, and Jimmie Foxx (*center*), the slugging first sacker.

Williams was taking his position. The slim, tall Californian was the talk of Boston; a natural hitter who batted fourth in the lineup after Foxx and was already among the league leaders in runs batted in. Coleman also enjoyed watching Williams on defense, where he chatted good-naturedly with patrons and could sometimes be caught practicing his swing with an invisible bat. When he jogged out to right and picked up his glove at the start of each inning, the crowd near him stood and applauded—an affirmation of their feelings for the confident, 21-year-old slugger. In the future, Williams would have a complex love-hate relationship with Boston fans, but at this point all was still fresh and new and good. Grinning, Ted tipped his hat.

In the second game, Williams hit a 420-foot shot right into a sea of his right-field admirers, part of a perfect 6-for-6 day at the plate (with two walks) in the doubleheader. Some of the loudest yells coming his way after the homer were delivered by one of Fenway's most familiar voices, Lillian "Lolly" Hopkins. Making the 100-mile roundtrip from Providence, Rhode Island, by train for each Red Sox home game—and many Boston Braves games as well—Hopkins always sat in the same seat along the first-base side with a group of friends known simply as "Lolly's Girls." She had a nickname of her own, "Megaphone Lolly," acquired for the gusto with which she shouted into the trusty red one she always had with her. And although Hopkins loved all the Boston ballplayers, her favorite was quiet, reliable second baseman Bobby Doerr. She'd shout "That's my Bobby!" when he stepped to the plate. She further showed her adoration by putting down her scorebook and tossing Tootsie Rolls in Doerr's direction for good deeds at bat or in the field.

This afternoon, Doerr matched Williams and rewarded Lolly's loyalty with a home run of his own, and the Red Sox split their twin bill with the Senators. Late in the second contest, with the Sox trailing, fans groaned as they saw a metal "18" slide into place by "NY" on the scoreboard. Although the Yankees had lost the first game of their own doubleheader in Philadelphia, they were well on their way to a lopsided 21–0 victory in the second contest that would enable them to maintain their six-game lead over the Red Sox in the AL pennant race. By year's end, the Yanks would

"In the afternoons, when everybody had left the ballpark, Mr. Yawkey would bring down a couple of .22 rifles, and he and [pitcher] Henry Johnson would run around shooting pigeons."
—Third baseman Billy Werber

claim yet another World Series championship, and the Sox would finish second.

This was a familiar refrain during the 1933–40 era at Fenway. Loaded with an array of All-Star talent purchased by the deep-pocketed Yawkey, and blessed with other players who had developed in their growing farm system, the Sox excited fans with their power display but never had quite enough pitching or depth to overtake their nemesis from New York and the other top American League clubs. Yawkey's lavish 1934 upgrade of Fenway, centered around the tall left-field wall marked as 315 feet (but really a little less) from home plate, would result in a team tailor-made for the ballpark's most unique feature. A slew of right-handed batters could tattoo the Wall with regularity but often hit into long outs during the 77 games they spent away from Boston. Still, the combination of a competitive team and a beautiful, revitalized ballpark would be enough to bring the big crowds back to the Sox' side as America emerged from the Great Depression and Europe edged closer to war.

Tom Yawkey was only 30 when he bought the team. This woman is not his longtime wife, Jean, who served as club president after his death. It is his first wife, Elise. In 1944, Yawkey married Jean a month after his divorce.

The Fenway Millionaires

Thomas Austin Yawkey was just the savior Bob Quinn was seeking. The heir to a mining and lumber fortune held in trust until his 30th birthday, Yawkey had grown up around baseball as the adopted son of an uncle who owned the Detroit Tigers in the early 1900s. Detroit star Ty Cobb had been like a father to Yawkey, whose own parents had died when he was young, and Cobb encouraged the young businessman to buy a ballclub when the opportunity presented itself. Yawkey heard in early 1933 that Quinn was looking to get out of Boston, and he let him know he was interested. Soon the legal wheels were in motion for a deal.

Quinn's main provision for the sale was that Yawkey find an experienced baseball man to help run the team. Although the Red Sox had brought Quinn much heartache—punctuated by their 43–111 record and dismal attendance marks the previous season—he still cared about the franchise and didn't want to see it fall apart completely. Bos-

After Billy Werber averaged 27 steals a year for the Red Sox from 1933 to 1936, it would be more than 35 years before a Red Sox player topped the mark even once.

"We'd be there when the gates opened. . . . We would be there for both games of the doubleheader right down until the last man was out, no matter the score or anything else. We might even be the last people in the ballpark."

—Ken Coleman, on attending Sunday doubleheaders at Fenway with his father

ton's other big-league club, the National League's Braves, was vastly improved and had outdrawn the Sox over the previous three seasons. The new owner could not afford to lose any more ground in this turf war for the city's baseball allegiances.

To help turn things around, Quinn suggested that Yawkey seek the counsel of Eddie Collins, a former standout second baseman for the Philadelphia A's and Chicago White Sox who possessed a keen mind for the game and (like Yawkey) an Ivy League education. It was the perfect choice; Yawkey had attended the same prep school as Collins, and he looked to the future Hall of Famer as an idol almost on par with Cobb. With Collins in place as vice president and general manager, Yawkey purchased the Red Sox—and with them, Fenway Park—for $1.2 million in May 1933. It had been a little over two months since his birthday had made this "gentleman sportsman" one of the country's wealthiest individuals, worth a reported $20 million.

Eddie Collins worked for friend Tom Yawkey and the Red Sox until his death in 1951. Today, a plaque honoring Collins adorns the main entrance to Fenway Park.

Overnight, the fortunes of the Red Sox and their ballpark went from the poorhouse to the penthouse. The stock market crash of 1929 and the long economic malaise that followed had impacted all of baseball, with attendance and profits down throughout the major leagues and owners scrambling to stay solvent as their own business interests sank. Younger and more in the black than any of his new peers, Yawkey had access to vast amounts of money at a time when his fellow owners needed it desperately. He was also willing to pay top dollar for top players and then give them bigger salaries than they could get elsewhere. And while he may have been largely unknown to Bostonians when they first read about the sale, he would not wait long to make an impact.

Fans were thankful that the Red Sox had added numbers to their uniforms in 1931, for it helped them keep track

Eager fans climb a Fenway billboard's legs to peer into the park in 1937. The date may have been June 20, when an over-capacity crowd of 37,195 watched a Boston-Cleveland doubleheader..

of the many new faces joining the team during the first few years of Yawkey's tenure. Utilizing Collins's expert acumen to identify the best talent available, the new owner acquired a quartet of future Hall of Famers—first baseman Foxx, shortstop Cronin, catcher Rick Ferrell, and pitching ace Robert "Lefty" Grove. He also signed other standouts, including right-handed hurler Wes Ferrell (Rick's brother), speedy third baseman Bill Werber, and outfielder Doc Cramer. The cost to the Red Sox? An assortment of mostly forgettable players and a boatload of cash, all of which gave Yawkey status as baseball's Daddy Warbucks and earned the team new nicknames such as "Yawkey's Gold Sox" and "The Fenway Millionaires."

For the next two generations, through good times and bad for the Red Sox, Yawkey would be the name atop the letterhead at Fenway Park. He split time between a posh New York City apartment, a vast South Carolina plantation complete with its own wetlands and hunting preserve, and (in season) a suite at Boston's Ritz Carlton hotel. Yet he seemed happiest taking batting practice on the Fenway diamond, talking with players in the locker room, and sitting in his box overlooking the field. Including the years that his wife, Jean, served as owner following Tom's death in 1976,

Catcher Rick Ferrell, shown on a Perez Steele postcard, was the first player that Tom Yawkey obtained to bolster his team. Ferrell responded with an All-Star season in 1933 and provided solid defense and a .300 bat for several more (although his brother, pitcher Wes, hit more homers).

and an additional decade when the Jean R. Yawkey Trust and its executors were in charge after Jean's 1992 passing, the Yawkeys would control the Red Sox for nearly three-quarters of a century. Over that time, they would become as synonymous with the team as its ballpark—which today resides on a portion of Jersey Street that was renamed Yawkey Way.

Remodeling and Rebirth

The park, as much as the team, was due for extensive overhauling when the new owner came aboard. At the same time that he had Collins reshaping the roster, Yawkey set about transforming the venue into what would officially be called "New Fenway Park." The reconstruction job, which took place during the fall and winter of 1933–34 at an estimated cost of $1.25 million to $1.5 million, was done with the cooperation of Osborn Engineering in Cleveland, the same firm that had helped with the original Fenway erection more than 30 years earlier. Coming when it did, in the depths of the Great Depression, the project was not just a renovation to Bostonians; it was a revelation. President Franklin Roosevelt created the Works Progress Administration (WPA) in the mid-1930s to help unemployed Americans get back on their feet. Through the WPA, laborers built everything from courthouses to dams to new roadways. Similarly, Yawkey's refurbishing of Fenway helped the citizens of Boston rebound, thus raising his stature in town.

As Glenn Stout and Dick Johnson explained in *Red Sox Century,* "Building New Fenway Park employed approximately 750 skilled union workers, used 15,000 cubic yards of concrete, 550 tons of steel, 100,000 bricks, 8,000 cubic feet of sod, and 500,000 feet of lumber, some of it undoubtedly harvested from the Yawkey lands. It was like Yawkey's own WPA

Yawkey's reconstruction of Fenway modernized the grand old ballyard in 1934. The most notable change was the addition of the massive wall in left field.

On January 5, 1934, a fire during the reconstruction effort damaged Fenway Park and surrounding buildings. The blaze may have begun when a small furnace, being used to dry fresh cement, overturned and ignited a canvas covering.

project and turned hundreds of workers and their families into Red Sox fans."

Construction began in December, after Fenway's fall tenants—the Boston Redskins of the fledgling National Football League—finished their season. Yawkey's ambitious goal was to have New Fenway completed by Opening Day, 1934, and workers would have to labor through a cold New England winter to accomplish it. Crews used more than three dozen miniature furnaces to keep concrete from freezing. But when the intense heat generated by those kilns drew close to the wooden support structures into which the concrete was poured, it proved to be a disastrous combination.

Early in the afternoon of January 5, 1934, a "hot air explosion" (according to early reports) started a fire in the framework beneath the brand-new bleachers. First igniting the canvas covering the furnaces, the fire quickly spread to the wooden scaffolds. A police detail of 300—the largest deployed in years by the city—rushed to the scene, and several firefighters were injured while saving the bulk of the ballpark. "The flames started in and destroyed the wood work of the new bleachers in the process of construction in the centerfield area," the Associated Press reported. "Only effective action by firemen prevented the flames from spreading to the first and third base pavilions."

Just as with the blaze at Fenway eight years earlier, blustery weather was a negative influence. After destroying the new bleachers, wind-aided flames quickly spread to neighboring tire companies, auto dealers, and garages, causing explosions that "spread terror in the neighborhood and increased the danger to firemen," according to the AP. Insurance covered only part of the $250,000 in damage, and early newspaper reports cited a deal Yawkey had made to play games at Braves Field if Fenway renova-

A place as classy as the New Fenway demanded appropriate attire and, for some, a cigar—even if the stogie was a panatela, not a Churchill.

Getting to Fenway was no problem. There were plenty of cabs, ample automobile parking (at least for the first few decades), and brand-new streetcar lines.

tions were not completed by the Red Sox' home opener on April 17. Yawkey, however, vowed to make the deadline, and those who remembered the '26 Fenway fire couldn't help but notice the contrast in the club's reaction to this latest calamity. Whereas a cash-strapped Bob Quinn had been forced to leave portions of the ballpark literally in ashes, a cash-happy Yawkey planned to finish his repair job on schedule with no evidence of damage.

Employing three shifts of workers around the clock meant plenty of overtime, which gained Yawkey even more popularity with struggling Bostonians who needed the extra dough. Another much smaller fire on February 19 in virtually the same spot of the new bleachers as the January blaze stalled things yet again. That fire was determined to be arson—carried out, police speculated, as part of a planned bankroll theft that never transpired. Again Yawkey was unwavering, and he hired private armed guards to watch over the rest of the job.

His perseverance paid off, as nearly 33,000 fans arriving at New Fenway for Opening Day against the Washington Senators were treated to a beautiful venue. The wooden right-field bleachers had been rebuilt in concrete and extended into center field, and new concrete grandstands stood proudly in both right and left. The main grandstands running down the first- and third-base sides of the field had been largely redone, and topped with roofs. Thinking to the future as Charles and John I. Taylor had done with the initial design in 1911–12, Yawkey had the steel in these roofs reinforced so that upper decks could be added atop them later.

Reporters covering the opener for Boston's numerous daily newspapers spoke glowingly of the revisions. The open-air press box, situated high above home plate, was impressive as well, featuring a buffet-style lunch area where hungry scribes could partake of draught beer and

> "You never knew what would happen—pop-fly homers down the line, a ball ricocheting off the wall or bouncing off the [left-field] door. Center field, whoa. A guy could make a circus catch—or fall down and miss an inside-the-park homer. Nothing was uniform. Pal, let me tell ya, that was the miracle of the place."
>
> **—Former Speaker of the House Tip O'Neill, who represented Massachusetts' 8th and then 11th districts**

sandwiches before grabbing their portable typewriters and banging out their game stories. Western Union telegraphers stood by ready to grab each page as it was finished. They would send the stories via Morse code to editors at the newspaper offices, where the words would be fitted into lead type and then fed through the presses for inclusion in the next edition.

A Wall Rises

Of all the changes that the reporters wrote about, the most ink was spent describing what they had observed in left field. The 45-degree hill known as "Duffy's Cliff," which had been a defining characteristic of the park since its inception, had been largely flattened out. The 25-foot wooden wall behind it was replaced with a metal and concrete version that was taller (37 feet, 2 inches) and wider (231 feet) than anything seen in a ballpark before. The massive, 9,000-square-foot fence immediately became Fenway's defining feature. Striking fear into the hearts of pitchers and delighting right-handed batters who took aim at it from just over 300 feet away, this partition would be woven into the fabric and strategy of every game played at Fenway.

A common refrain cited in one form or another in the 1930s was passed down through the years, and it still says it best: The Wall can "giveth" (turning routine fly balls that sneak over its top into home runs) and it can "taketh away" (turning screaming line drives from potential homers into doubles or even "loud" singles when they slam against its surface and bounce back to waiting fielders).

With the Wall in mind, Yawkey, Collins, and Red Sox scouts sought to fill their lineup with right-handed batters who

Whiskey, razor blades, and vitamin pills; Fenway's left-field wall was nothing if not inclusive. The Wall would be ad-free from 1947 to 1999.

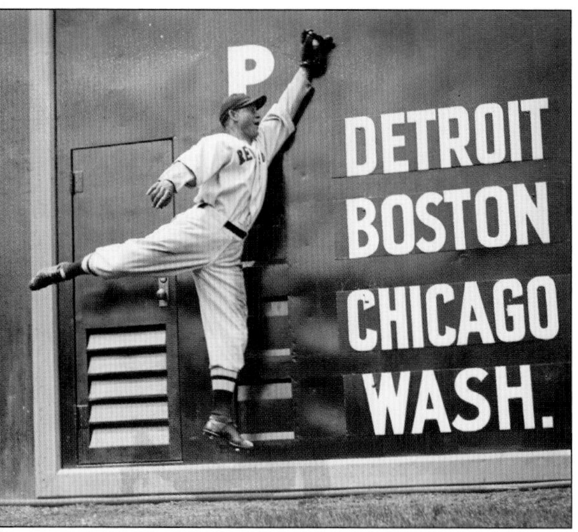

Although this photo was posed (not a genuine action shot), it provides a close-up look at the famous scoreboard and that mysterious door.

could regularly strike the ball off and over this imposing barrier. Left-handers, who more typically hit to right field, had a far tougher challenge in the revamped ballpark. Though only about five feet high, the fence in right-center field was 402 feet from home plate. As a result, many lefties would try to adapt their swings, taking aim at the inviting opposite-field target.

In addition to its impact on the game, the Wall served as an information source. It featured a huge new scoreboard that was run manually by workers who watched the action through narrow slits in its surface. Throughout each contest, these operators slid three-pound, metal, 16″ × 16″, alpha/numeric signs into place. The signs denoted the teams, pitchers (by number), line score, and other scores from around the American and National Leagues, which they picked up by radio and telegraph. Abbreviations—"NY" for the Yankees, "CLEV" for the Indians, and so forth—were used to denote the 16 big-league clubs, and with a quick glance fans in this pre-iPhone era could find out the score, inning, and pitchers at any AL or NL contest. Colored lights signifying balls (green), strikes (red), and outs (red) on the scoreboard also lit up as needed. "H" and "E" lights let patrons know if a questionable play had been ruled a hit or an error by the official scorer in the press box.

The scoreboard, which was in play and an additional source of bone-crunching body slams by leaping outfielders, wasn't the only thing adorning the Wall's face. The fence served yet another purpose for Yawkey: revenue generator. As with its smaller predecessor, the Wall was covered with colorful advertisements displayed above and around the scoreboard. The most popular were for Calvert Whiskey ("Clear Heads Choose Calvert"), Gem Razor Blades ("Avoid 5 O'Clock Shadow"), and Lifebuoy Soap ("Avoid B.O."). Depending on the outcome of a day's game, the illustration of a smiling ballplayer showering with Lifebuoy beneath the credo "The Red Sox Use It" might prompt a retort of "...and they still stink!" from smart-aleck fans. One thing nobody did, however, was refer to the Wall as the "Green Monster." For the

The Babe greets children at Fenway in 1933. Ruth always loved kids, whether they were street urchins or boys like these handsomely attired youngsters.

In this colorized photo from the early 1940s, it's hard to take your eyes off the ads in left field, which were more a distraction for fans than hitters. In 1940, the Red Sox were the only AL team to both score and give up more than five runs per game.

first 12 years of its life, its tin facing was a wide array of colors.

From the start, there was a sense of mystery about the Wall. Fans saw the small door beside the scoreboard and wondered, like Dorothy and her friends at the gates of Oz, what it was like back there. No photographs of the interior appeared publicly for decades, and those privileged few who had the chance to take a look found no Emerald City awaiting them. The cramped, dark space more closely resembled an old prison cell, with dirt floors, a few bare light bulbs, rough concrete walls, and no bathroom. It was cold in the spring and fall and stiflingly hot in the summer, but those who spent the baseball season there were the envy of all their friends. No prison cell ever had that kind of view.

Departures and Arrivals

It did not take long for Tom Yawkey to see the benefits of a revamped Fenway. In addition to providing a more comfortable and attractive setting for fans, the alterations had increased the park's seating capacity from 26,000 to 36,500 (a 29 percent boost). And although the Red Sox lost their April 17 opener to Washington, 6–5 in 10 innings, they drew 101,000 fans for their first five home games. An impressive feat on any level, this was even more noteworthy when one considered that it represented more than half of the team's attendance mark for the entire 77-game home season just two years before.

Those big crowds, however, were merely a warm-up for Sunday, April 22, when a record gathering of 44,631 jammed Fenway to see Babe Ruth's Yankees square off with the Sox. This was a decade before fire laws prohibited sports arenas and theaters from intentional overcrowding, but the park was so full that 8,000 more fans had to be turned away and mounted police called in to restore order. Ruth had—fittingly—been the first player to hit a ball over the new left-field wall the day before. He told reporters, with his typical bravado, that "I was more than happy to get that homer this afternoon, for they've been telling me that it's harder to hit them in the rebuilt Fenway Park. Listen, pal. It's just as easy as ever."

Four months later, with his skills quickly eroding due to age and girth, Ruth returned to Fenway for what fans expected would be his last visit in a Yankees uniform. An estimated 48,000 were on hand for an August 12 doubleheader, the largest gathering ever to see the Red Sox play in Boston (the paid attendance was 46,766). "Its enthusiasm overflowed all bounds," *The New York Times* reported of the crowd. "It also overflowed on the playing field in a solid mass from the right field foul line to the centre field flagpole, while outside the portals of the park some 15,000 more stormed and fumed in the streets because they could get no nearer to the scene."

He did not homer, but Ruth did have a single and double in the first game and two walks in the second. After the second base on balls, the Babe left the diamond in the sixth inning for a pinch runner as the crowd roared. He walked off with tears in his eyes, perhaps knowing that he would never again play at the ballpark where he had first shined two decades before. This was the case (save for a few exhibition games), but the Babe remains firmly etched in Fenway's record books. Through 2010, he and Mickey Mantle still held the mark for most homers at the ballpark by an opposing batter (with 38 each). As a pitcher, the Babe's .659 winning percentage and 2.19 ERA remained tops among all Red Sox left-handers with 100 decisions and 1,000 innings.

Despite Ruth's departure, plenty of talent still remained in the American League, and Yawkey made sure that many of these players wound up calling Fenway home. Rick Ferrell, the starting catcher in the first All-Star Game after coming to Boston in 1933, was a .302 hitter during his five seasons with the Red Sox. Brother Wes was runner-up for the league MVP Award in 1935, when he went 25–14 on the mound and batted .347 with seven homers at the plate. Bill Werber led the league in stolen bases in both 1934 and '35 and could slug the ball, too. And Doc Cramer was a fleet-footed center fielder and a consistent .300 hitter.

In addition, Yawkey spent his riches on three of the biggest stars who ever played the game. First on board was

Jersey City Defeats Birds, 2-
4TH VICTORY FOR LEFTY GROV

Johnstown Wins By 10 Lengths

BASEBALL
International League

National League

American League

Jersey City Beats Birds By 2 To 1

By HUGH TRADER, JR.

RENINGER FANS 7

Belmont Park Results

Lincoln Fields Results

Wins His Fourth Game

Lefty Grove (above) won his fourth game of the season today when he pitched the Boston Red Sox to an 11-4 victory over the Washington Senators.

SUFFOLK DOWNS RESULTS

Pitches To Trium Over N

Navy Stickm

Lefty Grove, pictured in *The Baltimore News Post,* had near-Hall of Fame career stats when he joined the Red Sox in 1934. He left his role as staff ace to become a supremely effective spot starter. The win here on May 27, 1939, was his fourth of the 15 he would net that season.

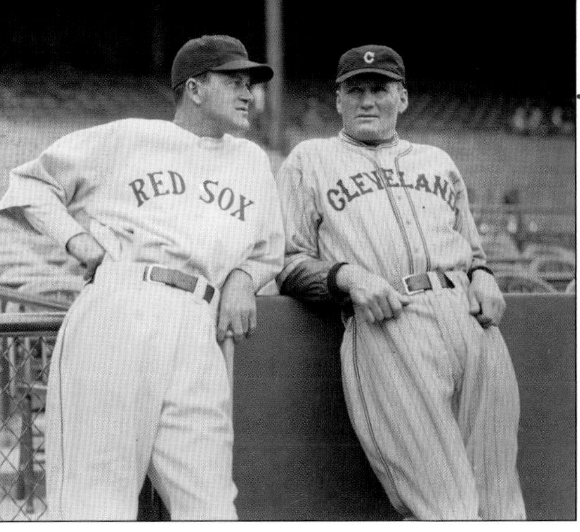

Joe Cronin, shown in conversation with Indians manager Walter Johnson in 1935, was the Sox shortstop/manager for a dozen years. A frequent All-Star in the field, he skippered Boston to four second-place finishes and one pennant.

Robert Moses "Lefty" Grove, who had been the American League's top pitcher with seven straight 20-win seasons and seven strikeout crowns for the Athletics before joining Boston's rotation in 1934. He promptly developed a sore arm, and after an 8–8 season it was rumored that A's owner/manager Connie Mack had offered Yawkey his $125,000 back. Yawkey stuck it out with Grove, and it paid off. Although he was never again the workhorse he had been for Mack, "Mose" became a crafty once-a-week pitcher who developed a forkball to compensate for lost velocity and was practically unbeatable at Fenway, going 50–14 at home from 1935 to '41. Grove led the league in ERA four times during the stretch, and in one three-year period he notched 20 consecutive victories in the shadow of the Wall.

Grove was also a fun-loving guy around the Fenway clubhouse. "You had to understand Lefty Grove," remembered Werber. "Grove was very fond of Mr. Yawkey, and Mr. Yawkey was very fond of him. Yawkey would come in there, and Grove would see him—Grove was a big fella, about 6-foot-3, 220 pounds, all muscle and bone—and he would grab hold of Yawkey and say, 'Come here, you little son of a bitch!' Then he would lift him off the floor and dance him around. Yawkey liked that camaraderie."

Joining this crew in 1935 was Joe Cronin, who had doubled as shortstop and manager for the Washington Senators. Cronin took on both roles for the Red Sox after Yawkey forked over a record $250,000 and incumbent shortstop Lyn Lary to Washington owner Clark Griffith. Like Grove, Cronin got off to a rough start in Boston. He made three errors in one of his first home

Brain in the Bullpen

The Red Sox may not have won any pennants during the late 1930s, but Fenway fans could still lay claim to having baseball's greatest mind in their midst. Backup catcher Moe Berg, who spent most of his time warming up pitchers or helping clubhouse boy Donald Davidson with his Latin homework, was a graduate of Princeton University and Columbia Law School who was quoted as saying, "I'd rather be a ballplayer than a Supreme Court Justice." Some may have questioned his choice. He had a lifetime batting average of .243, and it was said that he could "speak eight languages but hit in none of them."

Berg and Donald Davidson

A voracious reader who brought newspapers from around the world into the locker room, Berg would consider a paper "dead" and unreadable if a teammate touched it. And while he didn't get many opportunities to play, he handled his role with a good sense of humor. On August 9, 1939, after hitting his only double of the year off Fenway's left-field wall, he had sage advice for a rookie on the bench. "That's the way you are supposed to hit them, my boy," he told Ted Williams.

During World War II, Berg served as an undercover agent for the U.S. government, and among his missions was gathering information about Germany's nuclear program. *Said President Franklin Roosevelt, "I see Berg is still catching well."*

games at Fenway, which led to a showering of boos and a quick, tearful exit by his wife, Mildred. But an affable manner and a right-handed stroke that enabled him to pepper the Wall and drive in 90 to 110 runs a year helped turn around the fans, many of whom also shared Cronin's Irish-Catholic heritage.

Jimmie Foxx had no such growing pains after Yawkey plucked him and pitcher Johnny Marcum from the A's for $150,000 and two minor players in 1936. Perhaps the strongest man in the majors, "Double X" was a fun-loving gentle giant and a devastating right-handed hitter whose swing was perfect for Fenway's configurations. He totaled at least 35 home runs each season from 1936 to '40—leading the league twice—and in 1938 was named MVP after smashing 50 homers and pacing the AL with a .349 average and 175 runs batted in.

Double X was simply devastating at Fenway. His output in '38 included an incredible 35 home runs and 104 RBI in 74 home games, and he is one of just a handful of players to send a ball completely out of the park to the right of the center-field flagpole. Time and the huge shadow of Babe Ruth have since dimmed some of his accomplishments, but when Foxx ended an August 16, 1940, home game with a 10th-inning homer—the 494th blast of his career, passing Lou Gehrig's total—only Ruth had hit more.

Lillian Hopkins was another Fenway fixture who had a big year in 1938. Megaphone Lolly had been attending games regularly since the early 1930s, but it wasn't until that summer that she picked up her famous nickname. A fellow fan who had heard the nice lady in Section 14, Row 1, Seat 24 yelling herself hoarse each afternoon gave her the gift of a megaphone, and from that point on she was never without it. Cartoonists such as Gene Mack and Bob Coyne even started inserting Hopkins and her cone-shaped companion into some of their drawings, which appeared in the sports pages each day alongside the game stories.

Megaphone Lolly's fame spread in part because people were paying more attention to the Red Sox than they had in decades. Attendance at Fenway had taken a big leap. Getting beer back on sale at the ballpark after a long Prohibi-

Eagles Soar at Fenway

Although the Boston Redskins of the National Football League were a Fenway flop—drawing so poorly that their owner moved the franchise to Washington, D.C.—another local pigskin squad was a hit at the ballpark.

The Boston College Eagles, who called Fenway home for several seasons, were one of the nation's strongest teams in 1940 thanks in large part to triple-threat halfback "Chuckin'" Charlie O'Rourke. BC had already registered five shutouts and a 7–0 record when it played host at Fenway to Georgetown University, which entered the November 16 showdown on a 23-game unbeaten streak. The 40,000-plus fans who packed the ballpark saw BC recover from an early 10–0 deficit to take a 19–16 lead behind O'Rourke's passing attack. Then, pinned near his own end zone with a minute left, O'Rourke faked a punt and ran down the clock by darting back and forth, eluding tacklers before taking an intentional safety. Now up 19–18, the Eagles got a free kick and held on when a final Georgetown heave fell short beneath a darkening sky.

Two weeks later, another full house of 38,000 saw BC take on local rival Holy Cross, with a major bowl game awaiting the Eagles if they could win. Holy Cross, a huge underdog, battled the Eagles to a 0–0 stalemate and was minutes away from blemishing BC's perfect season when a fumbled punt set up an Eagles touchdown and a 7–0 victory. A month later, BC beat Tennessee in the Sugar Bowl to finish with an 11–0 record and a share of the national title.

In his day, the hyper-muscled Jimmie Foxx was second only to Ruth as a slugger. In six full seasons with Boston, he had 419 RBI in 420 Fenway games. "When Foxx hit a ball," Ted Williams said, "it sounded like gunfire."

Lolly Hopkins used her megaphone to cheer on her beloved Sox, but she wasn't averse to congratulating an opponent for a solid play as well. In this photo, she joins her gal pals at Braves Field.

These three Californians—Bobby Doerr, Ted Williams, and Dom DiMaggio (*left to right*)—were at the center of the Red Sox machine for years. All averaged well over .300 at Fenway, and none ever called another big-league park home.

tion-era hiatus didn't hurt, and there was plenty to drink to when the Sox rose all the way up to second place (behind the Yankees) in '38.

Next on the agenda for Yawkey and Collins was finding and developing young talent in the minor leagues, and here they hit pay dirt with three Californians acquired from the highly competitive Pacific Coast League. Second baseman Bobby Doerr was sure-handed with his glove from the start, and he developed into a consistent 20-homer, 100-RBI man. Bespectacled Dom "Little Professor" DiMaggio looked like a chemistry teacher but was a quick, brilliant centerfielder and leadoff man who played like a less powerful version of his brother Joe.

"They brought in the right field fence 20 feet and right away I was supposed to hit 75 home runs.... I thought I hit pretty good, .344 [in 1940], but I didn't hit the home runs I did the year before. I got a lot of catcalls and criticism. That just irked me enough so I got a little sour on everything and everybody."

—Ted Williams, on the alterations to the right-field stands, known as "Williamsburg"

Ted Williams, while no DiMaggio in the field, was one of the best hitters in the majors from the moment he debuted with Boston in 1939.

Foxx took the young Williams under his wing, and the pair formed a devastating power punch in the middle of the Boston lineup. In 1940, they were two of five Red Sox (along with Doerr, Cronin, and third baseman Jim Tabor) to hit more than 20 homers. The Fenway Millionaires held first place in the American League into late June before lackluster pitching eventually doomed them to fourth place. The staff was so depleted that even Williams took a turn on the Fenway mound, pitching the final two innings of a blowout loss to the pennant-bound Tigers in August and allowing one run on three hits.

By now, Ken Coleman's own dreams of Fenway glory had taken a big blow. A strong player in Quincy's youth baseball leagues, he was accidentally shot in the face in November 1939 by a neighborhood kid horsing around with a BB gun—blinding him in his left eye. During his recovery in the winter of 1940, Coleman spent a lot of time playing a game of "dice baseball" he had created himself. As he sat at the kitchen table, he was transported back to the Fenway bleachers, and he began doing play-by-play like he had heard Red Sox broadcasters Fred Hoey, Frankie Frisch, and Tom Hussey do on the radio.

He wasn't aware of it then, but Coleman was setting the stage for his future career—and many more trips to Fenway without the need for a ticket.

Welcome to "Williamsburg"

Although Ted Williams hit 31 homers as a rookie in 1939, Red Sox manager Joe Cronin felt the best was yet to come—if some changes could be made.

"Our long right field is ruining the value of Ted Williams, who hits the ball a mile—to right," Cronin told reporters that August. "They play him way back and catch most everything he hits. On the road, it has been different. He can shoot for the right-field fences in every other park.... He's leading the league in runs batted in, but he drives in twice as many on the road as at home."

The disparity wasn't nearly that dramatic—Williams totaled 17 homers and 77 RBI in away games during '39, compared to 14 and 68 at Fenway—but management still decided to give its young star an easier target. Prior to the 1940 season, workers constructed more bleacher seats and new home and visiting team bullpens in front of Fenway's existing right-field wall. These alterations cut the distance required for a homer from 402 to 382 feet in that part of the park.

Writers dubbed the new additions "Williamsburg," and Ted took the further step of gaining weight over the winter to help gain power. It didn't come right away; Williams actually hit *fewer* home runs (23) during the 1940 season, with just nine of them coming at home. But in the two years after that, he led the league with 37 and 36, with plenty of them taking up residence in Williamsburg.

CHAPTER 4

Near Misses

1941–1951

After the misery of wartime baseball, Red Sox fans flocked to Fenway when the stars returned. The Sox bashed their way to a 331–132 home record from 1946 to '51, yet they never did go all the way, losing a seven-game World Series in '46 and a playoff to Cleveland two years later.

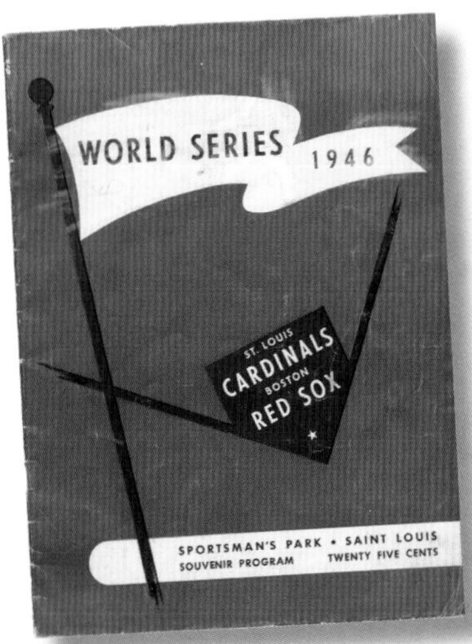

The Sox couldn't have come closer to a world title than in the 1946 Series, when they lost Game 7 in the bottom of the eighth on Enos Slaughter's "Mad Dash."

Elizabeth Dooley shifted nervously in her seat as she looked out at the scene in front of her. Everything was so green, it was almost as if you couldn't tell where the grass ended and the walls began. She had been going to games at Fenway Park all of her life, and she had acquired her own season tickets several years before. Never, she thought on this summer day in 1948, had the ballpark looked so beautiful.

As always, the left-field Wall was the first thing to catch her eye. Once covered in advertisements that pushed booze, soap, and razor blades, it was now painted a lush green that matched the shorter outfield fences. Sportswriters had started calling the Wall the "Green Monster," but Dooley thought it was more serene than scary. As a teacher, "Lib" knew that too much information could distract kids from a lesson. Similarly, with the ads gone from the Wall, she found it easier to focus on the game.

Dooley did not consider herself a fan. She called herself a "friend of the Red Sox," and the ballplayers shared this feeling. Before and after games, they sometimes stopped by her front-row seat, right behind the home team's on-deck circle, to sample the latest cookies the 29-year-old redhead had made for them. Now, as Dom DiMaggio walked by on his way to the plate, he gave Dooley a quick smile. The Sox were down 8–6 heading into the bottom of the ninth. But the way they had been playing, DiMaggio and his teammates were confident they could make up the deficit.

Lib was not so sure, and as she continued to fidget, her father offered her a peanut from the brown paper bag in his lap. Jack Dooley was now in his seventh decade as a Boston baseball fan; he had been going to Fenway since it opened in 1912. Changes had come, like the addition of the big Wall

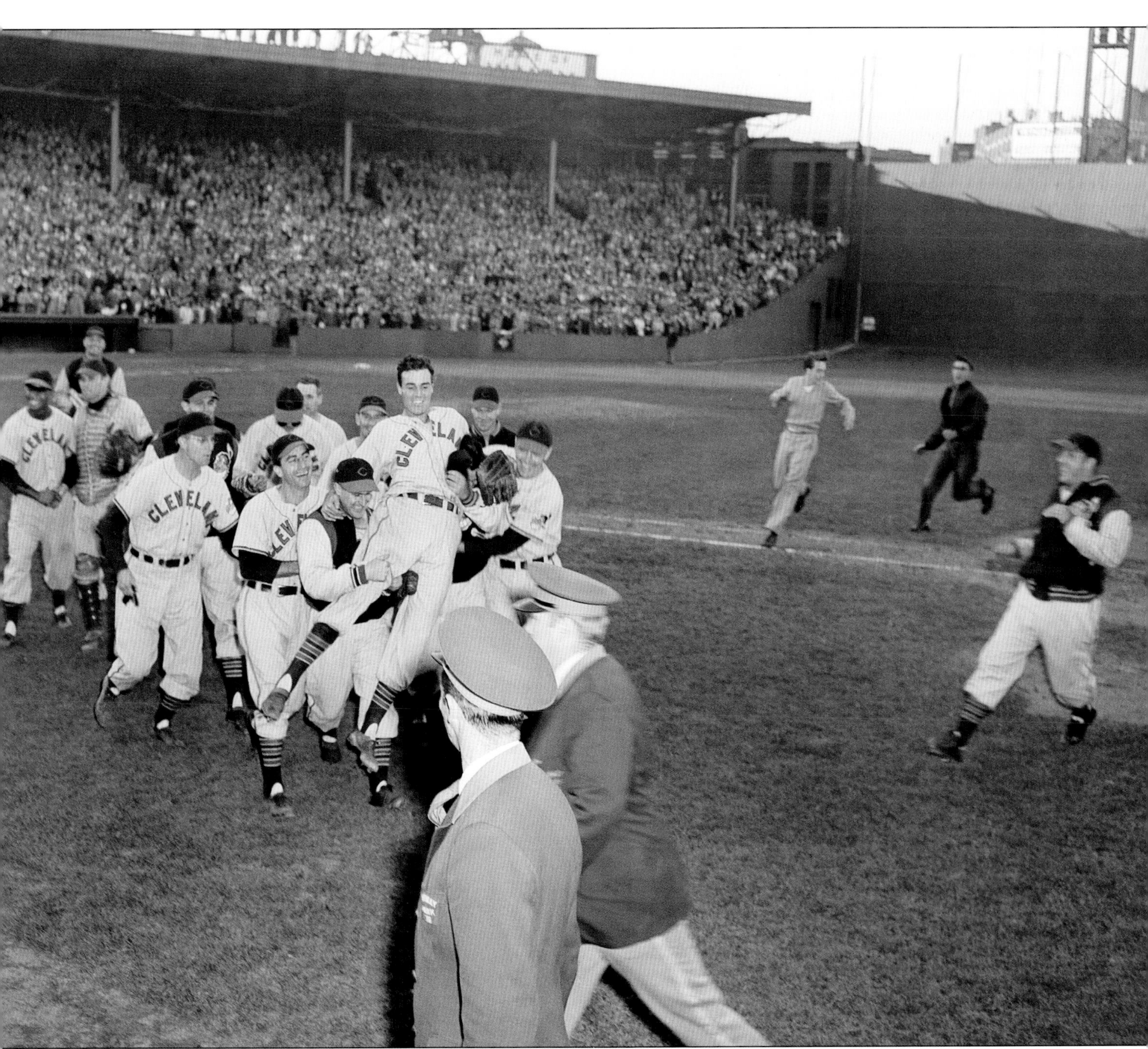

Indians right-hander Gene Bearden is carried off the field after shutting down the Red Sox on five hits in the 1948 AL playoff game.

In 1947, Fenway became the 14th big-league park to add lights. Here they shine at 4:30 in the afternoon because of smoke blowing down from Canadian forest fires.

in the '30s and the light towers (installed the previous year, 1947) that made night games like this one possible. Still, Jack felt a sense of continuity being in the same place where he had watched Tris Speaker, Joe Wood, and Babe Ruth excel.

Even the guy Jack bought his peanuts from this evening, Peter Davis, was the same vendor who had been peddling them from his cart in front of Fenway since the ballpark's first Opening Day 36 years earlier. Davis's son, George, was now at his side, and the younger man brought panache to his job by flipping the bags to customers after getting their nickels. Perhaps he saw this method as a good-luck charm. When he had joined his dad and started his tossing technique two years earlier, the Red Sox made the World Series for the first time in nearly three decades.

Now people were talking about the Series again, as the Sox were on a hot streak that had taken them from seventh place to within a half-game of the night's opponent, the American League-leading Cleveland Indians. Over in the National League, the Boston Braves were in first by a healthy 3½ games, so if the Sox could win this game, both Boston teams would be August front-runners for the first time since 1916. The Dooleys and countless other locals were hoping for an October showdown in which all one needed to travel to every game of the World Series was a dime for the Commonwealth Avenue streetcar.

Getting tickets, however, would be another story. Due to postwar prosperity, more folks than ever were venturing into the city for entertainment, and Fenway was a popular destination. The Red

Sox were on pace to set a new attendance record for the third straight year, and reserved seating for this evening's game had long since sold out. When 8,500 bleacher seats went on sale in the afternoon, lines outside Fenway's ticket office (located beside the park's main entrance) snaked for blocks down Brookline Avenue. An estimated 18,000 people were turned away, and one club official said the Sox could have sold 70,000 seats—more than twice the ballpark's official capacity, and way beyond its bursting point—if they had met everybody's demand.

In addition to a battle for first place and the novelty of a night game (one of about 15 on Boston's home schedule), another reason for the frenzied interest was Cleveland's starting pitcher: Leroy "Satchel" Paige. A Negro League legend, Paige had been added to the Indians roster in early July, making him the first African-American pitcher in AL history. The gangly, ageless right-hander entered action on August 24 with a record of 5–1. When the Indians took a two-run lead early on against the Sox, it appeared they would be able to maintain their hold on first place.

But Paige was soon knocked around as well, and the contest turned into a slugfest that Cleveland led 8–6 going into the bottom of the ninth. DiMaggio doubled to right-center leading off for Boston, and Johnny Pesky singled him to third. A deep fly ball by Ted Williams scored DiMaggio, and then Vern Stephens crushed the first pitch from reliever Russ Christopher for a two-run homer and a 9–8 Boston victory. Fans celebrated as if the Sox had just won the pennant, and the next day sports columnists postulated whether this would be the game looked back on as the key to a championship run.

Wishful thinking. Near misses were the order of the day for the 1941–51 Red Sox, who may have been the most talented team in baseball history to never win a World Series. While they did capture an American League championship in 1946, they lost a seven-game World Series to the St. Louis Cardinals that fall. In 1948 and '49, they were beaten out for AL pennants in the final game of each season. Several other second- and third-place finishes further frustrated Tom Yawkey's club, which despite

In 1949, the Red Sox needed to win only one of their final two games against the Yankees to land the AL flag. But they couldn't, making this "phantom" World Series pin an obscure collector's item.

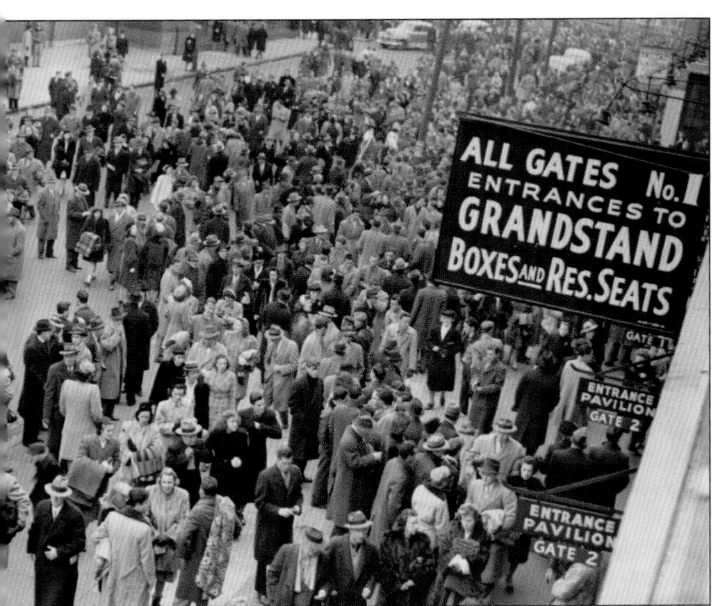

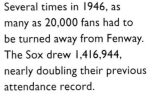

Several times in 1946, as many as 20,000 fans had to be turned away from Fenway. The Sox drew 1,416,944, nearly doubling their previous attendance record.

This stunning pennant dates from the postwar era, when interest in the national game soared to new heights.

having All-Stars at nearly every position and routinely crushing opponents at Fenway Park was unable to win when it mattered most.

Numerous reasons were blamed for the pattern. World War II depleted the Boston roster more than perhaps any other big-league team, removing four Hall of Fame-caliber players from the lineup in the prime of their careers. In addition, the failure by Yawkey and General Manager Eddie Collins to be trend-setters in breaking the game's racial barriers kept the Sox from signing some of the most dynamic players of all time. Moreover, management tailored the team too much to the confines of Fenway Park, leading to sub-par performances on the road. Finally, Yawkey paid his players *too* well, critics claimed, so they lacked the extra drive that athletes on more frugal clubs possessed to strive for World Series berths and the bonus money that came with them.

Likely it was a little of everything, along with a healthy dose of bad luck. But one thing was undeniable: While there was little for Red Sox fans to celebrate at the end of each season during this period, they had plenty to be excited about *each day* they came to the ballpark. War was raging on distant shores, and soldiers from New England and throughout the country were making the ultimate sacrifice. But Fenway served as an oasis—a place where anything was possible and the good guys usually won.

The 502-Foot Poke

Joseph Boucher was looking forward to a fun, uneventful time at the ballpark when he arrived at Fenway on June 9, 1946, for a Sunday doubleheader. He wound up with a big headache.

From his spot in the right-center-field bleachers—which were then true bleachers (benches), rather than individual seats—the 56-year-old construction engineer from Albany, New York, was some 500 feet from home plate. Imagine his surprise, then, when he saw a Ted Williams home run off Tigers right-hander Fred Hutchinson heading straight for him in the first inning of the second game. "All we could do was duck," he later recalled of seeing the ball emerge out of the glaring sun. "They say it bounced a dozen rows higher, but after it hit my head I was no longer interested."

The homer not only left its mark on Boucher's noggin, it crushed his straw hat as well. And if Boucher wasn't pleased, Boo Ferriss certainly was; the blast got him "headed" on the way to his 10th straight victory. Today, a red seat in a sea of green (Section 42, Row 37, Seat 21) marks the approximate spot where the 502-foot blast did its damage. Fans often stop by before and after games to take photos of Fenway's most legendary landing spot.

Seeking 300 and .400

The Red Sox of 1941 were a team in transition. The star players purchased by Yawkey in the early years of his ownership—Jimmie Foxx, Lefty Grove, Joe Cronin—were aging, and the young acquisitions of more recent vintage were emerging as stars in their own right. Bobby Doerr was now generally considered, along with Joe Gordon of the Yankees, to be the best second baseman in the American League. Though unimposing in appearance, Dom DiMaggio was a terrific defensive centerfielder with surprising pop. And Ted Williams—well, he had quickly become the center of the universe at Fenway Park.

"As a young person, I knew that every girl in the ballpark was madly in love with him. But I guess I was different. I looked at him as someone who didn't need any of us yet. So I said to him once, 'You go play ball, and when you're finished, then you'll know who your friends are.' So he kind of latched on to me—and we became like brother and sister."

—Season-ticket holder Lib Dooley, on bonding with Ted Williams at Fenway

Shifted over to left field in 1940, away from his adoring fans in right, Williams had found that the patrons who congregated in the shadow of the Wall were a bit more demanding. When he didn't go far enough beyond the promise of his outstanding rookie season to please the critics—hitting fewer home runs despite the addition of the shallower right-field fences of "Williamsburg"—he began hearing boos from the stands and reading unflattering things in the newspapers. Understandably hurt, he reacted impulsively and lashed back at his critics. He stopped tipping his cap and started talking about quitting baseball and becoming a fireman. Never did his nickname of "The Kid" seem more appropriate.

The defensive change had been made to minimize Williams's shortcomings. While he possessed a strong throwing arm, he was not very quick and had a

With Williams at bat, the shift is on. Three opposing infielders patrol the right side, daring the slugger to change his style. Cleveland manager Lou Boudreau had popularized the "Williams Shift" in 1946.

With the smallest foul territory in baseball, Fenway fans are right on top of the action. Snagging foul balls is a long tradition.

hard time chasing down balls hit to Fenway's deep right-field corners. He had committed 19 errors as a rookie, the most of any American League outfielder, and in left there was far less ground to cover. He worked hard to learn the ways of the Wall, how balls reacted when they hit off different spots of its concrete and tin surface or bounced around in the nooks and crannies of the scoreboard. For a bright young man who liked perfecting new skills—tinkering with cameras, making his own fishing lures—this was the type of challenge he embraced. While The Kid would never become an outstanding fielder, he would master the Wall.

At the plate, Williams made the slight changes necessary to reverse his drop-off in power. The Red Sox had an up-and-down start to the 1941 season, but Ted went on a 23-game hitting streak in May and June, during which he slammed nine home runs and raised his average from .308 to .425. Once again, the Yankees were playing at a pace that put them far in front of the pack, and by midsummer the major storyline at Fenway became a case of will he or won't he. It had been 11 years since any big-leaguer had batted .400, and fans and sportswriters began speculating whether The Kid could attain that magical figure.

For a while, Williams shared the national spotlight with Yankees superstar Joe DiMaggio, who was in pursuit of another offensive touchstone: Willie Keeler's record 44-game hitting streak. As DiMaggio neared and passed the mark—reaching 56 games before being stopped—Ted kept an interested party informed of his progress. "Ted was friendly with the man who operated the scoreboard in left field at Fenway Park, Bill Daley," Dom DiMaggio later explained. "Each time my brother would get a hit, Daley would holler out to Ted in left field through an opening in the scoreboard, and then Ted would yell over to me, 'Hey, Dom! Joe just got a double!'"

As Williams was continuing his own quest into midsummer, teammate Lefty Grove also got a great deal of attention. The legendary pitcher was now 41 and nearing the end of the line. His 20-game home winning streak was snapped in June, and after reaching 299 career victories he lost his next two starts in pursuit of No. 300 (a figure just 11 hurlers had then reached). Fenway fans feared that "Mose" might never attain the mark when he fell behind 4–0 on July 25. But the Red Sox rallied, and longtime teammate Jimmie Foxx—his own skills rapidly declining—came through with a tie-breaking triple in Boston's 10–6 triumph.

Grove would never win another game, and the Sox were nearly 20 arrears of the Yankees by early September. All eyes were now on Williams, and he didn't disappoint. Leaving Fenway for Boston's last road trip in possession of a .406 average, he finished with this same mark a week later after going 6-for-8 at Philadelphia—including his league-leading 37th home run—in a season-ending doubleheader.

With Grove (retired) and Foxx (released) both gone by the middle of the 1942 season, and manager Cronin reducing his own playing time due to the swift emergence of Johnny Pesky at shortstop, the torch had been fully passed. Williams, DiMaggio, Pesky, and Doerr would form the nucleus of the team for the next decade—and would become lifelong friends in the process.

Lost Years, Lost Chances

Unfortunately, this quartet would have three years of its on-field partnership taken away. America entered World War II after the December 7, 1941, bombing at Pearl Harbor, and while President Franklin Roosevelt encouraged professional baseball to continue for the good of morale, players throughout the majors were required to serve in the military if eligible. After a 1942 season in which they led the second-place Red Sox to their most wins (93) since Babe Ruth was a rookie—paced by the first of Williams's two "Triple Crown" seasons in which he led the league in average, homers, and RBI—Ted and Pesky joined the Naval Air Corps and DiMaggio the Coast Guard. Other Boston players quickly

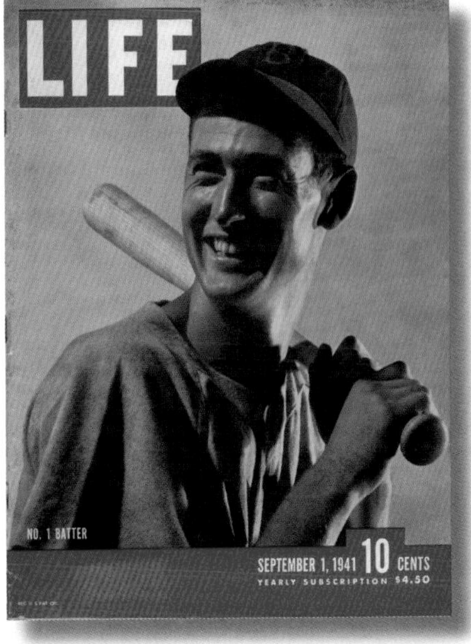

For this September 1941 issue, *Life* put Ted Williams on the cover even though its main story was Operation Barbarossa—Germany's invasion of the Soviet Union. Williams served as a fighter pilot during the war and missed the 1943 to '45 seasons.

After the Red Sox passed on him, Sam Jethroe (featured on this Bowman baseball card) went on to belt 49 homers and steal 98 bases in three big-league seasons—all (except for one at-bat) with the crosstown Boston Braves.

followed suit. Just when his club had seemed poised to challenge the Yankees in the American League, manager Cronin was left scrambling to replace half the roster.

All major-league teams were in the same boat, but the timing was especially devastating for the Red Sox. The heart of the team was pulled out right as it was jelling, and over the next three years a succession of raw youngsters, aging veterans, and assorted 4Fs (men unfit for military service) took their place at Fenway. Of the three holdovers from Boston's 1942 starting lineup who remained in '43—Doerr, third baseman Jim Tabor, and first baseman Tony Lupien—only Doerr was a consistent offensive threat. Moreover, just one starting pitcher—left-hander Tex Hughson, a 22-game winner as a rookie in '42—was of All-Star caliber. The team's farm system could not come up with replacements quick enough.

In the year before this talent exodus, only the Yankees drew better than the Red Sox among American League teams. But for the bulk of the war, attendance fell off more sharply at Fenway than at other AL ballparks. Even Boston's presence in a watered-down 1944 pennant race couldn't bring the big crowds out. Once Hughson and the team's two best hitters (Doerr and catcher Hal Wagner) got their calls to report for military duty late that summer, the Red Sox fell from contention.

The biggest winner at Fenway Park in '44 was President Roosevelt, who held his final campaign rally there on November 4, three days before securing his fourth term. "Our young men and young women are fighting not only for their existence, and their homes and their families," he told a crowd of 40,000. "They also are fighting for a country and a world where men and women of all races, colors, and creeds can live, work, speak, and worship—in peace, freedom, and security."

Roosevelt would not live to see the war's end or even the start of the next baseball season. But four days after his death on April 12, 1945, Fenway served as the venue for an incident that showed that the freedoms he spoke of were not yet guaranteed to all.

Three Negro League players—Sam Jethroe, Jackie Robinson, and Marvin Williams—were given an informal tryout with the Red Sox under the supervision of 79-year-old coach Hugh Duffy. The event was the result of a decade of work on the part of the Negro press, including Mabray "Doc" Kountze of the *Boston Guardian* and *Transcript.* The black press lobbied in print and closed-door meetings for the breaking of the unofficial color line that had kept African-American players out of the majors since the late 19th century. The mainstream media picked up the story when Isadore Muchnick, a member of the Boston City Council, threatened to block renewal of the license granting the Red Sox and Braves the right to play Sunday baseball unless they took steps to change what he called baseball's "pre-Civil War attitude toward American citizens because of the color of their skin."

General Manager Collins wrote to Muchnick that the Red Sox would gladly

"It's a great place to watch a ballgame, and to pitch in. I always thought the wall could help somebody as much as it could hurt them. Those line drives might be out of a park with low fences, but at Fenway you could hold them to a single or maybe a double. You might even be able to throw them out at second base, because the ball would get out there so quick."

—Pitcher Boo Ferriss, 33–12 lifetime at Fenway Park

grant a tryout if asked, so Muchnick and Wendell Smith of the *Pittsburgh Courier*—the leading African-American sportswriter of the day—rounded up Jethroe, Robinson, and Williams and brought them to Boston. Initially the Red Sox stalled, but further media pressure secured the April 16 tryout. The three performed well as Muchnick, Smith, Cronin, and a few reporters watched from the stands, but the ballplayers would later say they never felt they were given sincere consideration. Told by Duffy that they would hear from the Red Sox soon, they never did. And as they were leaving, according to *Boston Globe* writer Cliff Keane, an unseen voice from the back of the grandstands yelled, "Get those niggers off the field!"

Newspapers made only brief mention of the tryout (without the slur), and it soon fell off the radar. "The time just wasn't right," Jethroe would say in the early 1990s. But it was right for Brooklyn Dodgers President Branch Rickey when he signed both Robinson (later in 1945) and Jethroe (in 1948) to contracts. Each blossomed into a National League Rookie of the Year—Jethroe after being sold to the Boston Braves, making him the city's first African-American big-leaguer. And rather than break the color line, the Red Sox would be the last major-league team to cross it more than a decade later—after Robinson had already led the Dodgers to seven pennants and a world championship.

With this dark, unspoken cloud already hanging over the start of the 1945 season, things got worse in a hurry when Cronin, starting himself at third base out of necessity, broke his leg in the year's third game and quit playing entirely. An 0–8 start hinted at the seventh-place fin-

They called him "Boo," and he certainly scared AL batsmen, especially in Fenway Park. But arm injuries derailed Dave Ferriss, and he won his last big-league game at age 26. His lifetime record was 65–30, including 33–12 at Fenway.

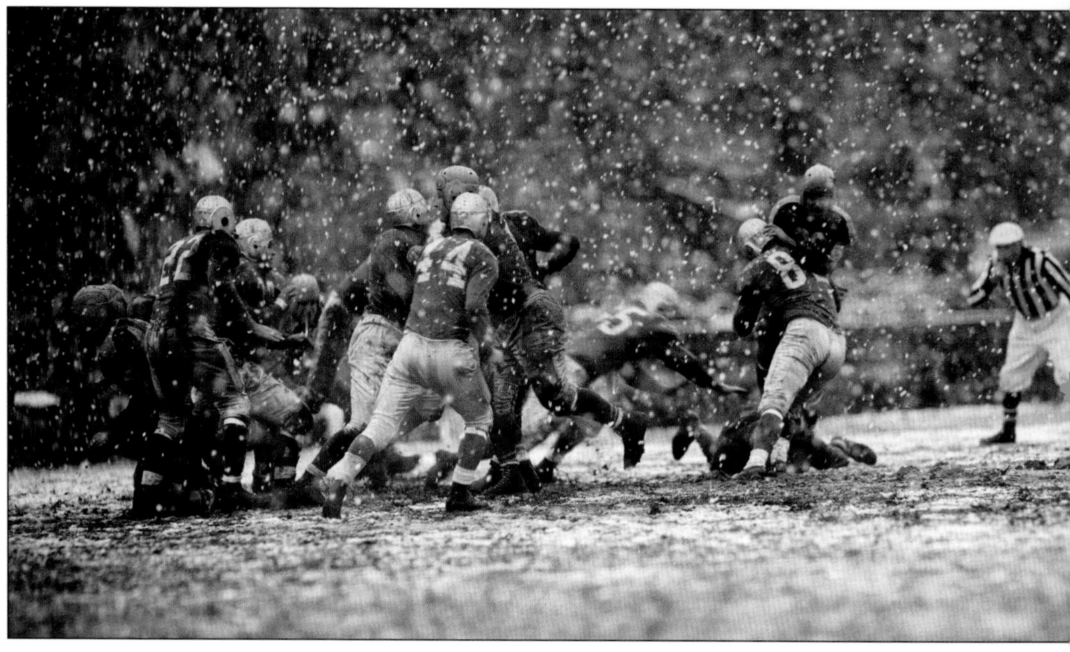

The NFL's Boston Yanks, who played their home games at Fenway, went 14–38–3 in their five years of existence (1944–48). Owner Ted Collins had named the team Yanks because he initially wanted the club to be based in New York and play in Yankee Stadium.

ish to come, but in mid-May the skies over Fenway began clearing a bit each time rookie pitcher Dave "Boo" Ferriss took the mound. Discharged from the service due to asthma, the right-hander from Mississippi threw 22 straight scoreless innings to begin his big-league career and won his first eight decisions—four by shutout. Home attendance shot up on the days he pitched. Despite a late-season asthma flare-up, Ferriss finished with a 21–10 record, making him the only Boston pitcher with more than eight victories for a 71–83 team.

The All-Star Game originally scheduled for Fenway in '45 was postponed a year due to wartime travel restrictions. But on July 10, the ballpark hosted one of seven exhibition contests between American and National League clubs held to benefit the American Red Cross and United War Relief funds. In Boston, this naturally meant a battle between the Red Sox and the NL's Braves, who had been getting together for "City Series" games at Fenway and Braves Field just before the regular season for decades. As 22,809 fans looked on, along with 846 servicemen and servicewomen, the Red Sox prevailed 8–1. More importantly, approximately $70,000 was raised for the cause.

It didn't count in the standings, but the lopsided win was good practice for what folks would be witnessing on a regular basis the next spring. The war was winding down, and Williams and Co. were about to trade uniforms.

Highs and Lows

The Fenway faithful had been patient for four years, and in 1946 they were rewarded for six months with the most entertaining and successful Red Sox team since the dynasty clubs of the 1912–18 era. Going an almost unfathomable 41–9 out of the gate, including a 15-game winning streak and a 28–4 start at home, Boston quickly distanced itself from the rest of the American League. A top-of-the-order quartet of DiMaggio, Pesky, Williams, and Doerr experienced a joyous reunion, producing runs at a better clip than any first four in baseball. New first baseman Rudy York flourished with 119 RBI while hitting behind this group. In addition, the pitching staff was deeper than ever with Hughson, Ferriss, Mickey Harris, and Joe Dobson winning in double figures and Earl Johnson leading a strong bullpen corps. Shining brightest were Williams (who earned his first MVP Award with .342, 38, 123 totals) and Ferriss (whose 25–6 record included a perfect 13–0 mark at home).

Despite a late-season slump that included six straight road losses before their pennant-clinching victory in Cleveland on September 13, the Red Sox finished with a 104–50 record and a 12-game advantage over second-place Detroit. Boston was a heavy favorite to win the ensuing World Series over the St. Louis Cardinals, in part because the Cards were expected to be drained after their hard-fought NL pennant race had ended in a tie with the Brooklyn Dodgers, necessitating a three-game playoff. In the end, though, the extra time did the Sox more harm than good. Boston management scheduled a pair of exhibitions at Fenway against a team of American League All-Stars to keep its club fresh, and midway through the first game Williams was hit in the right elbow by a pitch from Washington right-hander Mickey Haefner.

The seriousness of the injury was unclear heading into the World Series. And while Williams never used it as an excuse, his .200 average with no extra-

PAGE 20 — THE INDIANAPOLIS STAR

Great Pitching, 14-Hit Barrage Give American League Stars 12

Margin Most One-Sided In History Of Classic

By GAYLE TALBOT

Tribesmen Break Even In Twin Bill With Blues

By W. BLAINE PATTON, Sports Editor The Star

An Elevator Rescue

Charley Keller of the American League team scores after walloping a home run in the first inning of the game yesterday at Boston with the National League All-Stars. Ted Williams (9) tallied ahead of Keller. Bobby Doerr is at upper left, the catcher is Walker Cooper and the bat boy is in the foreground. (Associated Press Wirephoto to The Star.)

Cardinals Waive | **Hawks Handed** | **Red Sox Obtain**

The Indianapolis Star showcases a 1946 All-Star Game home run by New York's Charlie "King Kong" Keller, not one of the two by Ted Williams, who is about to congratulate Keller.

The '46 All-Star Game

For the Red Sox and their fans, the 1946 All-Star Game at Fenway felt in many ways like just another day at the ballpark. Four of the first five batters in the American League's starting lineup were Red Sox—Dom DiMaggio, Johnny Pesky, Ted Williams, and Bobby Doerr—and they were joined on the AL roster by four Boston teammates: Boo Ferriss, Mickey Harris, Hal Wagner, and Rudy York.

Williams, as he had a tendency to do at Fenway, stole the show. He went 4-for-4 with a walk, five RBI, and two home runs, the second of which he crushed in the eighth inning off Pirates hurler Rip Sewell's high-arcing, fast-dropping "eephus" pitch. The AL won the game 12–0.

Red Sox owner Tom Yawkey got another piece of good news when he learned that the City of Boston had reassessed Fenway Park at $900,000—up from $780,000. For the All-Star Game, the venue "never looked better," according to one reporter, as it featured a temporary press box on the roof capable of seating more than 300. With the Red Sox currently in first place, Yawkey hoped the extra space would be needed come October.

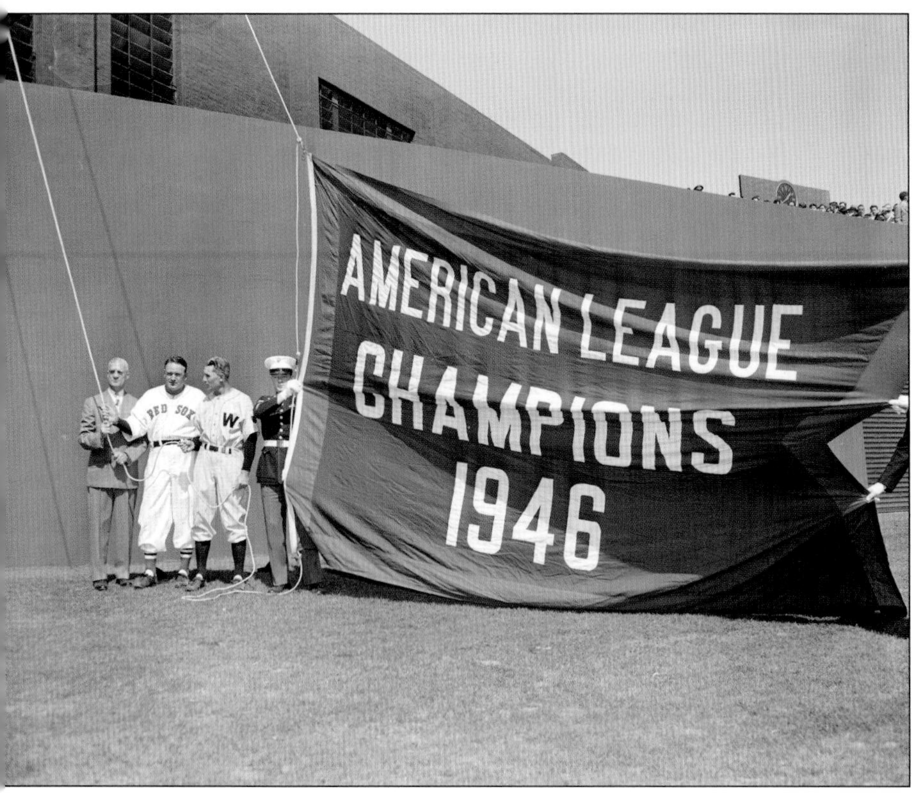

AL President Will Harridge joins Red Sox manager Joe Cronin and Senators skipper Ossie Bluege in hoisting this huge banner, which celebrates the Red Sox' first pennant in 28 years.

base hits or RBI over the seven games made it clear that he was not at full strength. Doerr (.409) was the only Boston regular to bat .300. While Ferriss ran his Fenway record to 14–0 with a Game 3 shutout, the Sox allowed the Cardinals to tie the series three times and force a winner-take-all finale at Sportsman's Park. Boston rallied from an early deficit to tie the seventh game 3–3, but St. Louis scored the title-clinching run in the eighth when a hard-charging Enos Slaughter went from first to home on a long Harry Walker single. It was the first time the Red Sox had ever lost a World Series—they had prevailed in five previous appearances—but the setback began a string of heartbreaking near misses.

The 1947 season was a washout, as injuries to pitchers Hughson, Ferriss, and Harris overshadowed Williams's second Triple Crown and the introduction of both the all-green Wall and night games at Fenway. Yawkey bumped Cronin up to general manager and brought aboard Yankee legend Joe McCarthy as field boss. McCarthy had captured seven world championships with New York, and his first two Boston clubs, in 1948 and '49, each won an impressive 96 games.

This was, however, two games too few. After a feverish summer-long battle between the Red Sox, Yankees, and Indians, Cleveland captured the 1948 pennant by defeating the Sox in a one-game playoff at Fenway—denying Bostonians their first ever "Subway Series" between the Sox and the National League champion Braves (who the Indians would beat as well). Then, in 1949, the Yankees did in their old skipper by taking the last two must-win games in the Bronx, when a victory in either contest would have given Boston the title. Fans who had lined up outside an empty Fenway for World Series tickets and listened to the finale on portable radios left empty-handed after Boston's ninth-inning rally fell just short.

Big challenges came in 1950, as a hard-drinking McCarthy resigned in midseason—reportedly for health reasons—and Williams injured his elbow making a leaping catch in the All-Star Game. The injury shelved The Kid for two months, but Boston rallied behind new manager Steve O'Neill to play .675

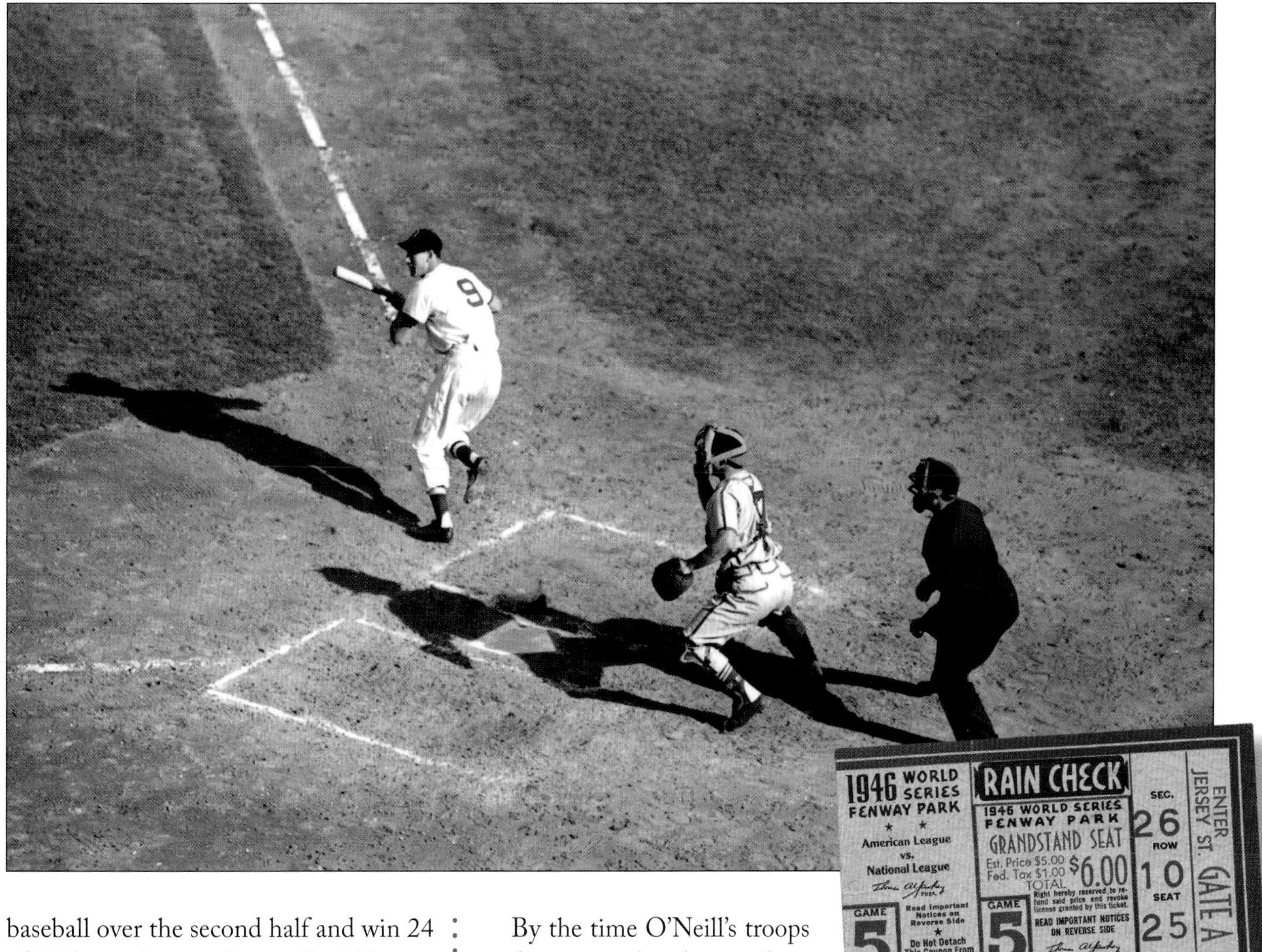

Occasionally, Ted Williams would attack the shift. Here he bunts toward third for a single in Game 3 of the '46 Series. It was one of Ted's five hits—all singles—in the Series. This ticket was for Game 5, a 6–3 Red Sox win at Fenway.

baseball over the second half and win 24 of 27 down the stretch to pull within one game of the Yankees in late September. This Boston club was the ultimate Fenway juggernaut, with nine regulars hitting .294 or higher, a .302 team average, three 120-RBI men (including rookie Walt Dropo), and a batting champion in Billy Goodman who couldn't crack the starting lineup. The Sox even had two 20-game winners in Ellis Kinder and Mel Parnell, but it wasn't enough. Four straight losses in the final week doomed them to third.

By the time O'Neill's troops made yet another late push to catch New York in 1951, even Boston's own front office staff was conditioned to expect the worst. Three mid-September losses prompted Red Sox officials to cancel reservations for out-of-town reporters to stay at Boston's Somerset Hotel during the World Series. When the Sox won six of seven, an attempt was quickly made to rebook the rooms. Conventioneers had already secured them, however, and when news of this breach of faith broke in the

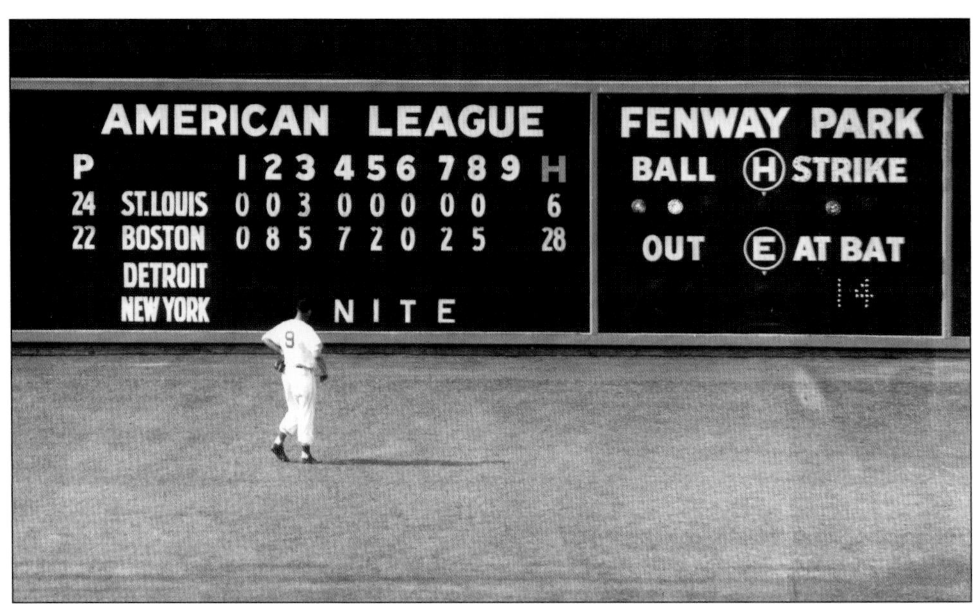

Fenway's obliging dimensions resulted in impressive slugging, as Ted Williams can see here. In this June 1950 game, Al Zarilla had four doubles, Bobby Doerr cracked three homers, and Williams and Vern Stephens belted two homers apiece in a 29–4 lambasting of the Browns. The day before, the Sox had beaten St. Louis 20–4.

The 1948 Playoff

Despite all the near-miss moments the Red Sox experienced from 1942 to '51, only one true winner-take-all game was played at Fenway Park during the period. And while most fans were not happy with the result, a few gentlemen didn't mind at all.

After finishing the regular season deadlocked with 96–58 records, the Red Sox and Indians squared off in the first one-game playoff in American League history on October 4, 1948. The Sox had earned home field advantage through a coin flip, but that was where their luck ran out. Boston manager Joe McCarthy shocked players and fans by giving the starting nod to journeyman pitcher Denny Galehouse, an aging, once-solid hurler who had a much less distinguished record than rested aces Mel Parnell and Ellis Kinder. McCarthy based his decision on the fact that Galehouse was a veteran right-hander who had pitched well against Cleveland earlier in the year, but the move backfired when the Indians bombed him early en route to an 8–3, pennant-clinching victory.

The Indians started celebrating by carrying their pitching hero, Gene Bearden, off the Fenway diamond, and as they neared their dugout they could see members of the Boston Braves standing behind it smiling. Most of the Braves, the NL pennant winners, admitted to cheering for the Indians even though it meant they wouldn't get a crack at beating their inner-city rivals in an all-Boston World Series. The reason? Cleveland's home park seated more than 80,000 fans, which meant a much bigger World Series bonus for teams sharing a portion of the gate receipts than they would enjoy at 34,000-seat Fenway Park.

papers, Boston promptly dropped 12 of its last 13 contests.

Reflecting on all these setbacks, sportswriters posed a theory that remains worth investigating: Were the Sox of this era geared too much to the confines of their home park?

Looking closely at the statistics of key right-handed batters, the Fenway Factor is undeniable. Doerr, for instance, had almost an identical number of at-bats at home and away during his 14-year-career, yet he hit 145 of his 223 career home runs with the Wall as his target. Dom DiMaggio was a sharpshooting .323 man in more than 700 games at Fenway—including an out-of-this-world .397 in 1950—but hit just .273 lifetime away from Boston. Vern Stephens, a slugging shortstop picked up by the Sox prior to the 1948 season, batted .347 at home but just .247 on the road in 1950.

The disparity extended itself to wins and losses. Not including the postseason, the Red Sox were 331–132 at Fenway from 1946 to '51, a .715 winning percentage; on the road they were 229–233, .496. The Yankees, in contrast, were more evenly balanced—a .680 team at home but a much more respectable .533 on the road over the same period. In an era when teams still traveled predominantly by train and road trips could last 15 games or longer, a few losses in a row away from home could snowball quickly into a serious slump. Each year from 1948 to '51, the Red Sox had significant road slides that caused them to fall far back in the standings. If they could have avoided them, and won just a few more times away from Fenway, it might have been Boston celebrating three straight world championships instead of New York.

Of course, as Doc Kountze would have been quick to remind folks, having Jackie Robinson and Sam Jethroe in Red Sox uniforms wouldn't have hurt, either.

Johnny Pesky, honored on this Bowman card, was one of those natural hitters the Sox always seemed to have, leading the league in hits three consecutive seasons. The right-field foul pole was nicknamed "Pesky's Pole" by Mel Parnell after Johnny won him a game with a shot there.

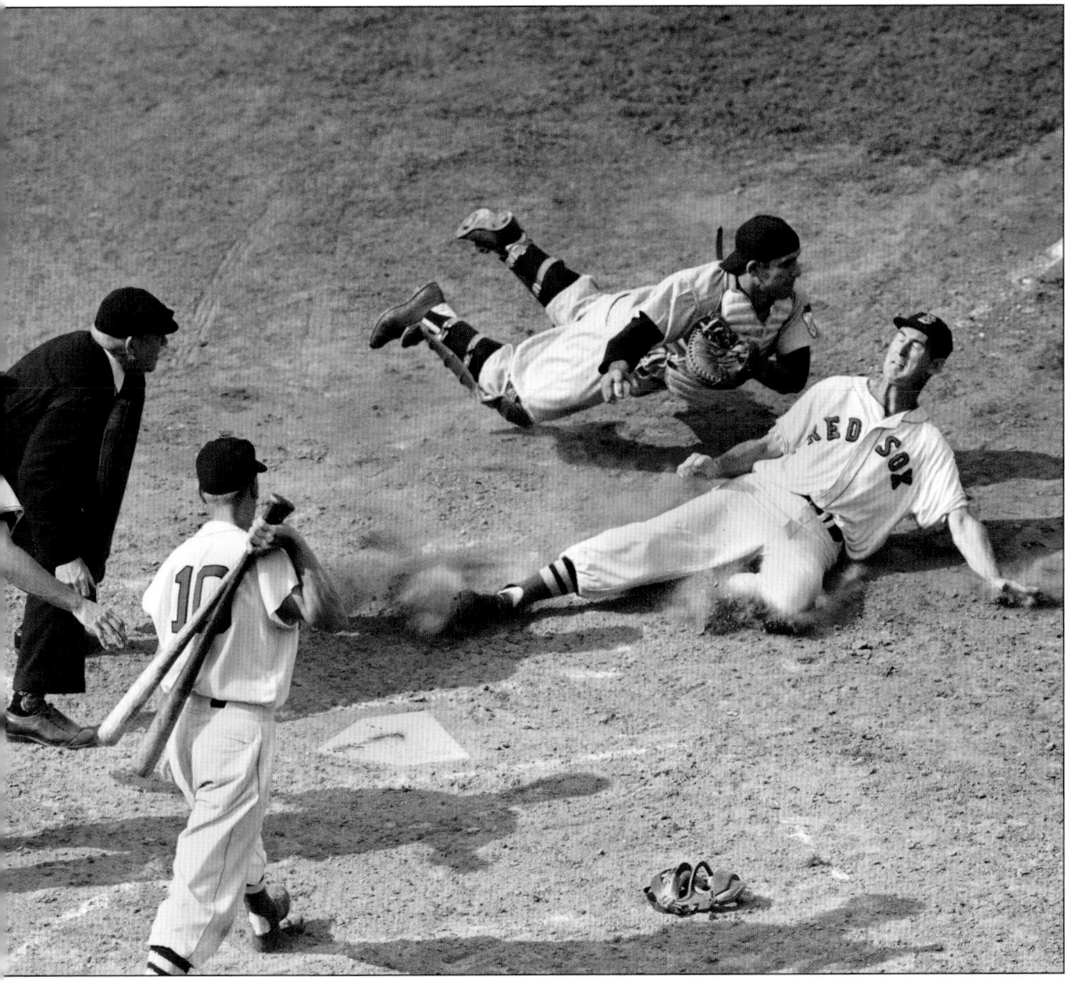

Ted Williams was called out on this 1951 play, but notice that Yankees catcher Yogi Berra has the ball in his bare hand, not his glove. This was one of a dozen Sox losses in their final 13 games that year, a stretch of futility that dropped them to third place.

CHAPTER 5

There's Always Next Year

1952–1966

During this 15-year stretch, the Red Sox never finished higher than third place or won more than 84 games. Yet fans had a blast at Fenway, whether they were cheering new heroes or dropping water balloons onto Landsdowne Street from the top of the bleachers.

Frank Malzone was excited for the chance to see and play in Fenway Park for the first time. Now he just had to *find* the place. After spending the previous night at the suburban home of his new Red Sox teammate, Dick Gernert, Malzone traversed the roughly 10 miles to Kenmore Square through twisting, turning roads and those strangest of all New England driving oddities: rotaries.

"They told me, 'Don't worry, you can't miss it,'" Malzone said with a laugh, recalling his Fenway debut on September 20, 1955. "They figure you know where you're going, but I'm from New York City, so I *didn't* know. I was used to numbered streets, and it wasn't until I got near the ballpark and saw the lights that I knew I was all right."

It's fitting that this 1950s Red Sox pennant features a huge right-handed slugger dominating Fenway Park. That's the way it was with Boston—for better or worse.

After using Fenway's light towers as a compass to guide him on the final approach to Jersey Street, Malzone got his first look at "that thing in left field everybody was talking about"—the Green Monster. When he entered the home clubhouse, he spotted his name on the Red Sox lineup card, playing third base and batting seventh. Malzone had gotten in as a pinch-runner three days before at Yankee Stadium, which was a thrill in itself for a guy who had grown up in the Bronx, but this was his first chance to really *play* in a big-league game. In the end, would find it much smoother than negotiating rotaries.

After grounding out in his first at-bat, Malzone cracked four straight hits—two singles, a double, and another single—in the first game of that afternoon's doubleheader. That earned him a promotion to fifth in the order for the second game, in which he collected two more hits and his first career RBI. "A 6-for-10, not bad for my first full day," he said, admitting that the per-

On Opening Day, 1952, these energetic young fans practice their "Hit it here, Ted" waves as they wait on Lansdowne Street for Gate C to open.

Vic Wertz, Frank Malzone, and Pete Runnels (*left to right*) were typical stars of the 1950s Red Sox: productive hitters on a team that perennially spun its wheels.

formance took some of the sting out of an embarrassing moment. "After my first hit, a single up the middle, coach Del Baker tells me at first, 'Okay, this guy [pitcher Bill Wight] has some pretty good moves. I say, 'Thanks, I appreciate that,' take two steps off the bag, and boom! He throws over and gets me. It turns out he had the best move in baseball! I might be the only guy ever picked off after getting his first hit in the majors."

Malzone likely didn't hear too many boos after his gaffe, because hardly anybody saw it. The Sunday twin bill drew a "crowd" of just 2,101 to Fenway, small pockets of patrons scattered amidst row after row of empty seats. The turnout was emblematic of the team's fortunes. Tom Yawkey's club was finishing up a solid 84–70 season, but by the mid-1950s it was no longer going into each late September with a legitimate shot at reaching the World Series. Even before being swept by Baltimore on this day, the Sox were nine games back and officially eliminated from pennant contention.

Small turnouts like this one, while still an anomaly in 1955, would become much more commonplace in the years to come. Red Sox fans who had come to expect exciting stretch drives would suffer through eight straight losing seasons from 1959 to '66, a period that included the retirement of Ted Williams—Fenway's greatest drawing card and the last link to the strong postwar clubs of the late '40s.

Even in those lean years, Fenway fans had plenty of All-Star caliber players to watch. In addition to Malzone, who was a terrific run producer and defensive third baseman, the lineup during the second half of the '50s included the splendid outfield of Williams, Jackie Jensen, and Jimmy Piersall as well as second baseman Pete Runnels—runner-up to The Kid for one batting title and a two-time champion himself. Pitchers Frank Sullivan and Tom Brewer were consis-

After rookie Jimmy Piersall (*pictured*) and combative Yankees infielder Billy Martin tangled in the shared runway to the team clubhouses in 1952, Yawkey gave each team private access. Piersall cracked an AL-high 40 doubles for Boston in 1956.

Mike "Pinky" Higgins (*center, in uniform*) managed the stuck-in-neutral boys of Fenway in the 1950s. Due in part to his refusal to take chances or try new ideas, the team floundered under his control.

tent double-figure winners. Dependable catcher Sammy White handled them and the rest of Boston's mound corps through nearly 1,000 games during the decade. The early 1960s would bring outfielders Carl Yastrzemski and Tony Conigliaro, first baseman Dick Stuart, "Steady Eddie" Bressoud at shortstop, and pitchers Bill Monbouquette, Earl Wilson, and Dick Radatz.

Talented individuals all, these performers failed to add up to a productive whole. There was always a problem, usually a lack of pitching depth, that kept the Red Sox from rising above third place in the 1950s and fighting to escape the cellar by the early '60s.

Suspect leadership didn't help. The manager and general manager for much of the period was Mike "Pinky" Higgins, a heavy drinker known for his narrow views on integration, but even Terry Francona would have faced a major challenge getting this club over the top. The Yankees of Mantle, Maris, Ford, Berra, and Howard were the latest custodians of a 40-year Bronx dynasty that stretched all the way back to Babe Ruth (thanks, Boston), and it was often clear to fans on Opening Day which club was likely to win the American League pennant.

"We had good ballplayers, and I thought on the field we had a pretty good ballclub," Malzone explained. "But let's face it. I played 11 years with the Red Sox, and unfortunately the Yankees won the pennant nine times. They not only had great ballplayers, but they knew *how to win.* That's big. When a player gets it in his mind that he can win, it never leaves him. It goes the other way, too."

Too often for Malzone and his teammates, it went the other way. And by the time the Sox bottomed out with a 62–100 season in 1965, the ballpark that had once been the jewel of the American League was seen as something of an albatross. Even though Boston usually won more than it lost at Fenway, the Red Sox were so dreadful on the road that the victories they piled up on Jersey Street had far less meaning.

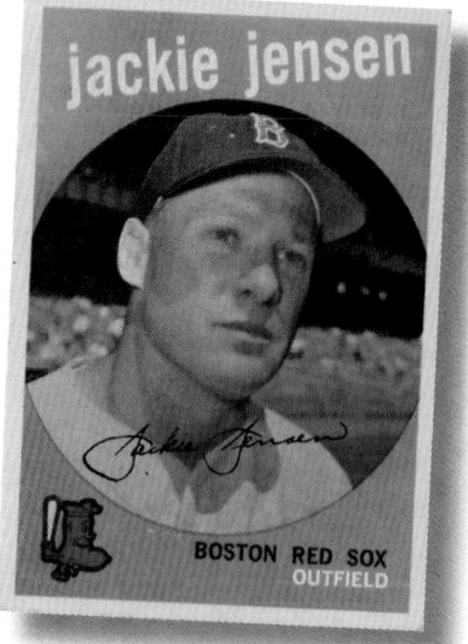

Shown here on a 1959 Topps card, Jackie Jensen had been a football star in college. In seven Sox seasons, he belted 170 homers. However, a dreadful fear of flying cut short his career.

Without Ted Williams, who missed all but 43 games in 1952–53 while serving in the Korean War, Fenway Park just wasn't the same. Attendance was flat, and the Red Sox finished sixth and fourth while he was away.

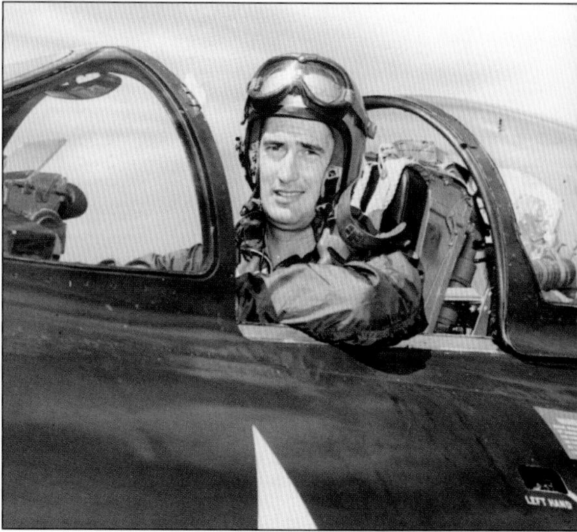

The whispers that their cozy home hurt more than helped the team grew louder. Speed and pitching were becoming increasingly important elements to success in the modern game, and slow-footed, one-dimensional sluggers like Stuart, who could mash balls up and over the Green Monster, were no longer enough. As the ballpark passed its 50th birthday, and he his 60th, Sox owner Tom Yawkey found himself wondering if a new venue might be needed to turn his fortunes around.

Goodbyes and Greek Tragedy

The stretch in which the Red Sox were arguably one of baseball's three or four most talented teams, a period that peaked in the late 1940s, began its rapid descent in September 1951 when second baseman Bobby Doerr announced he was retiring due to a bad back. Doerr was still near the peak of his powers—he had hit .294 with 27 homers, 11 triples, and 120 RBI the year before while leading the league in fielding—but he decided to hang it up rather than undergo a surgical procedure that carried the risk of permanent disability.

Next to depart the Fenway landscape in early 1952 was the masterful Ted Williams, who was called back to the Marines to fly jets in the Korean War. The Kid played just six games that April before reporting for duty, and the premature departure of him and Doerr—two future Hall of Famers in their early 30s—left gaping holes in the Boston lineup.

Rather than retool with big boppers as they had in the past, Yawkey, general manager Cronin, and new manager Lou Boudreau decided to gut the remainder of the club in favor of a youth movement. Fenway favorite Johnny Pesky and 1950 Rookie of the Year Walt Dropo were sent packing as part of a nine-player trade

Ted's "First" Last At-Bat

His final swing is one of baseball's most hallowed moments, but Ted Williams had another parting shot at Fenway that was just as clutch.

On April 30, 1952, Williams played his last game for Boston before rejoining the Marines the next day to fly jets in the Korean War. He was 33, and most speculated (including Ted himself) that if he served the expected two years, his playing career would be over. Before the contest, The Kid was given a new Cadillac and a "Memory Book" signed by 400,000 fans. He participated in a moving ceremony in which the entire crowd of 24,764 and players from both teams joined hands—with Williams clutching that of wounded Korea veteran Fred Wolfe—and sang "Auld Lang Syne." Ted even waved his cap.

The game seemed anticlimactic . . . until the seventh inning. With the score tied 3–3 and buddy Dom DiMaggio on first, Williams hit a curveball from Dizzy Trout into the right-field bullpen. The Red Sox won 5–3, and Ted was the hero—naturally. He also wasn't done. After flying 39 combat missions in Asia, he returned to hit 197 more home runs for Boston through 1960.

> "I never had any problem with the guys who like to go to the ballpark and rag ballplayers. As long as they don't get personal with the family, they can have their fun. They pay their money, they can do what they want."
> **—Third baseman Frank Malzone**

with the Tigers in June of '52. Centerfielder nonpareil Dom DiMaggio retired the next spring at a still productive 36 when it became clear that Boudreau wanted the proud seven-time All-Star to back up rookie Tom Umphlett.

Over the next several years, while a few of the "can't miss" kids who entered the lineup such as catcher White and outfielder Piersall shined bright, many more—particularly Umphlett, Gernert, and Milt Bolling—failed to live up to their early billing. Although the 1952 club bolted out strong with a 10–2 April record and held first place in mid-June, it fizzled quickly come summer and wound up in sixth place with a sub-.500 record. There were some wild moments at Fenway—such as an 11–9 victory over St. Louis in which a White grand slam completed a six-run ninth inning comeback against the great Satchel Paige—but the near-glory days were gone.

Boudreau had been hailed as a genius just a few years before, when as a young player-manager he led the Indians to huge October triumphs over both the Red Sox (in the American League playoff game) and the Boston Braves (in the World Series). Now on Boston's side, he suddenly didn't look so smart. His youth movement flopped, and he was fired after a dismal 1954 season in favor of former Sox outfielder Higgins.

The timing couldn't have been worse for the Red Sox, who for the first time ever had Boston all to themselves. The Braves, the National League franchise that preceded the Sox to town by more than 25 years but was usually considered

Dependable backstop Sammy White did all he could to keep the team on track, but Fenway attendance in the era plummeted. After drawing more than one million fans 12 times from 1946 through '58, the Red Sox hit the magic number only once in the next eight years.

The old Gruen Watch clock seen here was later changed to signify "Jimmy Fund Time" in the 1950s. It was later replaced by an electric scoreboard.

a poorer cousin to their inner-city rival, had struggled on the field and at the gate since winning the 1948 NL pennant.

The Red Sox routinely outdrew the Braves due to Tom Yawkey's pocketbook and a more fan-friendly ballpark. Braves Field, which sat beside the Charles River and the Boston and Albany Railroad a mile from Fenway, is usually described by those who remember it as "too big," "too windy," and "too smoky." Even touches such as fried clams, television monitors at the concession stands, and a "Knot Hole Gang" that allowed kids to attend games all summer for next to nothing couldn't reverse the trend. The chasm reached its breaking point in 1952 when the Braves finished seventh and played before just 281,278 fans, by far the worst attendance mark in baseball. That's the same year that Yawkey's club began to struggle mightily with the losses of Doerr, Pesky, and Williams, but 1,115,750 still came out to Jersey Street and cheered them on.

Faced with growing debts, and reportedly turned down by Yawkey when he proposed that they share Fenway Park, Braves owner Lou Perini announced he was moving his franchise to Milwaukee in March 1953. It was the first time a major-league team had shifted cities in 50 years, and it gave the Red Sox a perfect opportunity to quickly and dramatically increase their fan base. Instead, the reverse happened. Bostonians who no longer had the Braves to complain about realized that the American Leaguers were slipping as well. Despite the return of war hero Williams in 1954, attendance at Fenway dipped under one million for the first time in a decade.

There was, however, a glimmer of hope in a 69–85 season: young first baseman Harry Agganis. A multisport star, Agganis grew up a few miles from Fenway in Lynn, Massachusetts, and rose to All-American status on the football field at Boston University. The handsome, personable "Golden Greek" had given up a chance to quarterback the NFL's Cleveland Browns by choosing to stay near his large family and sign with the Red Sox for a $40,000 bonus. He made the big leagues within a year, and he started early in his rookie season.

One afternoon from that campaign stands out. On June 6, 1954, Agganis was due to receive his college diploma in a 4 P.M. ceremony at Braves Field (by then owned by BU). But first there was the matter of a 1 P.M. game at Fenway. Harry gave himself and the fans on hand a memorable present by smacking a game-winning home run against the Tigers before showering and donning a cap and gown for the one-mile drive up Commonwealth Avenue. The next day's *Boston Globe,* under a banner front-page headline applauding "HARRY'S HEYDAY," featured photos of him in both his baseball and graduation garb.

The muscular rookie hit a modest .251 with 11 homers for the year, but eight of them came at Fenway—where Agganis conquered the 380-foot distance to right field with power that reminded fans of fellow left-handed slugger Ted Williams. Agganis got off to a strong start in his second season, and was batting over .300 in mid-May, when he was hospitalized with chest pains that turned out to be pneumonia in his right lung. He rushed to get back on the field, and two hits at Chicago on June 2 raised his average to .313—tops among regulars on the team.

Boston was due to return to Fenway 12 days later, but Agganis was sent home early and hospitalized again when his

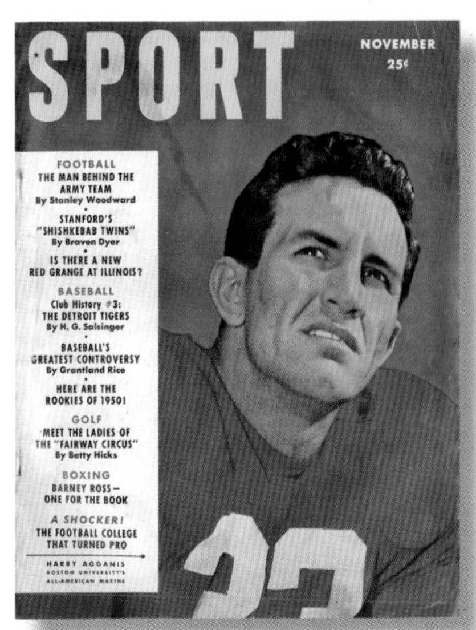

The Cleveland Browns actually waved $100,000 in front of Harry Agganis to make him their quarterback, but the local boy opted instead to join his beloved Red Sox. *Sport* magazine featured Agganis in their November 1950 issue.

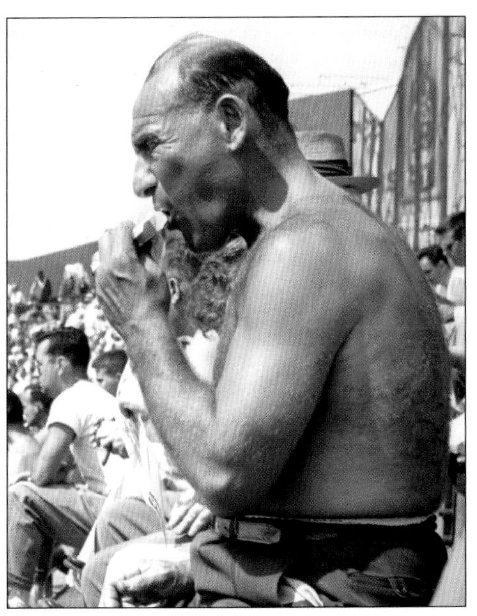

Contrary to popular opinion, Ebbets Field did not own the trademark on "Bleacher Bums." Fenway had its share of hot and hungry cheap-seat denizens.

The irony of this cherubic African-American bobble-head is that the Red Sox were notorious for ignoring black talent. In fact, they were the last MLB team to field a black ballplayer.

condition worsened. Early reports that he was rallying were premature, and he died suddenly on June 27, 1955, of a pulmonary embolism (a blood clot in his lung). The headlines this time read "NATION'S FANS PAY TRIBUTE TO AGGANIS." Nearly 20,000 friends and admirers, far more people than the Red Sox would draw in most home games that season, lined the streets of Lynn as the 25-year-old's body was driven from St. George's Church to its final resting place in nearby Pine Grove Cemetery. "He had it made," said Higgins, who attended the funeral with pitcher Frank Sullivan. "We thought he'd be our first baseman for 10 years to come."

The Buzz, the Bombers, and Balloons

The heartbreak of Agganis's death was completely unforeseen, but other problems that beset the Red Sox during the 1950s were of their own doing.

After the failure of Boudreau's youth movement, Yawkey was again attempting to rebuild his club with cash by throwing huge bonuses at unproven prospects—most of whom would never make it to the majors. And while other franchises followed the lead of such trendsetters as the Dodgers, Giants, and Boston Braves by signing African-American ballplayers, the Red Sox remained an all-white outfit for nearly the entire decade. Just as they had let future Rookies of the Year Jackie Robinson and Sam Jethroe get away in 1945 after their sham tryout at Fenway Park, they failed to capitalize on having exclusive first rights to a young Negro Leaguer named Willie Mays four years later. The man dispatched to scout him (Texan Larry Woodall) didn't feel like wasting his time watching black ballplayers.

The thought of Mays alongside Ted Williams in front of the Green Monster for a decade is tantalizing to say the least. And although the feelings of Tom Yawkey with regards to breaking the color line have never been fully proven, his confidant, Pinky Higgins, was reported to have said, "There'll be no niggers on this ballclub as long as I have anything to say about it." The team's idea of racial progress during the '50s was letting the Harlem Globetrotters play a game at Fenway in July 1954.

Thanks in large part to this attitude, the Red Sox of the late '50s settled into a stretch of mediocrity under Higgins. Along the way, a few individuals did shine, including Jensen (a three-time RBI champ and the '58 MVP), Runnels (a .320 batting average over five

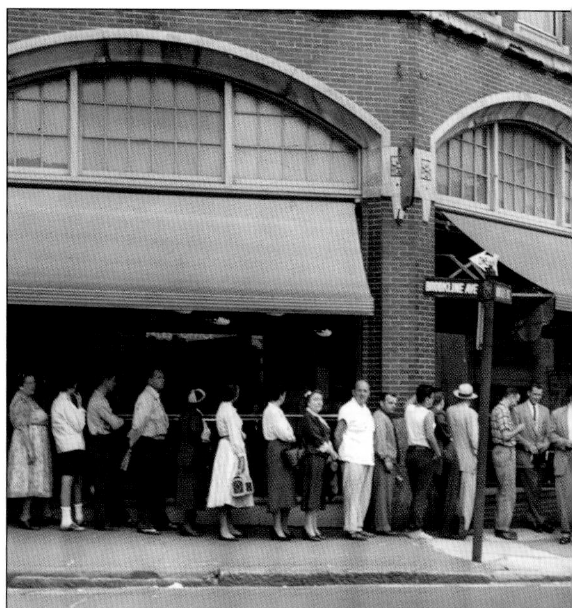

Boston seasons), and Malzone (three straight Gold Gloves at third base before Brooks Robinson put a stranglehold on the award). Shining above them all was Williams, who seemed to defy the aging process as his 40th birthday came and went. In 1957, he blasted 38 home runs and won his fifth batting title with a .388 average—the highest in the major leagues since his .406 mark. The next year, he was champion once again at .328, edging teammate Runnels in the last week of the season.

Electricity buzzed through Fenway each time Williams came to the plate. "When Ted was in the on-deck circle, that's when it started," recalled Pesky, the image still vivid in his memory more than a half-century later. "They would hoot and holler, and when he got to the plate he'd wiggle and waggle. They just loved him."

Part of the excitement was that fans never knew what The Kid might do. In 1956, for instance, Williams was fined $5,000 by Yawkey after a series of spitting incidents at Fenway. One of them was directed upward toward his adversaries in the press box after hitting his 400th home run, and several sideways spits were aimed at fans who had recently booed him for bad fielding plays. It was the fickleness of fans and their ability to treat a ballplayer like a hero one moment and a cad the next that most irked The Kid.

In another incident, Williams threw his bat in frustration after a called third strike late in the 1958 batting race—then watched helplessly as it soared into the third-base stands and hit Joe Cronin's 60-year-old housekeeper, Gladys Heffernan, in the head. The crowd booed as a distraught Williams ran over to apologize to the bloodied Heffernan, who as a huge fan of Ted's tried to comfort him even as she was being treated for a cut above her eye. Williams later cried in the dugout, but he pulled himself together to hit a key double in Boston's 2–0 victory and turn many of the jeers to cheers. That Christmas, he sent Heffernan an expensive piece of jewelry.

One group of Fenway visitors the Splendid Splinter *did* intend to harm were the pigeons that took up residence in the ballpark each summer. An avid hunter, Williams would occasionally take to the field with a rifle before the gates opened in search of his prey. In one day's tally reported by the *Boston Herald*, he shot down 40 of the annoying birds. Perhaps he imagined they were sportswriters or fickle fans.

Even when the Red Sox were losing badly late in a ballgame, Fenway

Fans wait in line for tickets in 1955. That year, a fan could sit in a Fenway field box for $2.10. The same seat today will set you back $130.

Even though Boston Garden hosted more events (and luminaries such as Winston Churchill and Elvis Presley), Fenway has offered soccer, football, basketball, memorial services, and even concerts, one of which the workers here prepare for.

patrons would stick around just to see if Williams could get another at-bat. For youngsters such as David Shulman, who grew up idolizing The Kid in the '50s, these moments were something to be cherished and could be recalled a half-century later. "When Ted was up," explained Shulman, "every at-bat felt like you were playing the Yankees."

This comment was telling of the feelings Boston fans had about their team's nemesis from New York. No matter how far the Red Sox fell behind the Yankees in the standings, fans like Shulman still packed the ballpark when the Bronx Bombers came to town. A week after the 1955 doubleheader at Fenway in which barely 2,100 fans saw rookie Malzone shine against the Orioles, nearly 30,000 turned out for a meaningless season-ending twin bill against New York. The rivalry at this point was clearly one-sided, and just as Babe Ruth and Joe DiMaggio before them, slugger Mickey Mantle and his teammates routinely made Fenway their home away from home. In 10 of 12 seasons from 1955 to 1966, the Yanks won more than they lost in Boston and went 69–51 overall (a very healthy .575 winning percentage).

With little or no hope for a pennant during these years, Red Sox fans sometimes found it a challenge rooting for the home team. "One Sunday in 1958, I just walked up to the ticket office and bought a ticket for a doubleheader," Len Levin remembered. "Jim Bunning was pitching the first game for Detroit, and the Red Sox were so dreadful that as the game moved along, everybody was rooting for Bunning to get a no-hitter. In the ninth inning, I kept hollering out to the Red Sox batters, 'C'mon, get a hit! Get a hit!' Everybody looked at me like I was a leper." To Levin's chagrin, Bunning got his no-hitter and a 3–0 win.

Other local fans who came to Fenway rooted against the Red Sox for purely ethical reasons—their favorite baseball team had left town. Jack Fabiano was just eight when his father came home from work one day and told him that the Braves were moving. "I thought it was some kind of cruel joke," the former Knot Hole Gang member recalled. "I was pissed, and I'm sure I cried." Still enamored with the game, he found a way to displace his resentment. "I started going to Fenway, but I'd say I was a Yankees fan because I was angry that the Red Sox had succeeded in driving the Braves out of town."

"On my way up to home plate, the whole stands, blacks and whites, they stand up and gave me a standing ovation. A standing ovation, my first time up! And the umpire said, 'Good luck, Pumpsie,' something like that."

—Pumpsie Green, recalling his first-ever Fenway at-bat on August 4, 1959

While the Red Sox front office had found reasons to ignore black baseball talent such as Pumpsie Green for years, the Fenway fans (for the most part) welcomed the new players. Green, who is pictured on a 1962 Topps card, debuted with the Red Sox on July 21, 1959.

Still, some youngsters would never think of hiding their loyalties—and would even endure personal pain to stand by their team. Ken Wright was 11 when he took the trolley in to Fenway from Roxbury to see a doubleheader against the Tigers on a scorching-hot summer's day. He had poison ivy on his feet, and he wore heavy, black shoes to protect them from the sun. The tactic didn't work, and his feet began to blister and sting as he sat in a 50-cent bleacher seat in deep center field. "I still stayed for both games, and the Red Sox won them both," he recalled proudly. "I cried on the trolley all the way home [because] my feet hurt so much."

Bill Nowlin devised more thrilling diversions to keep him occupied if the Sox were struggling. A preteen Ted Williams fanatic, he would bike several miles from his suburban home in Lexington to Arlington Square, take the bus to Harvard Square, and then catch a trolley for the final stretch to Fenway. There he and his buddies took up residence in the bleachers, back when they really were bleachers—long strips of wood with no back support and numbers painted on them.

"I'm not sure why they had numbers, because you could sit wherever you wanted—the park was half empty," Nowlin recalled. "There were so few people out there, and no center-field message board, so you could easily walk all the way up to the back wall of the bleachers and look down onto Lansdowne Street. We used to drop water balloons down on people. We weren't trying to hit them, but we wanted them to *think* we were trying to hit them. The perfect throw would be about 12 feet in front of someone. A couple times people got really upset, and actually bought tickets and came into the ballpark looking for us. But I had a reversible jacket, so I'd just turn it inside out to the other color and move to another section."

Pioneers and Legends

One place where a single color had always dominated was the Red Sox lineup, which through the 1958 season remained 100 percent Caucasian. By this point, the other 15 major-league teams had all fielded at least one African-American player. With two black athletes among their top prospects, infielder Elijah "Pumpsie" Green and pitcher Earl Wilson, it seemed only a matter of time before Boston did as well.

Green was invited to spring training in 1959, and although he had to live by himself 17 miles away from his teammates (the hotel the Sox stayed at in Scottsdale, Arizona, was segregated), the switch-hitter batted .327 with four home runs in exhibition play. Mabray "Doc" Kountz of the *Boston Chronicle* and other African-American sportswriters called for the team to keep Green on its roster to start the season, and many white journalists also took up the cause. When Higgins and his coaching staff chose to send him back for a second year at Triple-A Minneapolis, influential Boston columnists such as Harold Kaese of the *Globe* derided them for the decision. Jackie Robinson himself noted that "Tom Yawkey has owned the Red Sox for a long time and has missed a couple of pennants by a game or two. Maybe if he had a good Negro player on the team he might have won those pennants."

Two excellent books on the subject—*Shut Out* by Howard Bryant and *Pumpsie and Progress* by former balloon tosser Bill Nowlin—chronicle what happened next. The National Association for the Advancement of Colored People (NAACP) asked the Massachusetts Commission against Discrimination to look into the hiring practices of the Red Sox, and, when questioned, general manager Bucky Harris said the team had sent Green down to get more playing time.

To be fair, many seasoned observers—including Robinson and Ted Williams, who had befriended Green in Arizona—did feel Green might need a bit more seasoning, but this didn't stop at least one young white man from picketing outside Fenway with placards that read "Race Hate Is Killing Baseball in Boston" and "We Want a Pennant, Not a White Team." The *Boston Globe* reported the incident, which included a skirmish between the protester and several other white men near Fenway's front entrance. When it was discovered that the team didn't even have any black employees occupying jobs in and around Fenway, a few started popping up on the grounds crew and other departments.

Finally, after batting .320 over four months at Minneapolis, Green was called up to the seventh-place Red Sox in late July. The fact that Higgins had been fired as manager earlier in the month and replaced by the seemingly more accepting Billy Jurges was no coincidence. Upon reading a column by Larry Claflin of the *Boston Record-American* defending Green's skills, Higgins had reportedly spit tobacco juice on Claflin and called him a "nigger lover." Green met up with

The Red Sox would finish 13 games behind the pennant-winning Yankees in 1958, but August 17 was a good day. These fans cheered on their idol, who went 4-for-4 as Boston defeated the Bombers 6–5.

Jim Pagliaroni congratulates the joyous Earl Wilson after the latter became the first African-American AL pitcher to author a no-hitter, on June 26, 1962. A crowd of 14,002 watched Wilson top the Los Angeles Angels at Fenway.

the club in Chicago and saw his first action on July 21 as a pinch-runner at Comiskey Park. He started the next day at shortstop, and by the time the Red Sox returned home after a 13-game road trip he was batting .292. By this point, Green even had a roommate; the Sox had called up Earl Wilson a week after him.

The two African-American players made their Fenway debuts on back-to-back days. Green led off in the first game of a Sunday doubleheader against the Tigers on August 4, and he reacted to a fine ovation from the crowd of 21,304 with a triple off the Green Monster. He had a hit and run scored in each game that afternoon, and he even got a phone call in the clubhouse from Jackie Robinson. Wilson, a right-hander with a great fastball but trouble controlling it, started on August 5 against the Athletics and allowed five runs in less than two innings.

Despite intense media and public scrutiny, Green reacted to his status as Boston's trailblazer very well. His hot bat earned him a start in all eight games of his first homestand with the team, during which he hit .363—including a 4-for-5 performance against Whitey Ford and the Yankees. Most fans took to his hustling style, and he didn't worry about those who couldn't look past his color. "Sometimes terrible things would be yelled out, racial epithets," he recalled later. "I told people I had enough troubles trying to hit the curveball. I wasn't going to worry about some loudmouths." Wilson, a Louisiana native who had pitched minor-league ball in such segregated cities as Montgomery, Alabama, had the same attitude. "It never bothered me what people said in the stands in Boston," he said later. "What I heard in the South was much worse."

Neither of the newcomers wound up with stellar stats in 1959—Green cooled off to .233, while Wilson compiled a 6.04 ERA—but an important hurdle had been passed. And while Green

The 1960 Sox lost 89 games, the worst by the team in 27 years. Attendance barely slinked past a million fans. But the worst years were yet to come.

would never hit consistently enough to last as an everyday player, Wilson would emerge as a very dependable pitcher—going 12–8 in 1962 and pitching a no-hitter against the Angels at Fenway that June 26. Newspaper photos of Wilson smiling broadly as teammates slapped him good-naturedly on the back at game's end undoubtedly brought similar reactions in cafes and barbershops throughout Doc Kountz's Medford neighborhood. Wilson even hit a home run in the 2–0 victory, one of 10 he stroked at Fenway as one of the best hitting pitchers of his era.

Ted Williams made a subtle gesture that spoke volumes about acceptance by warming up with Green on the sidelines before games. By 1960, of course, just about everything Williams did was closely monitored by fans and sportswriters; The Kid had announced this would be his final season. Pinky Higgins was back as manager and the team was once again going nowhere—it would finish seventh at 65–89, its fewest wins to date under Yawkey's ownership—but Ted gave folks something to watch and read about.

Williams hit his 494th home run in the home opener versus the Yankees, passing Lou Gehrig to become fourth on the all-time list. Although assorted injuries limited his playing time, Ted's power stroke was as good as ever—at one point producing 12 home runs in 80 at-bats as he neared his 42nd birthday. He eclipsed third-place man Mel Ott with No. 512 in August (only Babe Ruth and Jimmie Foxx had more). His 25th of the year, hit at home off Washington's Don Lee, served as a bookend blast of sorts. As a rookie in 1939, Williams had homered off Don's father, Thornton, on another September Sunday at Fenway.

Attendance on Jersey Street had picked up somewhat over the summer, but a surprisingly small crowd of just 10,454 was on hand on September 28 for the final home game of Williams's career. Those who braved the dreary, cold day heard a nice little pregame speech from The Kid, in which he took a final dig at local sportswriters (he called them "the Knights of the Keyboard") and thanked "the greatest fans in America." As he stood a few feet away listening to the comments, Red Sox broadcaster Curt Gowdy was hiding a secret. Williams, a close friend, had told him that because the Yankees had already clinched the pennant, he had received permission from Higgins to not accompany the team to New York for the sea-

Frank Malzone's son Jimmy awaits his turn in a 1961 Red Sox father-son game. By the mid-'60s, the Sox had expanded the annual Fenway event to include daughters as well.

"They cheered like hell, and as I came around, the cheering grew louder and louder. I thought about tipping my hat, you're damn right I did, and for a moment I was torn, but by the time I got to second base I knew I couldn't do it."
—Ted Williams, recalling his last-ever at-bat (and home run) on September 28, 1960

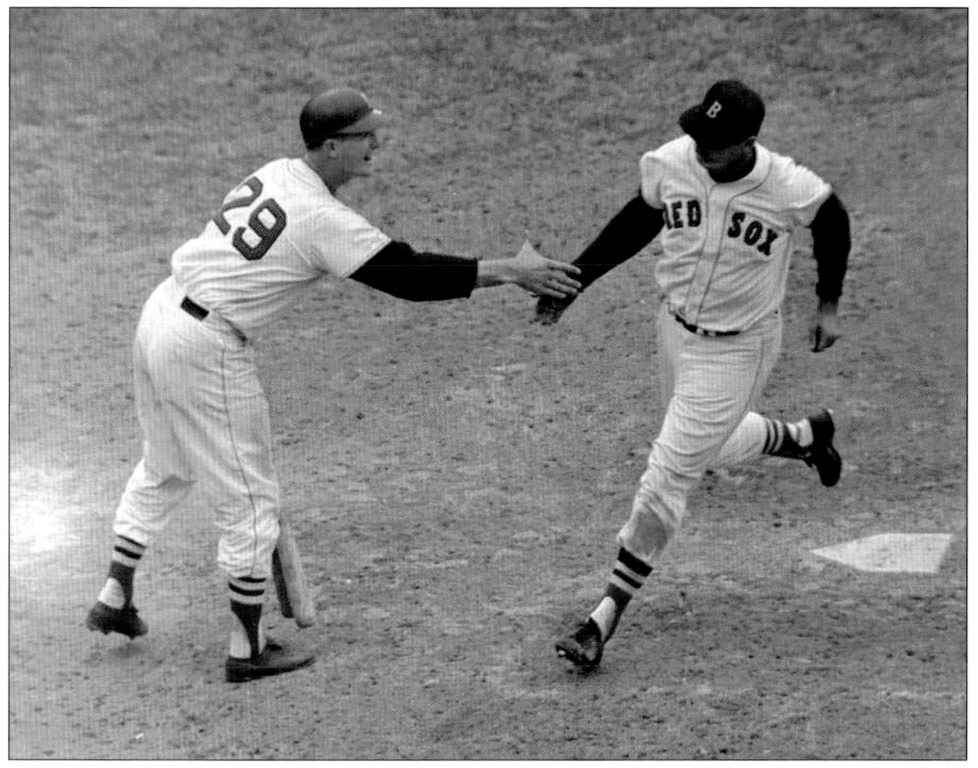

When Ted Williams crossed home plate after his historic farewell home run, he didn't offer Jim Pagliaroni much of a handshake, but Pag was delighted anyway.

son's final three contests. This would be his last game *period.*

Facing the Orioles, Williams walked in the first and then hit a pair of deep blasts to center and right field. The lights were turned on to defy the darkening skies, and when Williams came up again in the bottom of the eighth, the small crowd stood and cheered for two minutes. Williams took a ball, swung mightily and missed a high one from reliever Jack Fisher, and then connected on a fastball right down the middle. It was what fans call a "no-doubter," sending centerfielder Jackie Brandt back to the edge of the Red Sox bullpen. He leaped in vain, and the ball banged around a bit before falling into the pen. It's unclear exactly what happened to it next, but the daughter of Haywood Sullivan—the future Sox owner who, as a backup catcher, would have been in the bullpen at the time—says her father told her that he retrieved it and later gave it to Williams.

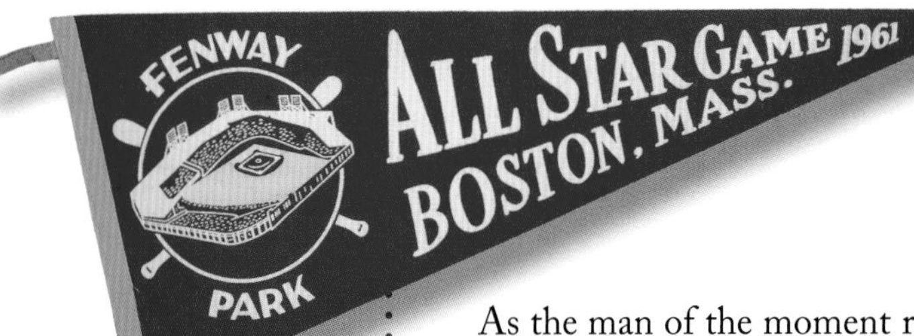

The second-ever All-Star Game at Fenway was also the second All-Star Game of that season. Pitcher Don Schwall, the lone Red Sox representative, allowed one run in three innings.

As the man of the moment rounded the bases, head down and expressionless, Gowdy could not control his enthusiasm from his radio booth above home plate. "A home run for Ted Williams in his last time at bat in the major leagues!" he yelled, and just like that the secret was out. Williams didn't tip his hat, and he refused to come back out and wave, despite a five-minute ovation, chants of "We Want Ted! We Want Ted!," and the pleadings of his teammates and even the umpires. A young novelist sitting in the stands, John Updike, would write an essay about the day entitled "Hub Fans Bid Kid Adieu" that appeared in *The New Yorker* three weeks later and in countless anthologies since. In it, the future Pulitzer Prize winner described Ted's reluctance to acknowledge the crowd succinctly and accurately: "Gods do not answer letters."

Fans did get a last chance to cheer him, however, when Higgins let Williams trot out to left to start the ninth inning and then immediately sent out Carroll Hardy to replace him. "They booed me all the way out, and booed him all the way in," Hardy later recalled. But Ted, his own man to the end, still made no gesture of appreciation as he jogged off the field and into the dugout and clubhouse beyond.

He had thanked the fans already; this moment would be for him.

All-Stars Fit to Be Tied

Fenway Park has been the site of many unique baseball moments through the years, so it seemed appropriate that it host a "first" in All-Star Game history.

There were two All-Star Games played each year from 1959 to '62, and Fenway hosted the second contest of '61 on July 31. The rosters served as a reminder of how far the Red Sox had fallen off in recent years. No members of the sixth-place Sox were elected by fans as American League starters, and pitcher Don Schwall (en route to the Rookie of the Year Award) was the lone manager's pick from Boston. The two teams were filled with big boppers—the AL had Mickey Mantle, Roger Maris, Rocky Colavito, and Norm Cash in its starting lineup, and the NL countered with Willie Mays, Orlando Cepeda, Ed Mathews, and Roberto Clemente—but the crowd of 31,851 wound up seeing a pitcher's duel rather than the expected slugfest.

The two teams combined for just nine hits, as seven hurlers including Schwall, Sandy Koufax, Jim Bunning, and Stu Miller registered 15 strikeouts between them. Knotted at 1–1 after nine innings, the clubs took for cover when rain came pouring down, and after waiting just a half-hour the umpires called the game and declared the first tie in All-Star history. The decision irked some fans who would have been willing to wait longer for a resolution—after all, tickets had cost up to $8!—but at least the final score kept the American Leaguers from losing their fourth straight game (until the next year).

The Wall's New Guardian

As the grandson of famed Royal Rooter John Fitzgerald settled into the White House during the spring of 1961, the son of a Long Island potato farmer settled into the left-field post at Fenway Park. And just as young Jack Kennedy had to deal with being compared to the American icon he had succeeded (Dwight Eisenhower), Carl Yastrzemski was scrutinized by fans who had spent the previous 22 years under the spell of Ted Williams. After reading about Yastrzemski's skills and his eye-popping minor-league stats all winter, the Fenway

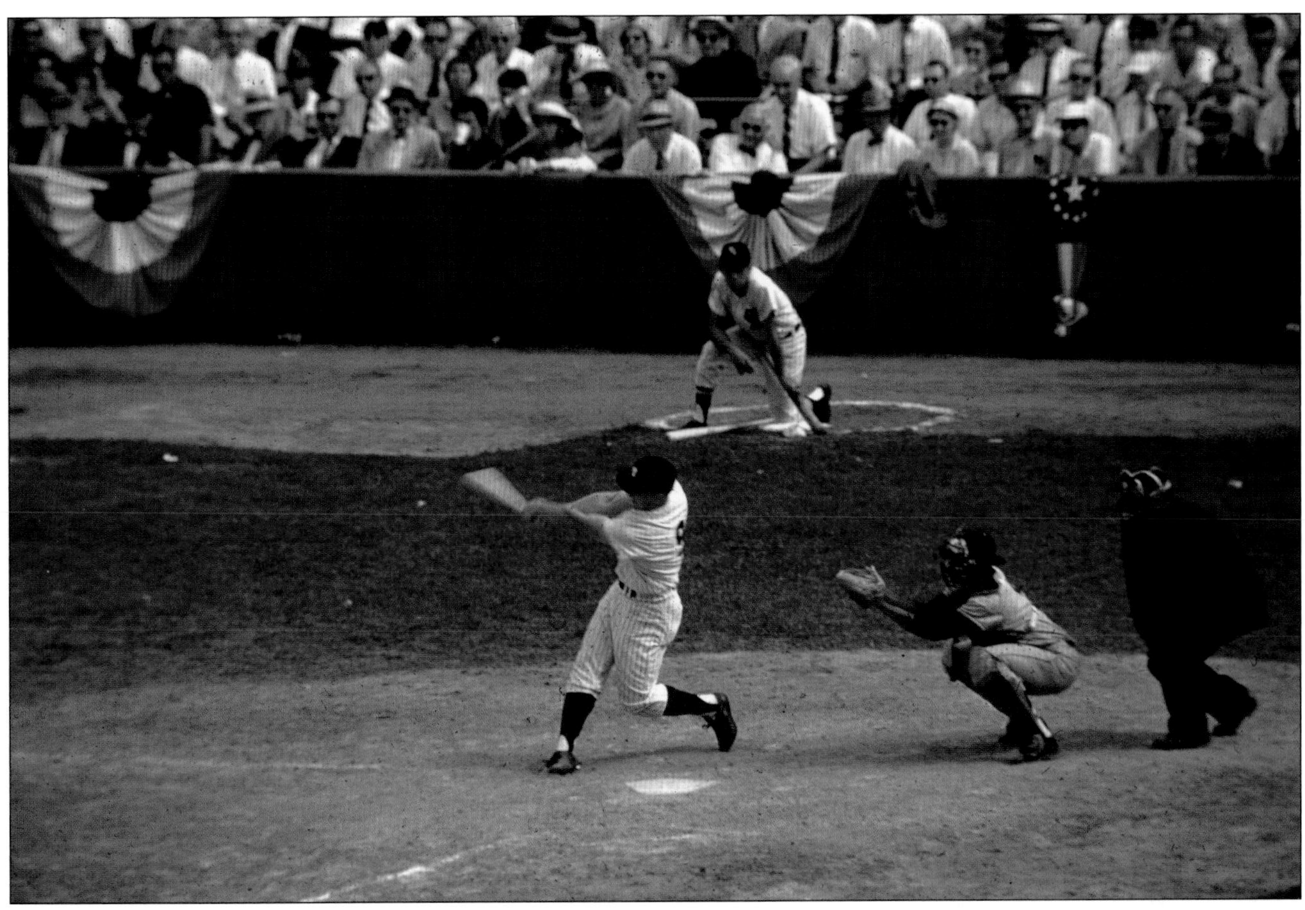

Faithful were anxious to see if the rookie wearing No. 8 could fill the cleats of the legend who wore No. 9.

The man bearing the scrutiny, however, said it never bothered him. "Ted Williams was my baseball hero when I was growing up, he and Stan Musial," recalled Yastrzemski. "But no, I didn't feel extra pressure as a rookie replacing Ted in left field. Some have suggested that, but it isn't true. There was pressure enough simply trying to make the grade in the majors."

Yaz singled off Kansas City's Ray Herbert in his first at-bat in the majors on Opening Day at Fenway, but by the end of June he was batting just .231. Tom Yawkey did the logical thing; he called Ted Williams in Florida and had him fly up to Boston to work with the rookie. The tips helped, and by year's end Yastrzemski was up to a respectable .266 and 80 RBI for yet another second-division club.

During the next five years, Yaz developed into one of the top players in the American League, winning the 1963 AL batting title and several Gold Gloves. A former infielder, he played the Wall better than his predecessor or anybody

Roger Maris, who was in the midst of breaking Babe Ruth's season home run record, aims for Fenway's right-field seats in the 1961 All-Star Game. On deck is White Sox shortstop Luis Aparicio, a future Red Sox.

Patriot Park

The Red Sox of the early 1960s never came close to a league championship, but another Fenway Park tenant during the decade did.

From 1963 to '68, the Boston Patriots of the American Football League rented out Fenway for the majority of their home contests, as Tom Yawkey tried to make up some of the money he was losing due to poor attendance figures for his second-division baseball club. Led by the likes of quarterback Babe Parilli, running backs Ron Burton, Larry Garron, and Jim Nance, and wide receiver/kicker Gino Cappelletti, the Patriots enjoyed several strong seasons on Jersey Street.

Perhaps the most entertaining Fenway game they played was a match-up with the Oakland Raiders on October 16, 1964. A chilly Friday night crowd of 23,279 watched both Parilli and Oakland quarterback Cotton Davidson toss four touchdown passes apiece. Trailing most of the evening, the Patriots scored 22 points in the fourth quarter and went ahead 43–40 on Garron's 11-yard scoring catch, only to have Oakland's Mike Mercer squeeze in a 38-yard field goal with five seconds left to account for the 43–43 final.

Overall, the Patriots went 10–3–1 during the '64 campaign, losing a chance at the AFL Eastern Division title with a 24–14 season-ending loss to first-place Buffalo at a snow-swept Fenway on December 20. Boston had won the East crown the year before, but it was sent packing in the AFL title game at San Diego, 51–10. By 1969, they were gone from Fenway as well, playing one year each at Boston College's Alumni Stadium and Harvard Stadium before getting their own new stadium in Foxboro, Massachusetts—and a new name, the New England Patriots—for the 1971 season.

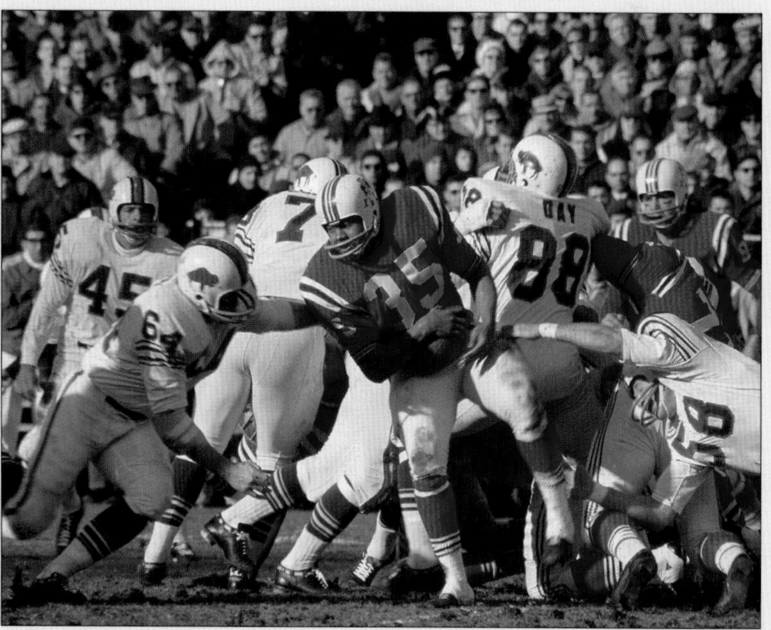

In a home game at Fenway Park, 260-pound fullback Jim Nance powers his way for extra yards against the Buffalo Bills on December 4, 1966. Nance twice led the AFL in rushing.

Yes, the Patriots were able to fit a full football field on Fenway Park's oddly dimensioned landscape. Of course, no shortstop wanted to field grounders late in the season, when the Pats and Sox shared the park.

else—routinely stealing away hits with leaping catches against the hard fence or deftly handling caroms and throwing runners out who attempted to take extra bases. Unfortunately, the team did not seem to be developing around him. Although players such as Malzone, Wilson, Monbouquette, and relief ace Dick Radatz shined, the Sox stayed under .500 each year through 1966 and their reputation as a "country club" of pampered, overpaid players grew.

Exhibit A for these underachieving Boston teams was first baseman Dick Stuart, a .260 hitter with great power, a terrible attitude, and defensive deficiencies that earned him such derisive nicknames as "Stonefingers" and "Dr. Strangelove" (a play on the popular movie *Dr. Strangelove*) from increasingly frustrated Fenway patrons. Things got so bad that fans took to cheering wildly when Red Sox starting pitchers were knocked from the game, because it meant Radatz—a 6-foot-6, 250-pounder nicknamed "The Monster"—was usually coming in. The hard-throwing right-hander routinely pitched two, three, or more innings out of the bullpen, and in 1963–64 he went 15–6 and 16–9 with 25 or more saves each season for dismal Boston teams.

Other than the brief moments of euphoria provided by The Monster—who thrust his arms over his head after each Red Sox victory he secured—the mood at Fenway Park lacked the electricity of

Right: Painters and other workmen apply the finishing touches to the new scoreboard behind the right-field bleachers one week before Opening Day, 1963.

Above: Dick "The Monster" Radatz, shown on this Topps card, should have been called "The Horse." In four-plus Red Sox seasons, he averaged 135 innings a year in relief.

On the last play of the game, Dave Morehead bobbles a ball but makes the play to keep his no-hitter intact on September 16, 1965. Only 1,247 fans saw it live.

Above: The Red Sox got a decent crowd for this game against the Kansas City A's on May 30, 1965. But as the losses mounted (100 in all), attendance diminished. *Right:* Ned Martin, Mel Parnell, and Curt Gowdy (*left to right*) broadcast a game from the Fenway bleachers in 1965. The turnout was typically sparse, despite the sunny weather. *Far right:* Sister Margaret Therese of Boston adds her voice to the encouraging crowd as the Red Sox battle Cleveland on Nuns Day, August 11, 1966.

"Yastrzemski was a great player; he could do everything. Ted played the Wall very well for a big guy, but Yaz was the best. He was a former infielder who went to the outfield, and it showed."
—Johnny Pesky, on Williams and Yastrzemski

the Williams years. Yaz, while an excellent player, was not flashy and not yet a consistent home run threat. Fans needed a new slugger on which to pin their hopes, and in the spring of 1964 they got one: rookie Tony Conigliaro. Like young Harry Agganis a decade before, "Tony C" was movie-star handsome and oozed with potential. Like Agganis, he had grown up a few miles from Fenway in East Boston. Signed right after his graduation from Lynn's St. Mary's High, Conigliaro played just one season in the minors before manager Johnny Pesky deemed him ready for the big leagues at age 19.

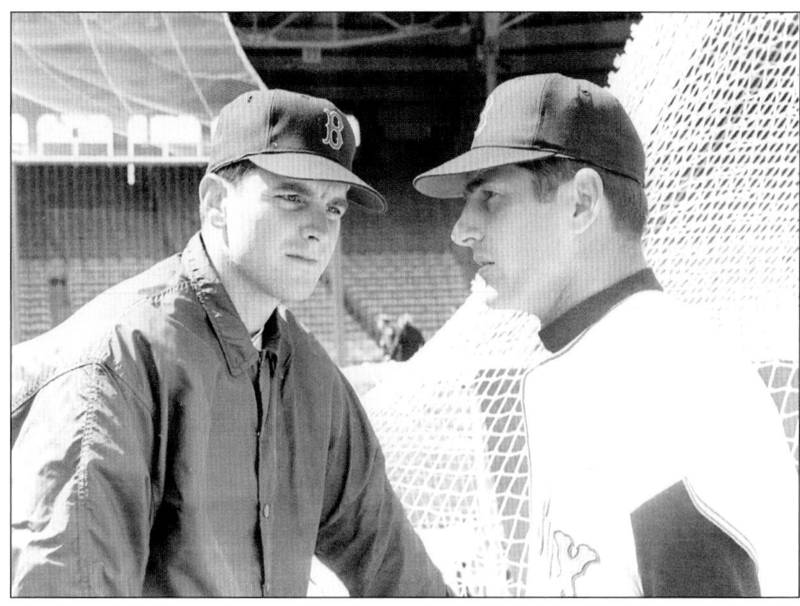

Tony C and Yaz. Boston fans hadn't seen such promising sluggers in quite a few years. Magic was on its way.

On April 17, 1964, another less-than-capacity Opening Day crowd of 20,213 at Fenway came out to honor recently fallen president John F. Kennedy and see the local kid's home debut. Game proceeds were going to fund the Kennedy Memorial Library, and JFK's brother Bobby threw out the first pitch. Along with Tony C's parents, his little brother Richie, and three generations of Kennedys, fans watching the somber occasion included Conigliaro's high school teammate Jim Driscoll and a group of his college buddies from Harvard. Among them was Jack Fabiano, the heartbroken Boston Braves fan who by now had fully turned his allegiances to the Red Sox. About 15 miles away, dressed in his Swampscott High baseball uniform, Conigliaro's other brother Billy left his own game to hear Curt Gowdy describe Tony's first trip to the plate against White Sox right-hander Joel Horlen.

Horlen's first pitch came in, Conigliaro swung, and the ball shot out toward left field—over the Wall, over the net above it, and onto Lansdowne Street. It was a "no-doubter" if there ever was one, and another occasion for hope. Fenway was now more than a half-century old. Perhaps, fans mused, Conigliaro and Yastrzemski would be the pair that would deliver the ballpark its first World Series championship since JFK's grandfather, Honey Fitz, was leading the cheers back in 1918.

CHAPTER 6

Rebirth and Rejuvenation

1967–1974

With Fenway attendance sometimes down to triple digits, owner Tom Yawkey considered tearing down the old park or moving the team. But everything changed in the summer of 1967, when fans flocked to see the Red Sox make an "Impossible Dream" come true.

The official 1967 Red Sox World Series press pin includes a nod to the home park.

This was the summer Arthur and Henry D'Angelo had been waiting for all their lives. Since coming over from Italy at age 12 in 1938, the twin brothers had worked together toward their dream of building a successful family business. And while they were not athletes themselves, their fortunes had always been directly tied to those of their adopted city's baseball team.

As teenagers during their first few years in Boston, selling newspapers outside Fenway Park after Red Sox ballgames—the first English words they learned were "two cents, mister"—they became experts in the art of fumbling through their pockets for change until fans anxious to get home just said "keep the nickel." The extra money allowed them to help support their parents and siblings. By the time Ted Williams & Co. came along in the early 1940s, the brothers had enough extra cash coming in to add ice cream, flowers, and shoe shines to their offerings.

World War II put a temporary halt to their progress, with the D'Angelos serving together in the infantry, but after the war both they and the Red Sox were ready for bigger things. The success of the 1946 pennant winners and Boston's renewed baseball fervor made the brothers' Fenway Park sales spot one of the hottest in town, and they realized that fans wanted to more visibly demonstrate their support for the team. The twins found suppliers who could make pennants and buttons with "Boston Red Sox" emblazoned on them, much like those Michael "Nuf Ced" McGreevy had produced for his Royal Rooters during the 1903 World Series. They also made sure that the "badge board" on which they displayed their wares was easily transportable. "By then the Sox had their own vendors, and when we

Red Sox players swarm pitcher Jim Lonborg after Boston defeated Minnesota in the 1967 season finale, clinching at least a tie for first place. At this moment, the crowd begins to descend onto the field.

snuck into Fenway Park they'd kick us out," explained Arthur D'Angelo with a laugh more than 60 years later. "Even on the street across from the park, the cops would run us off."

The brothers tried adding T-shirts to their repertoire, but they didn't sell so well and were harder to carry when running from police. To placate the men in blue and account for their growing business, the D'Angelos opened their first store, a rented 250-square-foot space with room for three counters just across the street from Fenway's main entrance. But then, right when things were looking up, Bobby Doerr's unexpected retirement and Ted Williams's surprising recall to the Marines in 1952 precipitated a youth movement by the Red Sox and a nearly 15-year stretch of noncontending teams occupying the home dugout at Fenway Park.

The D'Angelo brothers, Boston entrepreneurs, got in on the ground floor. They opened their memorabilia store across the street from Fenway Park's main entrance.

The big crowds stopped coming, and business fell off dramatically for the D'Angelos. During most of the mid- and late 1950s, the only items they consistently sold were anything related to Ted Williams, who after his heroic deeds in Korea had resumed terrorizing American League pitchers. To help make up for their drop in revenue, the brothers opened several dry cleaners in the Boston area, including one in Kenmore Square just a few blocks from the ballpark that was frequented by Ted and several of his teammates.

Now, seemingly overnight, things were looking up again. Under fiery new manager Dick Williams, a young Red Sox club that had finished a half game out of *last* place the year before was in the thick of a wild, four-team race for the 1967 American League pennant. Carl Yastrzemski had emerged as the best all-around player in baseball, and "Yaz" and local hero Tony Conigliaro were both among the league leaders in batting, homers, and runs batted in. The D'Angelos were selling "Yaz, Sir, That's My Baby" buttons as fast as they could get them made, along with "Tony C" pennants and any kind of hat, bracelet, or necklace you could think of with "Red Sox" emblazoned on it.

Like all of New England, the brothers were caught up in the excitement, and on August 15 they were among 27,125 fans at Fenway for a Tuesday night match-up with Detroit. The Red Sox went ahead 4–0 on homers by Yastrzemski, George Scott, and Reggie Smith, and as the brothers ran across the street to set up for the postgame rush, they could hear the boisterous crowd cheering each pitch of the Tigers' ninth. Once Dave Morehead finished off his six-hit shutout, the masses poured out of the ballpark and onto Jersey Street, many of them stopping in to buy a button or pennant before heading to their cars or the Kenmore Square trolley stop.

More than any place in Boston—and any place in baseball—Fenway Park was the place to be in the summer of '67. And while nobody knew it at the time, things would never be the same there again.

Sayonara Pinky, Hello Hope

The last time Morehead had pitched a shutout for the Red Sox, a little less than two years before, Fenway was in chaos on what would normally be considered a grand afternoon. On September 16, 1965, just 1,247 fans saw the young right-hander hurl a 2–0 no-hitter against the visiting Indians, and Morehead had to share the spotlight with news of a shake-up in the front office. Red Sox owner Tom Yawkey was frustrated by ever-dwindling crowds and his club's sixth consecutive losing season—they would wind up 62–100, their worst record since 1932—and word broke shortly after Morehead's masterpiece that Yawkey had fired Pinky Higgins as general manager.

All decisions regarding the roster would now fall upon team executive vice president Dick O'Connell, who unlike Pinky Higgins and Joe Cronin before him was neither a former Sox player nor an old buddy of Yawkey. The owner respected him, for certain, but the former Naval intelligence officer and Boston-area native was his own man and willing to make an unpopular trade rather than stick with the status quo or throw big bonuses at unproven kids. In addition to firing most of the scouting staff that had been around since the 1940s, O'Connell brought in former backup catcher Haywood Sullivan as his vice president and director of player personnel, and the two would work together to fix both the roster and the culture of the Red Sox.

The move to oust Higgins—which Yawkey told reporters was "the hardest thing I ever had to do in my life"—quite possibly saved the franchise as well as Fenway Park. A pair of games with the

The Citgo Sign

It is, in a way, the 3,600-square-foot heart of Fenway Park, pumping over and over as fans converge on the ballpark like blood coursing through veins of the city. Located atop the former Peerless Auto Sales and Services Building at 660 Beacon Street in Kenmore Square, and viewable above the Green Monster, this red, white, and blue sign advertises the Citgo Petroleum Corporation. Installed in 1965, it has become almost as familiar a fixture as the ballpark it hovers over—and a beacon in the night for drunken college kids and others trying to orient themselves around Boston's Back Bay.

Since replacing a shamrock-shaped neon Cities Services logo that had glowed for 25 years at the same spot, the Citgo sign has given Fenway sluggers a home run target for almost a half century, with the exception of four years (1979–83) when it was blacked out during the energy crisis. Citgo, owned and operated by the Venezuelan government, planned to take the sign down during this period, but public outcry and a 20-page report by the Boston Landmarks Commission defending it as a historic landmark saved the day.

The same electrician, Martin Foley of Hingham, has serviced the sign's blown-out bulbs from a trusty wooden swing since it was first put up. He aided in a $1.5 million renovation in 2005, during which more than 1.7 miles of stripes of LED lights replaced 5,878 glass neon tubes. This alteration cut the sign's energy consumption in half. When Boston Mayor Thomas Menino flipped the switch to turn the refurbished version on, he was aided by former Red Sox shortstop Luis Aparicio, a Venezuelan native.

The Citgo sign towers over the left-field wall.

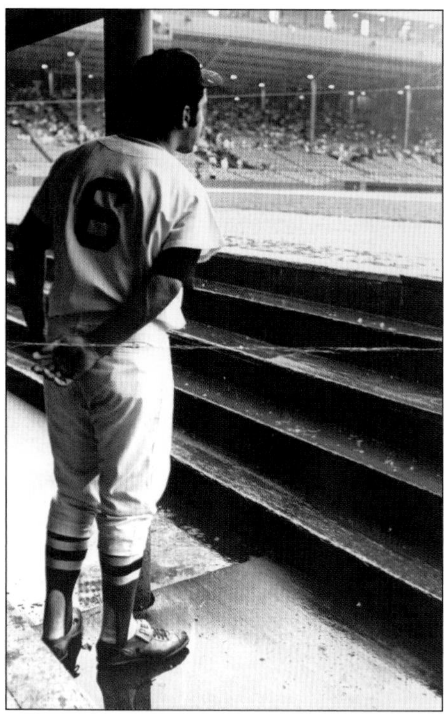

The once-lovely old park was not wearing well. Here, Red Sox shortstop Rico Petrocelli gazes at the field as water rolls into the dilapidated dugout.

California Angels in the waning days of the '65 season drew "crowds" of 461 and 409; there were nearly as many people working the 33,500-seat ballpark as there were paying to enter it. For several years before this, Yawkey had been considering proposals to tear down Fenway or move his moribund team. Last refurbished in 1934, the park was showing its age and lacked adequate parking for the growing number of fans who had moved from the city to the suburbs.

"The field itself was beautiful, but the building around it was a dump," said second baseman Mike Andrews, who joined the Boston club in 1966. "Coming down the runway from the clubhouse to the field, there were these old wooden slats on the ground covering puddles where the water always leaked in, and an old wooden shelf that players put their cigarettes and gum on. Guys would come in angry after they made an out and destroy the thing and send the cigarettes flying. The clubhouse was nothing, and we didn't even have any place for our wives."

Much of the Boston area was undergoing a period of urban renewal, which included the construction of new government buildings and highways. A Stadium Commission supported by the Massachusetts State Legislature looked into the prospect of building a new multisport arena like those going up in St. Louis and Houston, possibly with a retractable roof, which would support bigger crowds for football and postseason baseball. The commission was headed by Billy Sullivan, the former Boston Braves public relations whiz who now had a very vested interest in the matter as owner of the Boston Patriots football club. Sullivan's team played a majority of its home games at Fenway Park, where many fans had to sit in makeshift bleachers and Yawkey had full control over scheduling—a fact that often left the Patriots scrambling to find alternate home venues in September.

Other proposals suggested dramatically altering Fenway to fit in line with other construction already underway in the city. When a new turnpike was built alongside the railroad tracks that ran right behind Lansdowne Street in the late 1950s, there was talk of tearing out Lansdowne, pushing back the Green Monster, and adding a covered parking lot that would run up to the edge of the highway. "I'd like to see the Red Sox stay in the city," Cronin, then general manager, said of this proposal. "And I'd like to move back the fence so we'd have a more symmetrical park." Many local sportswriters were also convinced that fashioning a ballclub around Fenway was keeping the Sox from winning. For evidence, they pointed to 1965, when Boston led the American League in home runs and still lost 100 games.

Rumors also persisted that Yawkey wanted to sell the struggling club or move it to greener pastures, but for years he denied them. In 1960, as the Sox

"If this city is to remain a major sports center, a new stadium must be built somewhere in the Boston vicinity. Otherwise, it appears inevitable the city will lose both the Red Sox and the Patriots."
—Tom Yawkey in early 1967 (he would change his mind by September)

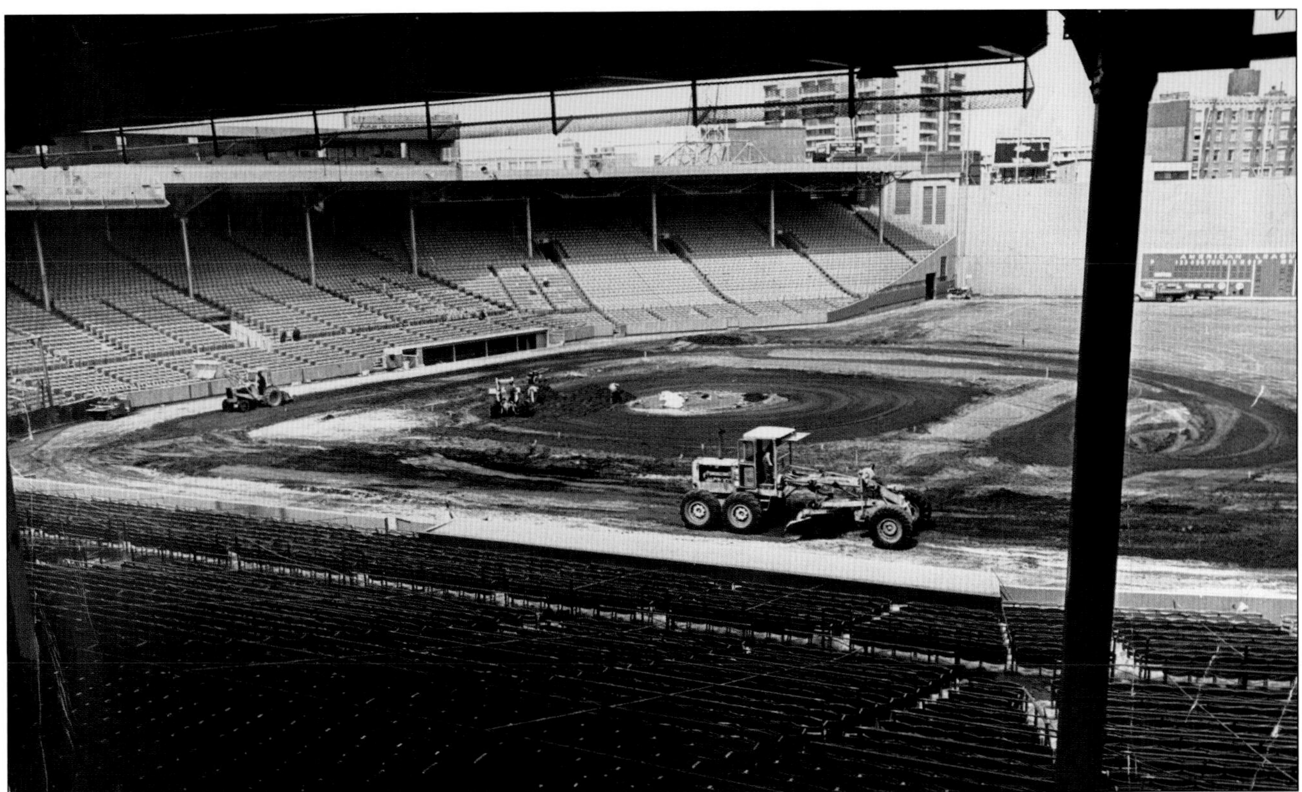

Even though they were talking about tearing Fenway down, the playing surface stayed pristine. Groundskeeper Joe Mooney, who would join the Red Sox in 1970, would ensure the field's prime condition for decades.

were limping to a seventh-place finish during Ted Williams's final season, the Associated Press and other news services reported that a syndicate of 10 Boston-area businessmen represented by attorney Herbert Abrams had offered Yawkey $5 million to sell. Abrams backed up the story, and Dick O'Connell, then business manager for the Red Sox, said it was only the latest of many bids that "come along sometimes as often as every two or three weeks." Yawkey claimed he knew nothing about the offer, and he issued a written statement saying the team was not for sale.

The rumors grew louder by 1966, when attendance continued to dwindle even as the team showed signs of improvement. Hard-hitting rookies George Scott (at first base) and Joe Foy (at third) joined veteran outfielders Conigliaro and Yastrzemski in the lineup. Young pitchers

Arthur D'Angelo, whose family fled the dictatorship of Benito Mussolini, rose from Boston street peddler to owner of the world's largest souvenir store.

Jim Lonborg and Jose Santiago continued developing, and Boston went 45–43 from July 1 on—yet still averaged barely 10,000 fans per game.

The D'Angelos never gave up. Arthur's days would usually start at 5 A.M. He'd spend a full morning and afternoon overseeing operations, employees, and machines at the family dry cleaning stores, and if there was a night game he'd be at Fenway until midnight working the store there—sometimes with just a few sales to show for the effort. He was now married with four sons, and Bobby the oldest began accompanying his dad to the ballpark after grade school and on weekends. "I grew up at Fenway," Bobby would recall later. "Me and my friends used to play Wiffle ball on Jersey Street right in front of the ballpark, and since we knew the ushers at every gate, they'd let us in whenever we wanted. There was almost nobody there anyway."

This Topps card was issued for Joe Foy, one of three talented young African-Americans in the 1967 Sox lineup. Foy was tough in the clutch and always in the middle of any fracas.

Filling the Seats

This certainly seemed to be the case on Opening Day, 1967, when just 8,234 showed up at Fenway on a 40-degree afternoon to see the Red Sox beat Chicago 5–4 behind four RBI from shortstop Rico Petrocelli and a strong start from Lonborg. The home club even stole three bases, almost unheard of on Boston's slow-footed, wait-for-a-homer teams of the past. They were young—the average age of the eight everyday starters was less than 24—and in new manager Dick Williams (just 37 himself) they had a hard-driving, crew-cut leader who was not afraid to bench players or shake up his lineup.

These clearly weren't the same old Red Sox. For one thing, Scott, Foy, rookie centerfielder Reggie Smith, and ace reliever John Wyatt were all African-Americans. By mid-June, around the time most Boston clubs of recent vintage were settling in near last place, the '67 Sox were within five games of first. The stadium talk persisted, however, and on June 21 Yawkey dropped a bombshell when he told reporters that he would move his team out of Boston unless a new facility was built.

"This is not a threat; this is a matter of fact," he said. "I cannot continue indefinitely under present circumstances. I am losing money with the Red Sox and no one—unless he's a damn fool—likes to lose money." The owner said he had lost $3 million during the previous five years, and everyone from Massachusetts Governor John A. Volpe to NFL Commissioner Pete Rozelle—who had said the Patriots might also have to leave Boston if they didn't get a new stadium to play in—applauded Yawkey's candor.

What nobody was counting on, however, was that the Red Sox would actually keep winning. The 10-team American League was shaping up to be a free-for-all, and the Red Sox stayed in the thick of things through the summer. Ten straight victories in July made believers out of many skeptical fans, and with Lonborg emerging as the AL's best starting pitcher and Yaz, Tony C, and Scott among the league's top hitters, Boston had a quartet of first-tier stars. Savvy veteran pick-ups by GM Dick O'Connell—pitcher Gary Bell, infielder Jerry Adair, and catcher Elston Howard—were significant on-field contributors and steadying hands in the clubhouse.

Three days after Morehead's August 15 shutout of the Tigers, the Sox took the field at Fenway for a Friday night contest with California just 3½ games from the top. The evening started uneventfully, but in the bottom of the fourth a smoke bomb thrown into left field delayed play and cast an eerie, smoky haze over the steamy ballpark. Conigliaro stepped up against Angels starter Jack Hamilton as things started to clear, taking his usual aggressive stance by leaning over home plate. This gave him little time to react when Hamilton's first pitch tailed up and in on him.

"When the ball was about four feet from my head, I knew it would get me," Conigliaro recalled in his autobiography, *Seeing It Through*. "I threw my hands up in front of my face and saw the ball follow me back and hit me square in the left side of the head. As soon as it crunched into me, it felt as if the ball would go in one side of my head and come out the other; my legs gave way and I went down like a sack of potatoes."

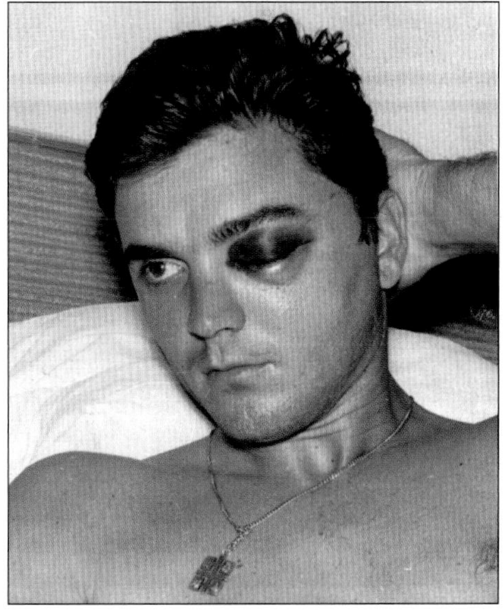

This is what Tony Conigliaro looked like the day after his left cheekbone was shattered by a high, hard one. When he returned in 1969, he was partially blind in his left eye, yet he still put up 20 homers. The next year, he slugged 36 for Boston.

The crowd of 31,027 fell silent as Tony C lay motionless at the plate, with on-deck man Petrocelli whispering in his ear that everything would be okay. Lib Dooley, the daughter of original "Royal Rooter" Jack Dooley and then in her 23rd year as a season-ticket holder, saw the scene unfold from her familiar front-row seat behind the Red Sox on-deck circle. She would never forget the crunching sound the ball made as it hit Conigliaro (nor did anybody else who heard it). Before each of the more than 2,500 games she attended after this one, Lib said a prayer, asking that no other player get hurt.

Billy Conigliaro, the little brother who had heard Tony's first Fenway at-bat and home run over the radio, saw this plate appearance live. "The whole

> "There were no other parks in the league where the fans were so close. You could almost reach out and touch them."
> **—Second baseman Mike Andrews**

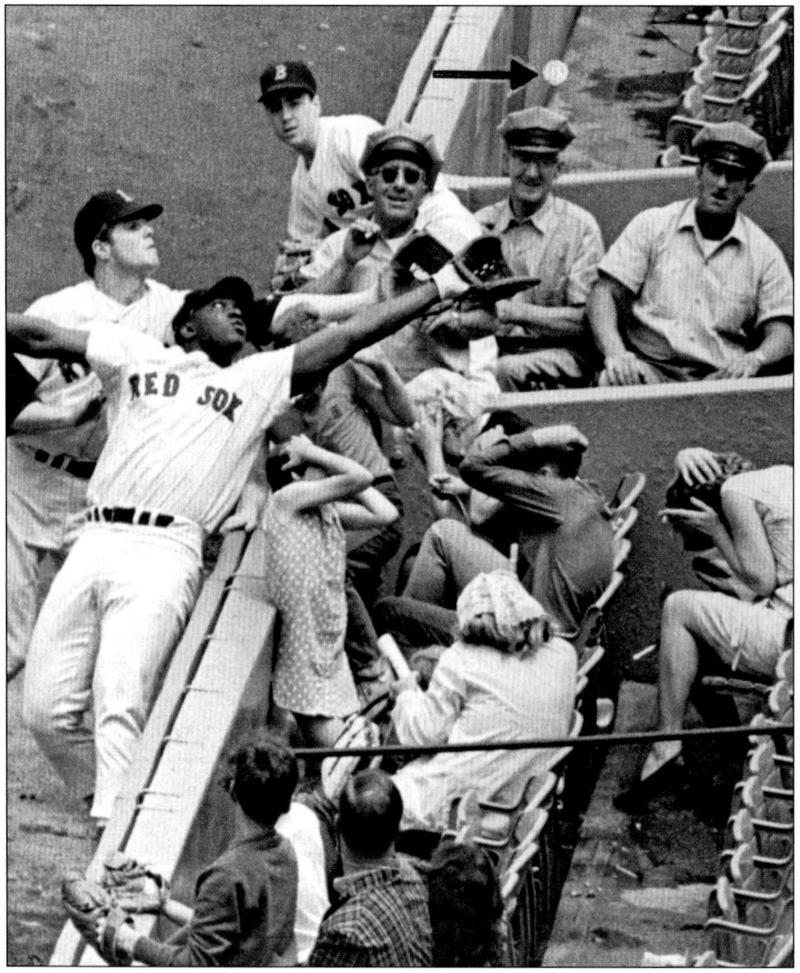

First baseman George "Boomer" Scott (*right*) and second baseman Mike Andrews try to snag a foul pop. Look at all the empty seats in the first and second rows. Had they all stepped out for a Fenway Frank, or was this another dismal turnout?

family was there; we didn't know until afterwards how bad it was," he remembered. "He got hit all the time. We just figured he'd get up and brush it off like he always did." He didn't, and as Conigliaro was carried away on a stretcher, there was good reason to think the pennant chances were going off with him.

The Red Sox, however, were resilient. Conigliaro would be lost for the year with a crushed left cheekbone and severely damaged left eye, but the team won eight of its next nine and on August 26 took sole possession of first place. September would see the Sox move in and out of the top spot numerous times as they battled California, Detroit, and Chicago in one of the closest pennant races in history. Boston claimed numerous come-from-behind victories over the span, and Yastrzemski enjoyed an incredible stretch drive in which he hit .523 (23-for-44), fielded spectacularly, and delivered one key hit after another during the season's last 12 pressure-packed games.

Suddenly, the empty seats that Yawkey had been worried about were no longer an issue. Fenway's stands were routinely packed, as older fans in ties and sport coats cheered alongside longhaired teenagers in jeans waving "Go-Go Red Sox!" banners. "It was almost like one of those time-lapse videos where you see the stands filling up to the point where they are jammed," Andrews said of the ballpark's transformation. "It was so exciting every game, just something very special to be a part of. There was no booing. We were growing together, and the fans were behind us."

Everybody seemed to be in a festive mood on Jersey Street, and the team's last-gasp tendencies earned it a catchy nickname—the "Cardiac Kids." Although Boston's Roxbury neighborhood, just a few miles from Fenway, erupted in a race-related riot that summer (one of many that raged in the U.S.

Carl Yastrzemski not only won the 1967 Triple Crown, but he also led the AL in runs, hits, total bases, runs produced, on-base percentage, and slugging average while playing Gold Glove defense.

during the "Long, Hot Summer"), photos appeared in the sports pages showing black and white Red Sox players hugging and mugging for the cameras. It was a display of brotherhood never seen in Boston baseball before, and it no doubt appealed to the college-age fans now coming out to the ballpark in droves.

Field of Dreams

In late July 1967, *Boston Globe* sports columnist Harold Kaese first referred to the Red Sox pennant chances as an "Impossible Dream." A song of that title written by Joe Darion had been featured in the Tony-award winning show *Man of La Mancha* a few years before. It described a quest by protagonist Don Quixote to "follow that star... no matter how hopeless, no matter how far." It was a perfect anthem for the Red Sox in their passionate, unlikely pursuit of a World Series berth. The phrase picked up steam near the end of the season, and in the future this club would forever be known throughout New England and beyond as "the Impossible Dream team."

Less than three months after saying he'd move the Red Sox unless a new park was built, Tom Yawkey had a change of heart. On September 6, with the team closing in on a new franchise home attendance mark—their final count of 1,727,832 would lead the American League—the owner told longtime *Record American* columnist John Gillooly that "[new] stadium or no stadium, the Red Sox won't move one inch away from Boston so long as the decision, if any, is mine."

Yawkey must have been feeling good about his choice a few weeks later. On September 30, just a year after finishing 72–90, the Red Sox beat the Minnesota Twins at Fenway 6–4 to tie them atop the AL standings at 91–70 and create a loser-go-home finale the next afternoon. Lonborg, 21–9, faced Twins ace and fellow 20-game winner Dean Chance, and the morning papers noted Lonnie's 0–6 lifetime record against Minnesota. Arthur and Henry D'Angelo managed to get two box seats for the game, and they walked right past the knowing ushers with a homemade stool and Arthur's ticketless son Bobby. Then, as they took their seats, they put down the stool so Bobby could join them.

The Twins and Chance held a 2–0 lead early on, until Lonborg surprised everyone with a bunt single leading off the fifth to spark a five-run rally. The

Hall of Fame Opens Doors to New Trio . . . Page 5

The Sporting News

AUGUST 5, 1967

DICK WILLIAMS

Page 5

Converted Card

SHANNON ON SPOT

Page 7

History Repeating?

BOUDREAU HAILS CUBS

Page 10

PGA King

JANUARY REIGNS

Page 45

College Stars

CHALLENGE TO PACKERS

Page 47

Red Sox manager Dick Williams stripped Carl Yastrzemski of his captainship, saying, "There's only one boss here." Williams, showcased here on the cover of *The Sporting News,* was tough and gruff, but he built a team worthy of Boston pride.

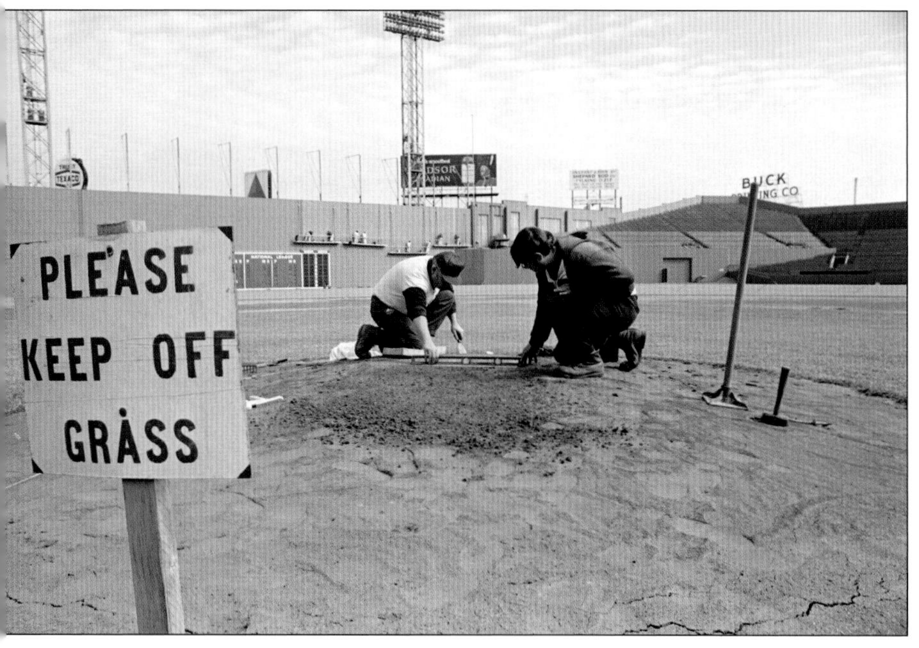

It's 1973, and grand old Fenway is getting rattier and stinkier, but you can bet that infield will still look divine.

crowd of 35,770 chanted "Go! Go! Go!" throughout the 24-minute frame, with many of them holding up signs with messages such as "Yaz Is God" (he responded with a two-run single). In the ninth, when pinch hitter Rich Rollins stepped in to face Lonborg with two outs and the Red Sox up 5–3, they were on their feet screaming again.

Bill Nowlin, who as a preteen threw water balloons at Fenway between at-bats by his idol Ted Williams, was now a 22-year-old University of Chicago student who was hooked on the Cardiac Kids and had put off returning to school to attend the season's final four games. "I was at the finale with my sister Lisa, who was 15," Nowlin recalled. "I think we had standing-room tickets, but in the last inning I led her down into the lower box seats. We were on the third base side in front of Section 24, and the Red Sox security had no idea what was about to happen with the crowd. There were no police or ushers blocking the way; they just let a bunch of us go right down to the first couple of rows."

It had been nearly 50 years since the last time a championship of any kind had been clinched by the Red Sox at Fenway—the 1918 World Series victory over the Cubs—so it's fair to say that the cops and ushers didn't know what to expect. Besides, even if the Sox did hold on to win this game, it would only clinch *a tie*. If the Tigers swept their doubleheader with the Angels, they would face the winner of the Boston-Minnesota game in a playoff for the title. Surely fans wouldn't go crazy over a *possible* pennant.

Above home plate, Red Sox broadcaster Ned Martin readied to make the biggest call of his career. His partner, Ken Coleman, had already headed down to the home clubhouse to get equipment set up for his postgame interviews. Coleman, the Quincy, Massachusetts, native whose own teenage dreams of pitching for Boston were dashed by a BB bullet to his eye, had spent much of this glorious summer recalling Sunday doubleheaders enjoyed with his father at Fenway 30 years before. Wishing his dad could have lived to see this moment, he thought of his own son Casey, a Fenway concessions worker who, with this being his day off, had hoped to get into the game by flashing ushers his concessions pass. The elder Coleman had no way of knowing if Casey did in fact make it in, but he would later learn that the resourceful teen had done so by climbing atop a

> **"If we stayed out there we might get crushed, so one by one we wended our way into the dugout and through the tunnel to the clubhouse. It was there I finally gave the ball to Lonnie, who was one of the last to make it off the field."**
>
> **—Rico Petrocelli, on catching the last out of the 1967 regular-season finale against Minnesota and saving the ball for winning pitcher Jim Lonborg**

ticket booth and then over a fence after his pass had failed to gain him entry.

As Coleman readied things below, Martin described the last pitch from Lonborg to Rollins over the 44-station Red Sox Radio Network: *"Looped toward shortstop. Petrocelli's back. He's got it! The Red Sox win! And there's pandemonium on the field! Listen!"*

Martin's description was dead-on, as was his decision to stop talking and let listeners gather a picture in their minds of what was transpiring beneath his booth. The first seconds of the celebration actually started quite innocently, with Petrocelli, Andrews, Scott, and Howard running to the mound in an attempt to hoist Lonborg up in the air. They managed to do so, but in a few moments the pitcher could no longer see his teammates as they disappeared in a sea of fans that were descending on him like water running down a drain. Among them was Nowlin, who on impulse had leaped over the short wall separating the box seats from the field and was one of the first to reach Lonborg. "Somehow I patted him on the back, and then I felt this huge mob coming up behind me," Nowlin remembered. "I got out of there quick. It wasn't like he was going to invite me home for dinner; he looked terrified."

He was. Whatever Lonborg's plans were for that evening, they did not include exiting Fenway Park atop a human wave of strangers. "I realized I couldn't see anybody I recognized. Not a single person," the pitcher recalled. "The crowd starting moving toward the right-field foul pole, and I was trying to get back to the dugout. A lot of articles of my clothing were starting to disappear; the moment of jubilation had passed, and now the moment of anxiety had started to set in."

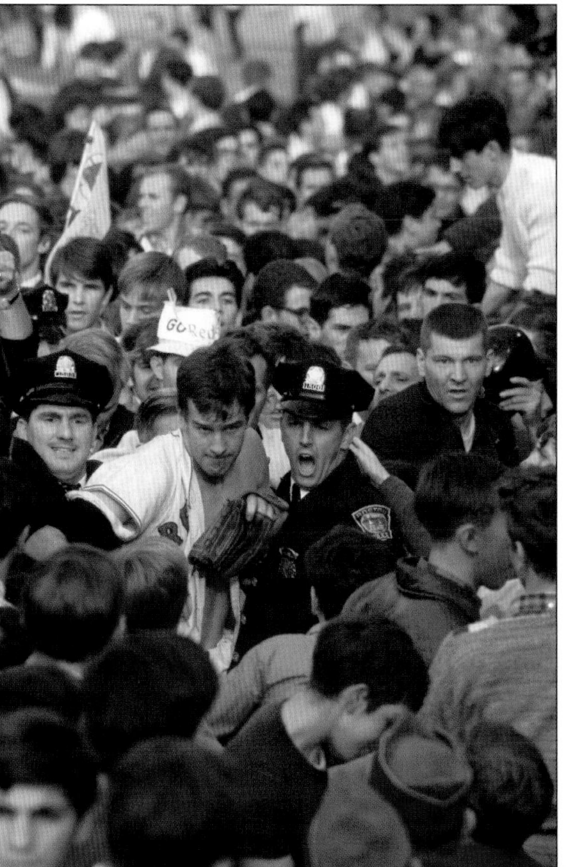

For a few harrowing moments, Jim Lonborg felt what it was like to be a rock star. After the pitcher defeated Minnesota in the 1967 finale, delirious fans tore at his clothes as he tried desperately to reach the dugout.

Somehow, security police managed to get a cap-less, shirt-ripped Lonborg off the field and into the clubhouse, but thousands of fans—including Casey Coleman—were left to mill around the field unattended like the second coming of the Royal Rooters. It's understandable why the revelers were in no hurry to leave.

Despite his earth-rumbling season and appearance on the cover of *Life*, Yaz was not the unanimous selection for AL MVP in 1967. A New York writer voted for Minnesota's Cesar Tovar, a .267 hitter. (Sox-Yankees enmity ran deep.)

While the Red Sox now give daily tours of Fenway and numerous in-season opportunities for people to stroll, picnic, or play catch on the hallowed field, no such options existed back in 1967. This was likely the first time most of these fans had ever set foot on Fenway sod, and they wanted it to last. Some reached down and tore out a handful for a memento, while others ventured out to left field and grabbed steel name or number plates from the front of the manual scoreboard. Behind home plate, one especially zealous group of about 20 men crawled up the protective netting that ran from the backstop to the press box for no apparent reason. Luckily, none of the Spiderman wannabes was reported hurt.

What was ironic about all this bedlam, which Ken Coleman later compared to the moment in *The Wizard of Oz* when Dorothy exits her black and white house and enters the Technicolor world of Munchkinland, was that it was premature. The Tigers had already beaten the Angels in the first game of their doubleheader, and if they won the nightcap, Detroit and Boston would square off at Fenway the next day to determine the American League champion. All the Sox had clinched so far was second place.

Back in the clubhouse, Boston players huddled around radios and listened to Tigers broadcaster Ernie Harwell describe the last portion of the second Detroit-California game. When Dick McAuliffe of the Tigers hit into a double play to end the 8–5 Angels win, the room exploded in a mixture of joy and relief. Earlier, the players had doused themselves with beer, but now they used the real thing—champagne provided by Tom Yawkey. Before the evening ended, Yawkey would nearly double Yastrzemski's salary to $100,000, making him one of the highest-paid players in the league. In going 7-for-8 in the last two pressure-packed games, Yaz had secured the Triple Crown with .326, 44, 121 totals, and cameras recorded him being hugged and kissed by his manager. Off to the side, Tony Conigliaro—still sidelined since his August injury—was overcome with emotion and sat quietly crying by his locker.

Heavy underdogs in the World Series against the St. Louis Cardinals, the Red Sox wound up surprising everyone again by pushing the National League champs to seven games. Lonborg had a one-hitter and a three-hitter in two complete-game victories, but Cardinals ace Bob Gibson bested him in the finale, 7–2, when Boston manager Williams was forced to counter with his best hurler on just two days rest. Gibson's third win of the series earned him the MVP Award over teammate Lou Brock, who hit .414 with seven stolen bases, and Fenway fans

Game 2 of the 1967 World Series was close until the seventh inning. Yaz's three-run poke (his second of the game) jolted the Sox to a 5–0 lead as they knotted the Series at a game apiece. Here is a rarity—a swing and a miss by Yastrzemski.

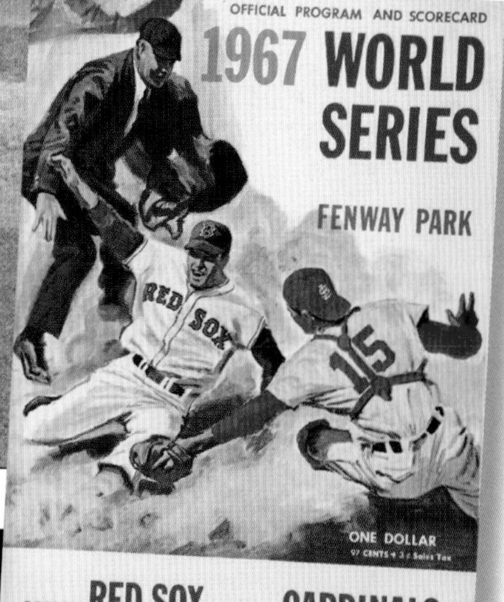

OFFICIAL PROGRAM AND SCORECARD
1967 WORLD SERIES
FENWAY PARK
ONE DOLLAR
BOSTON RED SOX ST. LOUIS CARDINALS

This was the first World Series program that Red Sox fans had seen in 21 long, hard seasons.

In Game 7, the Cardinals' Julian Javier slugged a three-run homer off a weary Jim Lonborg in the sixth inning, giving St. Louis a 7–1 lead. Cards pitcher Bob Gibson, who homered himself in the game, went the distance and won 7–2.

showed their class by loudly cheering both these future Hall of Famers when they came up to bat in the ninth inning. A few minutes later, as it filed quietly out, the crowd watched Gibson and his teammates celebrate on the Fenway diamond—quite a contrast from the wild events of a few weeks before.

Despite this disappointing ending, the 1967 season has not been treated by history in the same way as the near-misses of other years. It was so fun and surprising a ride that the final outcome did little to detract from the total package. For many Red Sox fans of a certain age, one of their most treasured possessions is likely a well-worn copy of *The Impossible Dream* LP album that came out after the '67 World Series. A retrospective on that magical summer, narrated by Ken Coleman, the record features audio clips from actual game-day broadcasts interspersed with reflections on the campaign set to verse.

When originally broadcast in Boston as a documentary on WHDH-TV Channel 5, this homage included footage of an empty, litter-strewn Fenway that showed just how stark and unglamorous the ballpark looked during this period in its history. Other than the left-field scoreboard, which featured an attractive addition on which the starting lineups of both clubs were listed in lights, Fenway appeared tired and old—with rusting railings, uncomfortable-looking wooden seats on which the back slats seemed too far apart, and concrete walkways worn dark by decades of cigarette ashes and shoe soles. The dugouts looked like something out of the low minor leagues, and a sad little team logo above an exit ramp was the closest thing to window dressing.

Then, in an instant, the scene changed. The stands were full. The players sprinted out of the dugout and took their positions on the diamond as the crowd cheered the start of a game. Fans were waving pennants and wearing bright white hats emblazoned with "Go Red Sox!", and their bright shirts offered a rainbow of colors to blot out the gray.

It was clear what had happened. The Sox had started winning, the fans returned, and the park was reborn.

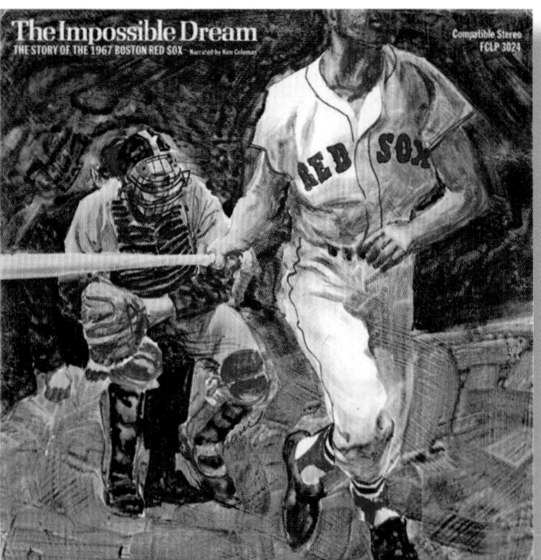

The Impossible Dream album, narrated by Red Sox broadcaster Ken Coleman, delighted New Englanders throughout the 1967–68 off-season. You can still hear clips from it online.

Chasing Tigers and Birds

Just as they had after the 1946 World Series loss to the Cardinals, New Englanders assumed that the '68 Red Sox would be contenders for another post-season berth. But as had been the case a generation earlier, the team failed in its American League title defense due in large part to injuries. An off-season

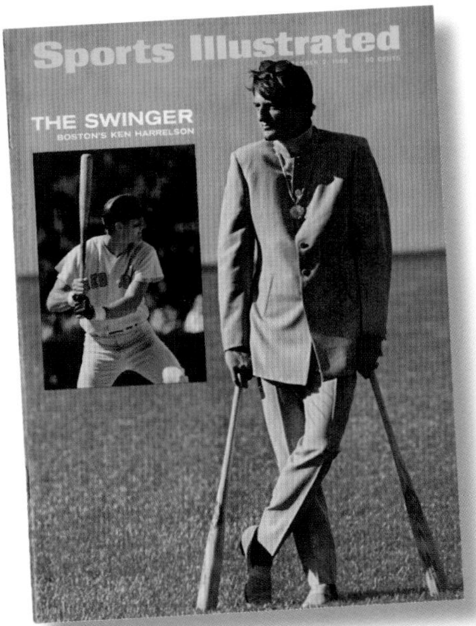

skiing accident that caused severely torn knee ligaments limited Lonborg to a 6–10 record in 1968, and No. 2 starter Santiago went down in midseason with elbow tendonitis. Conigliaro wound up missing the entire season as his eye slowly healed, yet he found it impossible to put baseball out of his mind: His Kenmore Square apartment overlooked Fenway Park.

Despite these setbacks and the fact that Boston's respectable 86–76 record in '68 left it 17 games behind a juggernaut 103–59 Tigers squad at season's end, the magic of the previous season's club had carried over to Fenway. The little ballpark on Jersey Street was now the "in" place to be for college kids, families, and seasoned fans alike. Attendance climbed to a new team record of 1,940,788, more than every club in baseball but the two pennant winners, Detroit and St. Louis. It was no longer just the Yankees who brought in big Fenway crowds for weekday afternoon or late-season contests, either. The games with less than 2,000 fans were a thing of the past—as was most talk of a new stadium.

A new hero arrived on the scene in Ken Harrelson, an outfielder brought in late the previous summer to replace Conigliaro. Harrelson emerged as a fan and media superstar in 1968, as much for his Nehru jackets, dune buggy, and flashy cleats as for his 35 homers and 109 RBI.

Sports Illustrated cover boy Ken Harrelson, known for his cool duds, prominent schnoz, and powerful swing, became a Red Sox after he called Kansas City A's owner Charlie Finley "a menace." The A's released him in August 1967, and he immediately signed with Boston.

Pele Played Here

In addition to its last season as the home of the Boston Patriots, Fenway played host in 1968 to another football—make that *futbol*—team.

In the summer of 1968, the Boston Beacons called Fenway home for their first and only season in the North American Soccer League. The club struggled to a last-place finish in the league's Atlantic Division, and most of its games on Jersey Street drew fewer than 5,000. The one exception was a 7–1 exhibition loss on July 8 against three-time World Cup hero Pele and his Santos team from Brazil. A crowd of 18,431 watched as, according to the Associated Press, "time and again, Pele dribbled past the defense or hit his teammates with pinpoint passes as the Brazilians dominated the action." Boston's 9–17–6 record suggests it wasn't just Pele who had this success against the Beacons.

Boston Beacons (*dark jerseys*) hosting the Baltimore Bay

> "It's hard to put into words how I feel about Fenway Park and the Boston fans. Everybody is so warm and friendly and they just took me in as part of the family. Maybe that's what it's like to watch a game at Fenway Park, everybody belonging to one family."
>
> **—Outfielder Ken "Hawk" Harrelson**

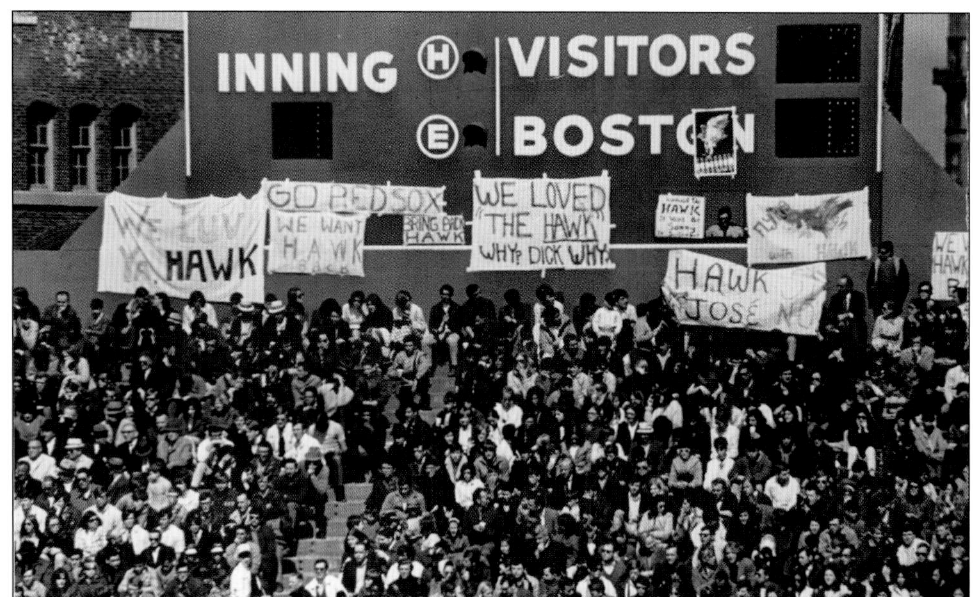

After Ken "Hawk" Harrelson was traded in April 1969, Fenway fans vented their displeasure. A year earlier, the popular outfielder had led the league in RBI while playing errorless defense in the outfield.

Members of the "All-Time" Red Sox lineup, as selected by fans, are honored prior to a game on July 5, 1969. Going down the line from left to right are Bobby Doerr, Frank Malzone, MLB Commissioner Bowie Kuhn, Joe Cronin, Lefty Grove, Birdie Tebbetts, Carl Yastrzemski, and Ted Williams, now the manager of the Washington Senators. Williams doffed his hat to a standing ovation when he came on the field.

Nicknamed "Hawk" for his prominent nose, Harrelson was a swinging bachelor who developed a cult following in the Fenway bleachers. The D'Angelo brothers sold cartloads of "Don't Knock the Hawk" buttons, stickers, and bracelets, and business was so good that the twins moved out of their little rented space and bought a big store on Jersey Street right across from Fenway's main entrance.

The dismal sub-.500 years were behind the Red Sox. Dick O'Connell's strong trading skills and Haywood Sullivan's player development acumen assured that a steady stream of talent from the farm system and other big-league clubs would keep the Red Sox in the 85- to 90-win class for the foreseeable future. Unfortunately, after the Tigers came back to earth in 1969, Boston had to spend most of the next six years looking up in the standings at an outstanding Baltimore Orioles team.

Led by clutch hitters Frank Robinson and Brooks Robinson; stellar defense from Brooks, Paul Blair, Mark Belanger, and Davey Johnson; and a starting rotation led by 20-game winners Jim Palmer, Dave McNally, and Mike Cuellar, the Orioles reached the playoffs five times from 1969 to '74 under Hall of Fame manager Earl Weaver. Major League Baseball split both the American and National leagues into Eastern and Western divisions in '69, and it added a best-of-five Championship Series in which the division winners would battle for a spot in the World Series. Logic dictated that the Red Sox, with just five teams to beat for the AL East rather than nine, would have a much better shot at the postseason. Unfortunately, logic did not account for the Orioles. The Sox finished 22, 21, and 18 games behind Baltimore from 1969 to '71, placing third each year. "Wild card" teams were still decades in the future, so Fenway's red, white, and blue bunting stayed in storage between Opening Days.

The most optimistic Boston fans knew deep down that Baltimore was nearly unbeatable over 162 games, and while people kept coming out to Fenway in great numbers—the Sox led the league in attendance each of those three years—the feel-good atmosphere that had symbolized the team's and park's rebirth gave way at times to a cynical bitterness. Yastrzemski, the '67 AL MVP and leader of the Impossible Dreamers, remained a top-flight player, winning a third batting title in 1968 and just missing a fourth in 1970 when he hit .329 with 40 home runs. But when Yaz fell off dramatically to a .254 average and 15

Gene Monster

The Red Sox could not repeat as American League champions in 1968, but the red, white, and blue bunting that usually signals playoff baseball could be seen up around the ballpark for one night that summer.

Senator Eugene McCarthy of Minnesota, the presidential hopeful who was widely popular with liberals and college students, filled the ballpark well past its legal capacity for a rally on July 26. An estimated 40,000 turned out (with an overflow of 5,000 milling about outside) to hear McCarthy voice his support for local candidates and rail against racism and the war in Vietnam. Hundreds of balloons were released skyward as the candidate's motorcade entered stylishly from behind a garage door in the center-field wall. McCarthy said the wildly cheering crowd "reflects the confidence of the people to bring about changes when change is necessary." It was a great line, for sure, but he still lost the Democratic nomination to Vice President Hubert Humphrey.

The no-nonsense mentality that had served Dick Williams well as Red Sox manager wore out in 1969. The players simply got tired of it. Williams was canned with nine games to go.

homers in 1971, due in large part to a wrist injury that forced him to alter his swing, Fenway fans booed the captain so badly that he put cotton in his ears before heading to left field.

He wasn't the only one. A few years earlier, in 1969, Tony Conigliaro heard things like "Go home, blind man" when he struggled during stretches of a brave, productive 20-homer comeback season. And just prior to this, after O'Connell traded Harrelson to Cleveland to add pitching depth and make room for Tony C's outfield return, fans picketed outside Fenway and lashed out at the general manager.

To his credit, O'Connell ignored the criticism and continued seeking a perfect formula by blending young players up from the minors with accomplished veterans acquired by trade. Nobody was sacred. In 1971, he sent popular second baseman Mike Andrews to the White Sox for aging Hall of Fame shortstop Luis Aparicio, then plugged up second base by sending Tony Conigliaro (coming off a 36-homer year, but his eye failing again) to California for a trio that included future Gold Glove winner Doug Griffin. A year later, a huge 10-player swap sent a package including two more '67 heroes—George Scott and Jim Lonborg—to the Brewers for, among others, speedy outfielder Tommy Harper (who would set a Red Sox record with 54 stolen bases in 1973). O'Connell even fired manager Dick Williams when he felt his drill sergeant methods were wearing thin, putting amiable "player's manager" Eddie Kasko at the helm.

Not every move was a good one. For example, ace reliever Sparky Lyle went to the Yankees for first baseman Danny Cater, then promptly saved an AL-high

Billy Conigliaro (*right*), who was in the Fenway stands when his brother (*left*) was felled by the Jack Hamilton pitch, was his outfield partner when Tony returned. They combined for 54 homers in 1970.

Runner-up for Rookie of the Year in 1967, talented switch-hitting outfielder Reggie Smith was part of the influx of great young talent to emerge from the Boston farm system.

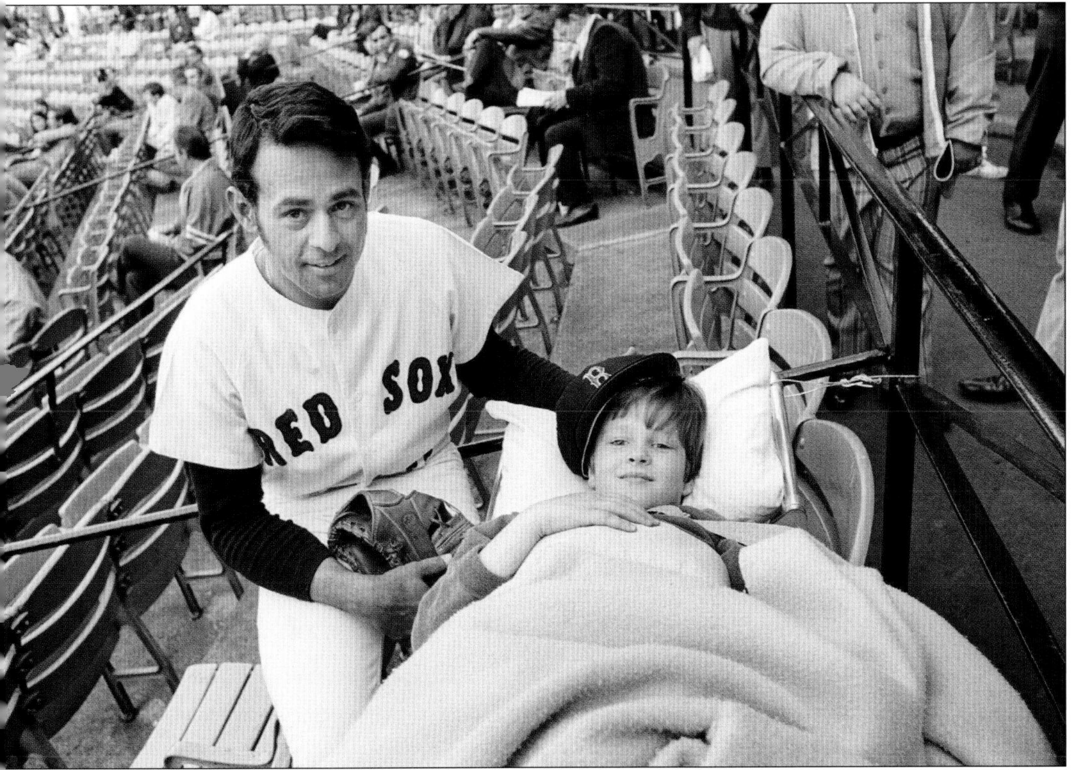

Luis Aparicio gives his cap to a boy who had fallen from a Fenway billboard, on which he had climbed to see Luis play. As a Red Sox, the aging Aparicio was a two-time All-Star.

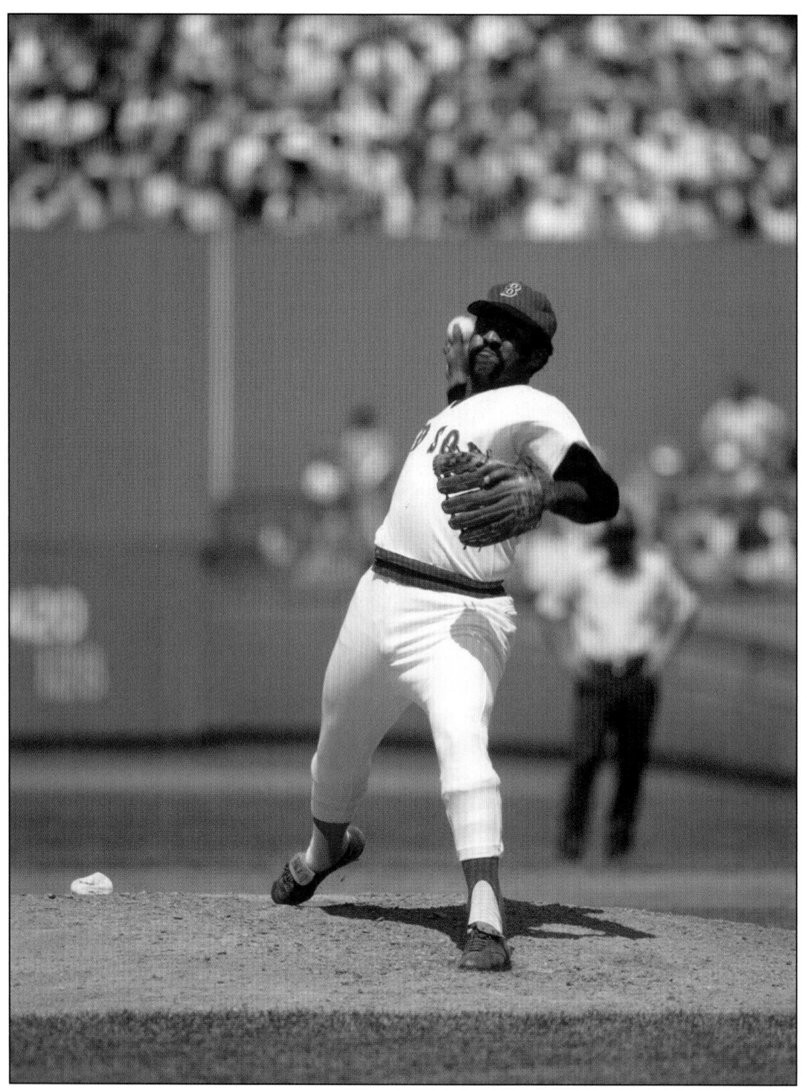

One of the most beloved Red Sox of all time, Luis Tiant used a delightfully twisty repertoire of baffling motions to mystify AL hitters. He was a three-time 20-game winner for Boston and 31–12 in September and October.

35 games while Cater hit .237. But O'Connell kept right on swinging. And in the summer of '71, he hit his biggest home run when he signed pitcher Luis Tiant off the scrap heap. The Cuban right-hander, a former 20-game winner for the Indians, had battled shoulder injuries and was thought washed up when the Braves released him at age 30. O'Connell got a good report from pitcher-turned-scout Lee Stange, however, and decided to take a chance.

Tiant initially pitched solely out of the bullpen, but when the Red Sox got off to a dismal start in strike-shortened 1972 he became first a swingman and then an ace. In August and September, he was almost unbeatable, going 11–1 with six shutouts (including four straight) in 12 starts. Along with freshman catcher Carlton Fisk, who would be named Rookie of the Year at season's end, "Looie" led Boston to the brink of an AL East title and paced the league with a sterling 1.91 ERA.

The pair became instant fan favorites that summer at Fenway. Fisk, who had grown up in New Hampshire, possessed a no-nonsense, take-charge attitude on and off the field. Tiant was a fun-loving leader who delighted crowds and befuddled batters with a seemingly endless array of windups, deliveries, and pitching speeds. When Yaz emerged from his yearlong power slump to hit eight home runs in September, it felt like 1967 all over again on Jersey Street. But the Sox had to finish on the road, and they lost two of three at Detroit on the final weekend to wind up one-half game behind the Tigers.

The 1973 season was highlighted by Harper's 17-homer, 54-steal year, 20 wins from Tiant, and 20 home runs from another O'Connell reclamation project—Orlando Cepeda, the first Red Sox designated hitter. Boston was close to the top all season, but in the end the Orioles again proved too strong to overcome. O'Connell shook things up once more, trading disgruntled star centerfielder Reggie Smith for veteran righty pitcher Rick Wise and outfield super sub Bernie Carbo. He also surprised many by releasing the still productive but aging Cepeda and Aparicio at the end of spring training in 1974.

Going with youth, the '74 Red Sox had five players under 25 (Dwight Evans, Mario Guerrero, Cecil Cooper, Juan Beniquez, and Rick Burleson) appear in 90-plus games. Veterans Yastrzemski and Rico Petrocelli—the last of the '67 holdovers—were the top two RBI men, and Tiant and left-hander Bill Lee combined for 39 victories at the top of the rotation. Even serious injuries that sidelined No. 3 starter Wise for almost the entire season and Fisk from late June on didn't stop the Sox from taking a commanding lead in the AL East.

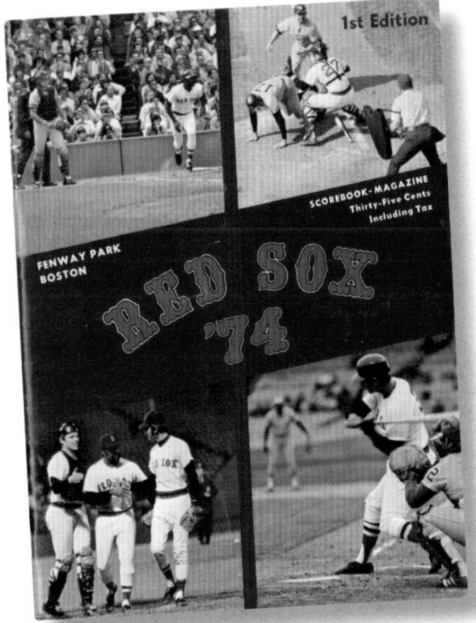

Despite rookie manager Darrell Johnson's positive attitude, the 1974 Red Sox blew a seven-game lead in August and finished third in the AL East.

When Tiant beat Vida Blue and the defending world champion A's for his 20th win before 35,866 raucous Fenway fans on August 23, Boston was in front by seven games and seemed poised to finally get over the hump and back into the postseason. Then the entire lineup went cold for three weeks, and after a 4–14 stretch (including eight straight losses, four by shutout) they had tumbled to third for good. The only consolation for the Fenway faithful in the waning days of another lost season was watching the continued progress of the team's young players—especially Cooper, Burleson, and a couple late-season outfield call-ups named Fred Lynn and Jim Rice.

New Englanders became acquainted with them in September. In October of the following year, nearly 36 million television viewers would get their turn.

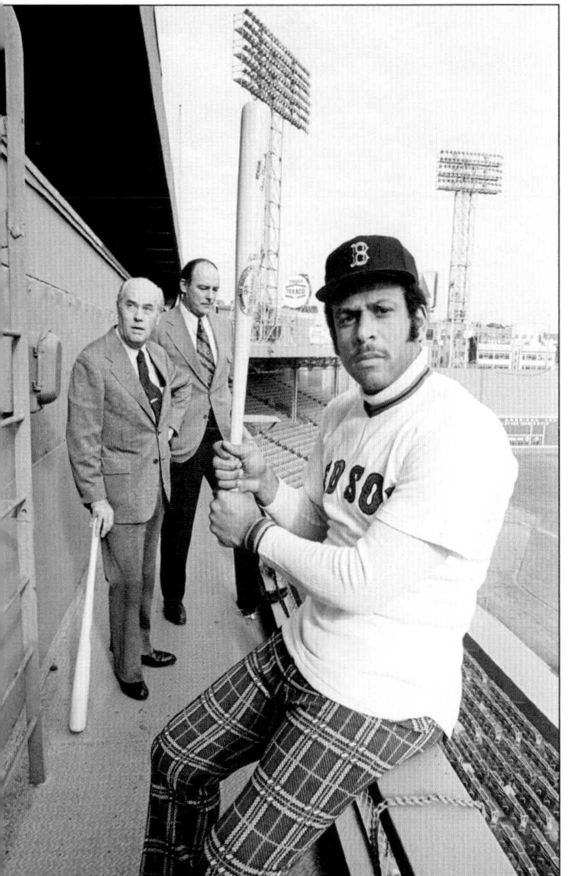

Five-time 100-RBI man Orlando Cepeda signed with the Red Sox as a free agent in January 1973 and became a full-time designated hitter in the first year of the DH. Red Sox officials Dick O'Connell (*left*) and Haywood Sullivan celebrated the deal.

CHAPTER 7

High Highs and Low Lows

1975–1985

When Carlton Fisk's 12th-inning home run banged off the foul pole in Game 6 of the 1975 World Series, New England erupted in unbridled joy. Alas, the Red Sox lost Game 7 the next day, launching another decade of frustration.

Everybody thought he was knocked out cold, or even worse, but rookie Fred Lynn was conscious the entire time. He just couldn't feel anything below his waist.

Moments earlier, Lynn had crashed into the concrete wall in center field at Fenway Park while in pursuit of a Ken Griffey fly ball. Now, as he lay crumpled at the base of the fence, just below the "379" sign, the capacity crowd of 35,205 was silent as it waited for him to move. Lynn had known he was going to hit the wall as soon as he felt the warning track dirt underneath his feet, and he knew it was going to hurt. But this was Game 6 of the World Series, there were two men on base in a tie contest, and the Red Sox had to beat the Cincinnati Reds to force a winner-take-all finale. In Lynn's mind, letting up his stride and fielding the ball off the wall wasn't an option.

The 1975 World Series reestablished baseball in America's hearts and minds. It matched two teams with storied pasts against each other in sensational fashion.

"I had played football at USC, and gotten hit hard a few times by middle linebackers, so I knew what it felt like," Lynn recalled. "Griffey had hit the same ball in Cincinnati and I tracked it down, but Fenway is a different animal."

As the moments passed to minutes, Lynn prayed for the feeling to come back to his legs. Outfield mates Carl Yastrzemski and Dwight Evans (who had backed up the play and thrown the ball in, holding Griffey to a triple) were at his side, and trainer Charlie Moss asked Lynn what day it was. He knew it was Tuesday, of course, but all he could really focus on was his lower body—which finally started tingling. In time, he felt good enough to stand up, and when he told Moss he was staying in the game and the trainer jogged off, the crowd roared its approval.

All throughout this 1975 season, his first full year in the big leagues, Lynn had been invaluable in the field and at the plate (he would become

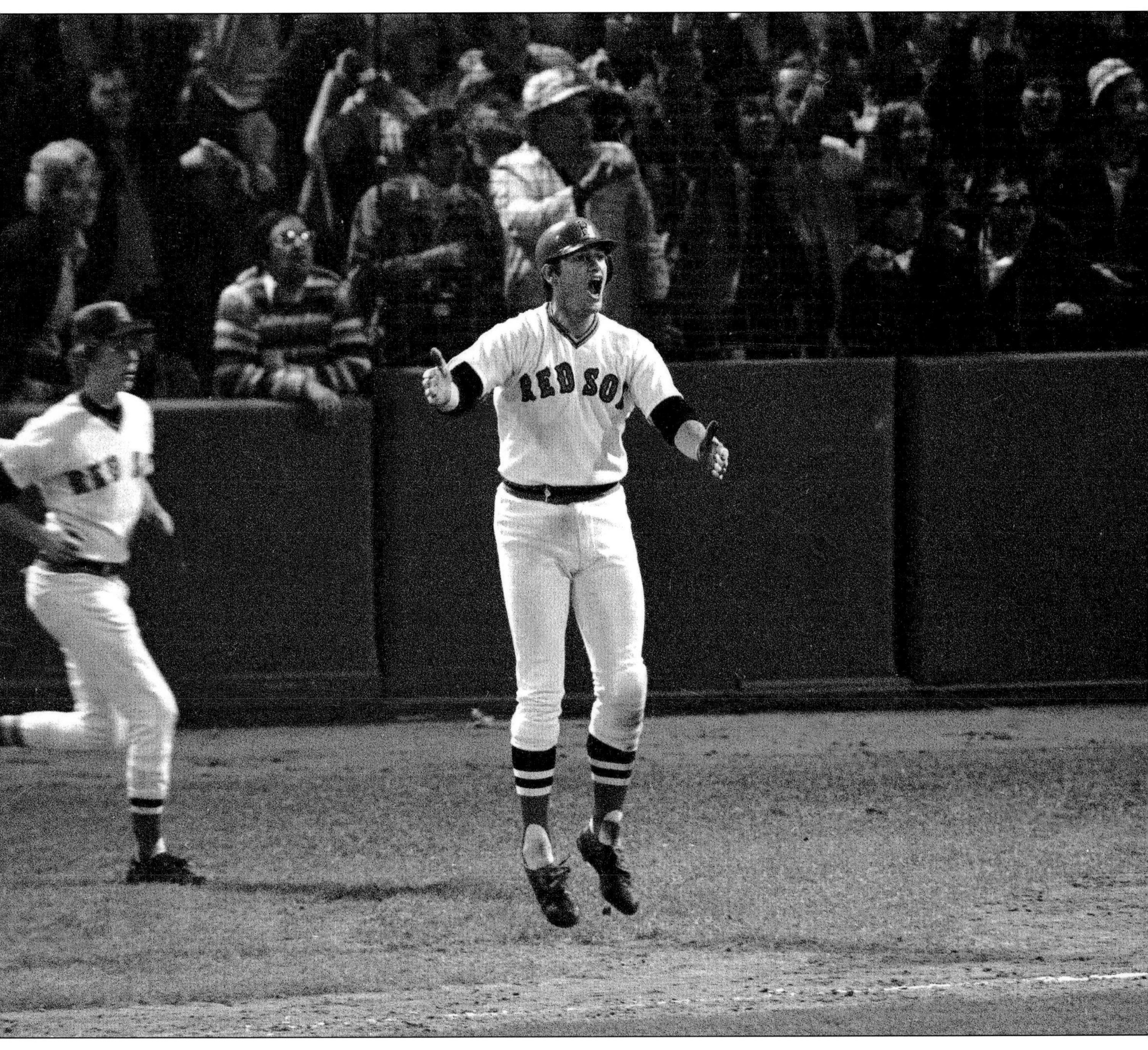

Carlton Fisk frantically tries to wave the ball fair in Game 6 of the 1975 World Series. In a few moments, Fenway Park organist John Kiley would begin the "Hallelujah Chorus" and several journalists would suggest that Game 7 be canceled. "How could it get any better than this?" they claimed.

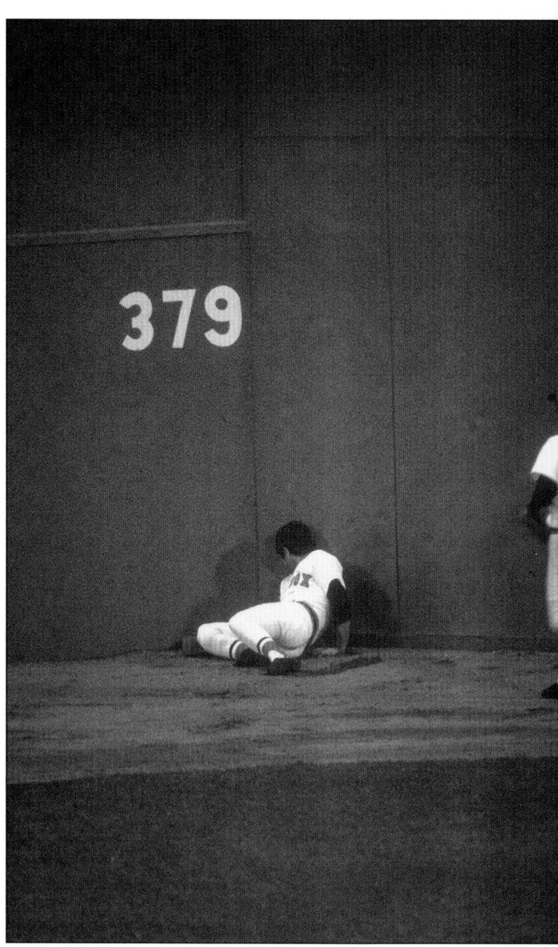

Fans held their collective breath until Fred Lynn finally moved after attempting to snag Ken Griffey's fly ball in Game 6. The next year, the outfield walls were padded.

You could get a box seat for the 1975 ALCS for only seven bucks, but prices were hiked for the next round. For the World Series, upper box seats at Fenway cost $15.

the first major-league rookie ever to win a league MVP Award). Tonight's game had been no different. In the first inning, with two men on base, he had smashed a Gary Nolan pitch for a home run to deep center, past the same spot to which he tracked Griffey's hit. The Reds had come back against Boston ace Luis Tiant, however, and Griffey's blow made it 5–3 Cincinnati in the fifth inning. Time was running short.

It got even shorter by the eighth, when Cesar Geronimo led off with a massive homer to make it 6–3 and chase Tiant, who had been going for his third win of the Series. The Fenway faithful showered the stout Cuban pitcher with the familiar chant of "Loo-ie, Loo-ie" as he walked off the field, knowing it was likely the last time they would be able to salute their hero until the next season. After pitching nearly 300 innings since April and 25 in the Series, the most beloved athlete in New England this side of Bobby Orr had run out of gas along with his team. Boston had fought hard against a fantastic Cincinnati club, but like the seventh game of the '67 World Series and the final days of '74, '72, '49, and '48, it appeared the Sox were going to fall short again in their quest for their first world championship in nearly 60 years.

Watching from the deepest, highest point of the center-field bleachers overlooking Lansdowne Street, 12-year-old Sharon Sullivan shivered beside her brothers Kyle and Marc. Their father was also in the ballpark on this night, but he had a considerably better and warmer view from the owner's box. Dad was Haywood Sullivan, vice-president of the Red Sox and confidant to owner Tom Yawkey. When the three kids told their father at the last minute that they wanted to go to Game 6, these were the best seats he could come up with—but it didn't really bother Sharon at all. Fenway felt like her second home.

She and her twin brother, Kyle, were just five years old when Haywood Sullivan—a former backup catcher for the Red Sox in the 1950s who had most recently managed the Kansas City A's—was invited by Yawkey and General

Manager Dick O'Connell to help revitalize the Boston team in the mid-1960s. Over the next decade, along with their big brother, Marc, Sharon and Kyle literally made Fenway their playground. They'd enter with their mom and take their "official" seats in the family section behind home plate, but when Mom turned around they'd be gone and off on another adventure.

The days they accompanied their dad to work long before game time were the most fun. "One time we took a couple friends in with us and played hide-and-seek for eight hours," Sharon, now Sharon Sullivan-Constantin, recalled. "I would often find myself hiding in the left-field wall, which would infuriate [groundskeeper] Joe Mooney because we had to run across the field to get to it and he hated anybody running on his grass. I'd also hide under Joe's desk in his little office, behind the beer taps in the grandstands, in the clubhouse tunnel, or in the clubhouse itself. If you were small enough, you could even squeeze into the smallest seat in the photographer's box, which hung down from the press box behind home plate. You needed a ladder to get to it, so I couldn't wear a dress."

The Sullivan kids knew every nook and cranny of the ballpark, and they helped keep it looking good when Mooney let them spread mulch and move sod. If they had told this detail to the bleacherites sitting nearby them on this night, it's doubtful that anybody would have believed them—just like they wouldn't have believed that Sharon knew Fred Lynn, who was now stepping up to the plate in the bottom of the eighth, on a first-name basis.

Lynn, showing no ill effects from his concrete headache, lined a single off the leg of pitcher Pedro Borbon. He moved to second on a walk to Rico Petrocelli, and from there he had a perfect view of pinch hitter Bernie Carbo as he stepped in two outs later against new pitcher Rawley Eastwick. Carbo, a former Reds outfielder who had belted a pinch homer earlier in the Series, was completely fooled by Eastwick's two-strike fastball, barely fouling it off with an awkward swing that Sox catcher Carlton Fisk would later deem the worst in major-league history. But then on the next offering, Carbo hit yet another ball to deep center field, and it was Griffey who had to watch this one go into the seats for a 400-foot, game-tying homer.

An admitted "flake," Bernie Carbo victimized his former Reds teammates with one of the most clutch homers in Series history—a three-run blast in the eighth inning of Game 6 that tied the game at 6–6.

Fenway exploded as Carbo bounded around the bases, lifted his arms to the sky, and pumped out his chest as he crossed home plate. "Bernie was the most stunned guy in the ballpark, and I was second," Lynn recalled. Given how the previous games in the Series had gone—three of five contests decided by one run, two in the last inning—the sudden developments seemed altogether fitting.

Boston nearly won it in the ninth, loading the bases with nobody out, but somehow Eastwick wriggled out of the jam. In the 11th, with a man on first and one down, Cincinnati's Joe Morgan hit a shot to right field that Dwight Evans tracked down and caught in midstride by reaching up with his glove just before the ball could reach the seats. Using the chest-high fence for momentum, Evans pushed himself off it and gunned the ball in as hard as he could to Yastrzemski near first base. Although his rushed throw was a bit off, causing Yaz to move into foul territory near the Boston dugout to grab it, shortstop Rick Burleson had the presence of mind to sprint over to cover first so Yaz could toss him the ball and double up Pete Rose to end the inning.

It was a beautiful and critical play, and Rose was fuming for making the third out. He knew already that the significance of this contest would go beyond the box score. When he came to the plate a few minutes earlier, he had turned to Fisk and said, "This is some game, isn't it?" Fisk agreed, not knowing he would soon make it that much more memorable.

The score was still 6–6 in the bottom of the 12th, the clock inching past 12:30 a.m., when Fisk led off for Boston. Standing beside Lynn in the on-deck circle as Reds reliever Pat Darcy took his warm-up tosses, the self-assured catcher told his teammate, "I'll get on, and you drive me in."

Some fans were still settling into their seats after grabbing post-midnight snacks as Fisk took Darcy's first pitch high for a ball. He then hit the next one on a rising trajectory down the left-field line, toward the foul pole that rose above the Green Monster. "It was a question of it being fair or foul," Fisk told reporters after the game. "The wind must have carried it 15 feet toward the foul pole. I just stood there and watched. I didn't want to miss seeing it going out."

Actually, Fisk did more than just watch. In an effort to circumvent the wind, he stepped out of the batter's box and began leaping, waving his hands in an effort to wish the ball into play. And while he, Lynn, and everybody else at

In 1975, the man who would retire with the most hits ever, Pete Rose, was at the peak of his career. Here he scrutinizes the Red Sox during a pre-World Series workout.

Four sets of eyes stare at Carlton Fisk's Game 6 fly ball. Would it sail past the right of the foul pole or the left? The answer was neither. The ball hit on the fair side of the pole and fell into left field.

Fenway was tracking the flight of the ball, the 36 million fans viewing the Series on NBC were treated to the raw emotion of Fisk leaping and pleading. The footage, shot by veteran cameraman Lou Gerard, gave birth to what became known in TV sports as the "reaction shot," and it's one of the most replayed images in sports history. All thanks to a rat.

The inside of the Green Monster was never the Taj Mahal, but by the mid-'70s it had become downright nasty—a dark, dirty, graffiti-covered pit in which a few rats sought solace from Joe Mooney's groundscrew. It was here where Gerard had set up his camera for Game 6, and his instructions from director Harry Coyle were to follow the path of the ball if it was hit toward him—or if not, then to stay zeroed in on Fisk.

Gerard was set to carry out the assignment until he spotted one of the Wall's furry freeloaders perched atop his camera. Shocked, he momentarily froze rather than swivel his camera to track the ball, and his lens stayed hooked on Fisk. It was up to Dick Stockton, calling the game for NBC viewers, to describe for them where the ball was headed: "*There it goes! A long drive! If it stays fair.... Home run! We will have a seventh game in this 1975 World Series!*"

In the end, Fisk's shot bounced off the foul pole and fell harmlessly back

Pitching in for Jimmy

When Red Sox management rebuilt Fenway's left-field wall after the 1975 season, they devised a unique way to rid themselves of the scraps. They mounted and sold them to fans to benefit the Jimmy Fund of Dana-Farber Cancer Institute.

It was a natural decision. Since adopting stewardship of the Jimmy Fund from the Boston Braves and owner Lou Perini when they moved to Milwaukee in 1953, the Red Sox have maintained it as an official team charity. A Jimmy Fund billboard was the only advertisement that Yawkey allowed in the ballpark for decades, and the Braves and Sox long played an annual exhibition game to benefit the cause—which aids children and adults battling cancer. The old-fashioned mailboxes spread throughout Fenway that serve as Jimmy Fund collection containers are a part of the ballpark's history, as is the Jimmy Fund insignia now adorning the Green Monster.

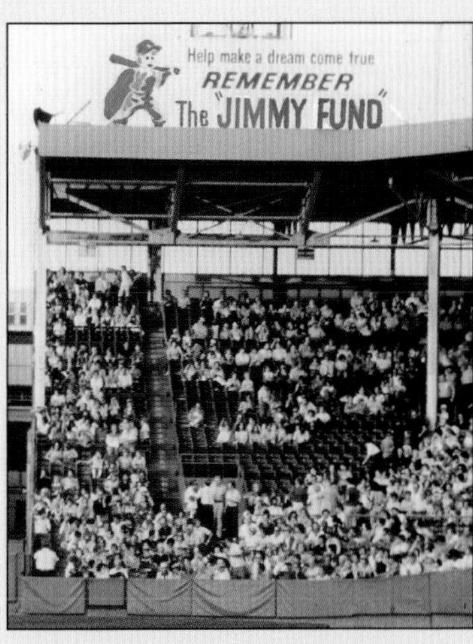

The special connection between ballplayers and fans being treated at Dana-Farber makes this partnership all the more special. Players routinely host young Jimmy Fund Clinic patients at Fenway Park, or visit them at the clinic less than a mile up Brookline Avenue. The 1967 "Impossible Dream" Red Sox were so moved by their owner's devotion to the cause that they even gave a full World Series share to the Jimmy Fund in honor of Tom Yawkey.

In Game 6, Joe Morgan (*right*) had the probable winning hit snatched from him by Red Sox rightfielder Dwight Evans. In Game 7, his little dink of a looping liner drove in the run that decided the Series.

down to left fielder George Foster as Fisk rounded the bases. Perhaps due to the crowd's sheer exhaustion, just a few overzealous fans outflanked a mild security presence to vault onto the field and slap Fisk high-fives as he rounded third and headed home to end what was then the longest game (four hours, one minute) in World Series history. Throughout New England, car horns honked, church bells rang, and kids with transistor radios under their pillows jumped on their beds. Fenway Park organist John Kiley broke into a succession of festive numbers such as the "Beer Barrel Polka"—this was long before rock music was piped into the park—and fans sang along.

Banging away at his portable typewriter above home plate, Ray Fitzgerald of the *Boston Globe* suggested in print that a seventh game was not necessary. How could anything top this? How could either of these teams lose? But the combatants were back at Fenway later the same day to settle matters. The Red Sox took a 3–0 lead early against a shaky Don Gullet, yet their missed opportunities at more runs came back to haunt them. After left-hander Bill Lee, the Sox' outspoken flake and the intellectual hero of Fenway's growing college-age fan base, took a shutout into the sixth, the Reds chipped away at Lee and his successors. They eventually went ahead 4–3 on a soft, ninth-inning single to center by Joe Morgan.

The Sox went quietly in the ninth, and after Yaz flew out to end the game and the fifth one-run contest of the Series, thousands of mostly disappointed

patrons rushed the field and ripped up patches of grass to remember this true Fall Classic. The Red Sox had lost, but Fenway and its fans had been winners.

Safe Oasis

If the Impossible Dream season of 1967 marked the beginning of Fenway's comeback, Game 6 of the '75 World Series served as its apex. Perhaps because the ballpark was so woven into the fabric of this incredible contest—Lynn running into the Wall, Evans reaching into the stands, Fisk waving his homer fair off the foul pole—it would forever be linked to this watershed moment in baseball history.

During the previous decade, professional football had eclipsed America's pastime in popularity. While 48 percent of Americans in a 1964 Lou Harris poll

> "You're playing on a field where the greats played. That's pretty special, and I know the fans feel it when they come in. They don't care that the seats are small or there is no parking."
> **—Centerfielder Fred Lynn**

named baseball as their favorite sport, just 17 percent did in 1975. Monday Night football, with bombastic broadcaster Howard Cosell at its epicenter, had become the equivalent of a weekly World Series, energizing citizens gathered in bars and living rooms nationwide. Some felt baseball was in serious trouble, no longer "hip" enough for the disco generation, but the Red Sox-Reds classic would be credited with reinvigorating the sport. Whereas in 1975 the Red Sox and Yankees had been the only two American League teams to average more than 15,000 fans per game, this number jumped to nine clubs just two years later.

By sweeping the three-time defending World Series champion Oakland A's in the 1975 American League Championship Series (ALCS), and then playing the equally powerful Reds to a near standoff, the Red Sox had established themselves as the AL's premier team. The shrewd trades and player development efforts of Dick O'Connell and Haywood Sullivan had resulted in a wealth of great talent, much of it under the age of 30. Catchy slogans such as "Fenway Fun in '71" and "The Place to Be in '73" were no longer needed to sell fans on a trip to Jersey Street, nor were ads that offered free valet parking service when they came to pick up tickets. This roster was incentive enough.

Reigning American League Rookie of the Year and MVP Fred Lynn, handsome and California cool, had a beautiful left-handed swing made for Fenway Park and played center field like a gazelle. Only a freshman season as astounding as his (.331, 21, 105, Gold Glove) could overshadow fellow '75 rookie Jim Rice (.309, 22, 102), whose sheer strength reminded many older fans of Jimmie Foxx and whose postseason absence with a broken hand may have cost Boston

Dwight "Dewey" Evans, shown here on his 1978 Topps card, had some snap in his bat, but he was best known as the best rightfielder in the AL—while playing the toughest right field. His arm was compared to Roberto Clemente's.

From 1975 through '79, Fred Lynn (*left*) and Jim Rice (*right*) routinely appeared in the AL's top five in offensive categories. Lynn hit .347 at Fenway for his career, while Rice ripped .320 at the ballpark.

Tagged "The Ace from Outer Space," Bill Lee had no problem warming up in a uniform that would have worked well on Mars. The Red Sox beanie was a nice touch.

the title. Rice played in left field alongside Lynn, and the two were dubbed the "Gold Dust Twins"—a nickname the D'Angelo family imprinted onto countless pennants, posters, and other items at their souvenir shop.

This dynamic duo was just the tip of the talent now summering at Fenway. Carlton Fisk, the Game 6 hero whose .331 average had helped propel Boston into the 1975 playoffs, was one of the best catchers in the game. His take-charge leadership, which included chewing out pitchers during his frequent mound visits, earned him the respect of both these hurlers and the fans. Fiery shortstop Rick Burleson had a great glove and steady bat, and right fielder Dwight Evans was a defensive standout with 20-homer power.

Carl Yastrzemski, the most senior member of the squad, had been revitalized after temporarily moving from first base back to left field to take Rice's place in the '75 postseason, playing like a man 10 years younger than his 36 years. Fellow Impossible Dream holdover Rico Petrocelli was fading at third base, but powerful, young Butch Hobson was being readied to eventually fill the spot. Pitching ace Luis Tiant was the heart and soul of the team, a prankster with a Fu Manchu mustache and ever-ready cigar who could be counted on for 18

Tony C's Last Comeback

The way the 1975 season ended at Fenway Park—with two of the most compelling World Series games of all time—has been well documented. Not as often recounted are the moving events that transpired in the *first* contest played there that year.

Henry Aaron, Tony Conigliaro

On Opening Day, April 8, Tony Conigliaro received a rousing ovation when he was introduced in the starting lineup for Boston's matchup against Milwaukee. The game was billed as the first American League contest for Henry Aaron, who before his trade to the Brewers that winter had established a new record with 733 lifetime home runs. Tony C, however, shined in *his* first game since an abrupt retirement four years earlier due to deteriorating eyesight resulting from his horrific 1967 beaning.

Singling in his first at-bat, Conigliaro later pulled off a double steal with his old teammate Carl Yastrzemski. Fans hoping for another big year from the "Impossible Dream" duo would be disappointed, however. While Yaz kept on going strong to October, Tony C found that while his eyes were better, his reflexes had been dulled by the long layoff. Although he hit Boston's first homer of the year, he was soon sent to the minors with a .123 average and retired shortly thereafter at age 30. That fall, just as in '67, he watched the World Series from the sidelines.

> **"It looks like a bunch of catacombs and old places, and the next thing you know you come out and there is this beautiful ballpark—a jewel sitting right in the middle of downtown Boston. You're like a mole that comes out and sees the sunlight for the first time. It's a pretty amazing sight. It's so quaint, and the crowd is always at full capacity."**
>
> **—Pitcher Bill Lee**

to 20 wins a year, including many in the clutch. Rick Wise and Bill Lee were also dependable starters, and Dick Drago and Jim Willoughby offered steady bullpen help.

It was a powerful team filled with strong, colorful personalities, and to showcase it in style, aging, ailing owner Tom Yawkey gave Fenway Park its biggest facelift since the 1930s. The left-field wall, stretching over to deepest center, was completely rebuilt with new steel panels and padding that assured that future players would not endure the same fate as Lynn in the World Series. The press box underwent significant renovations, including being completely enclosed for the first time.

And while the hand-operated scoreboard on the Green Monster remained in place, it was now complemented by a modern partner—a huge, \$1.2 million electronic message board at the back of the center-field bleachers. Messages typed on terminals, including up-to-the-at-bat statistics, trivia questions, and out-of-town scores that came in to the press box through a ticker-tape machine, would be typed into computer terminals and transferred directly to the board. Photos of players and in-game action would also be displayed.

Not surprisingly, this 40″ × 24″ addition was initially met with derision from fans. Modern stadiums in Kansas

When the old left-field wall was torn down, it was sold in chunks to raise money for the Jimmy Fund. This piece was signed by the field's two most famous residents, Ted Williams and Carl Yastrzemski.

The 1976 renovation of Fenway included this electric scoreboard, along with a rebuilt Green Monster and a more accommodating press box.

City and Pittsburgh had similar message boards in place, but such gadgetry seemed tacky for a traditional ballpark that people the world over had fallen in love with the previous October. What would be next, the Fenway faithful feared, "Pong" contests between innings?

Dick O'Connell tried to assuage concerns by explaining that the expensive new appliance would do little to change the Fenway atmosphere, and he insisted that it had nothing to do with an increase in most ticket prices. Fans were skeptical, and although they again came out in record numbers, the 1976 season would be remembered more for disappointment and sadness than anything else.

The Red Sox got off to a terrible start that had them under .500 in June, and on July 9 Tom Yawkey died in his sleep at age 73 from complications of leukemia. The only owner many Red Sox fans had ever known, with 43 years at the helm of the team and Fenway Park, he was eulogized as an influential, generous leader and lauded for his charitable endeavors toward such organizations as the Jimmy Fund of Dana-Farber Cancer Institute. His team's inability to win a World Series during his long tenure, and its failure to embrace integration earlier, were not dwelled on by a respectful press—likely in part due to the team's recent success as well as progress in developing African-American stars such as Rice and first baseman Cecil Cooper.

The franchise and Fenway Park would now be run by a trust controlled by an executor, one of Yawkey's business associates, and his widow, Jean. Writing about the late owner's love for Fenway, where the organ was silent for a night out of

In 4½ seasons as Red Sox manager, salty Don Zimmer won 90 games or more three times. But he never won a flag. Decades later, Zim would serve as bench coach on Joe Torre's hated Yanks.

respect, Edgar Driscoll of the *Globe* stated: "He spent more maintaining his small, old-fashioned ball park as an immaculate and safe oasis for baseball than most cities spend keeping up their large stadiums."

Shortly after Tom Yawkey's death, a season-ticket holder who lived in the Kenmore Square area recalled being awoken early one morning by a loud sound. Looking out her window, she saw a helicopter hovering over Fenway and something being thrown out the side. It has never been proven whether she saw the last wishes of the owner being carried out, but the facts are these: Yawkey was cremated in a private service, and other than perhaps the wild animal reserves on his South Carolina plantation, there was likely no place he'd rather spend eternity than Fenway Park.

Rivalry Redux

Shortly after the owner's death, the stretch of Jersey Street on which Fenway's front gates and ticket office were located was renamed Yawkey Way by a unanimous vote of the Boston City Council. On the field, the '76 Red Sox never could get on track. As is often the case in such circumstances, the manager took the fall. Less than a year after leading the Sox to the brink of a World Series title, manager Darrell Johnson was let go in late July and replaced by third base coach Don Zimmer. Although Zimmer salvaged respectability for the club with a strong record during a meaningless September, Red Sox fans found it difficult watching a refurbished Yankees team march to the pennant.

After being largely dormant for 20 years, during which first the Sox and then the Yanks underwent rebuilding periods, the rivalry between baseball's Athens and Sparta was reemerging with a vengeance. Gruff, chunky New York catcher Thurman Munson—the hardheaded leader and captain of his team—developed a dislike for likeminded counterpart Fisk, perhaps due to the extra attention his more classically handsome rival received from the media. The two brawled at Fenway in 1973 when Munson bowled over Fisk on a play at the plate, and the Red Sox proudly put a photo of them about to collide on the cover of the team's '74 yearbook.

Billy Martin took over as New York manager in 1976, and the rivalry went from hot to steaming. Martin always seemed to be looking for a fight himself, including with his own players, and was the perfect villain right down to his thin, black mustache. When the two teams met at Yankee Stadium in May 1976, a bench-clearing brawl precipitated by another play at the plate, this one involving Fisk and feisty Yankees outfielder Lou Piniella, left Boston pitcher Bill Lee with a torn ligament in his shoulder that required two months on the disabled list. The outspoken hurler called the Yankees "Brownshirts" and Martin "a Nazi," and the war escalated some more.

Fenway Park, which during its post-1967 revival had been primarily marketed

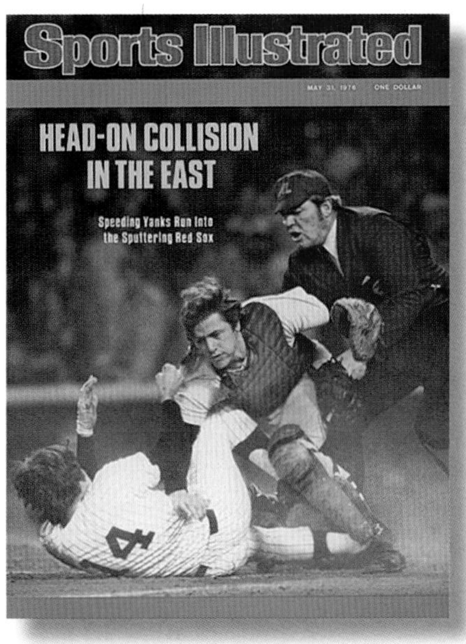

As this *Sports Illustrated* cover calls it, the'70s battles between the Sox and Yanks became the stuff of legend, particularly the Munson-Fisk brawl in 1973 and the torrid AL East race in 1978.

The toughs of Boston hung out in the bleachers in the 1970s. Blazing sun, multiple beers, and one infuriating call or play were enough to set them off. The Red Sox had to employ a crowd-control unit to maintain order.

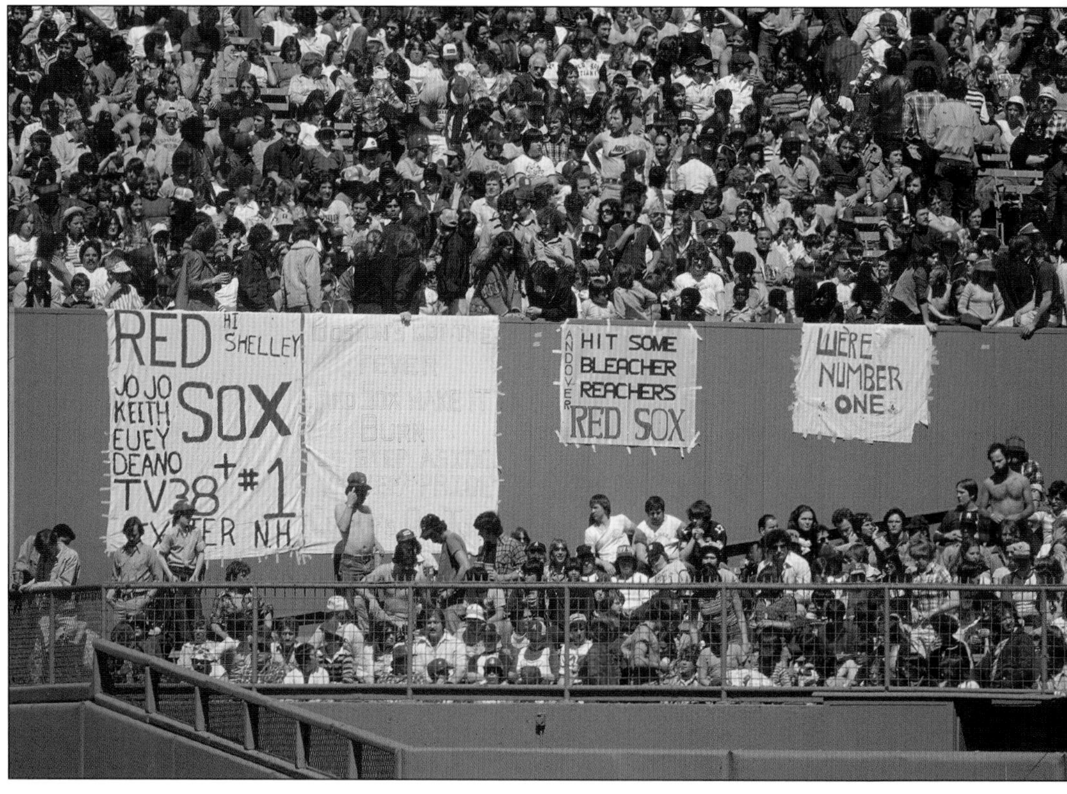

as a family-friendly environment, began taking on a tougher edge. The center-field bleachers, now largely home to young men between the ages of 18 and 25, was routinely the scene of fistfights fueled by both the sun—which hit this uncovered part of the ballpark hard each afternoon—and easy access to several beer stands. Creative banners began popping up, including "Sell Campbell, bring back $1.50 bleachers" when the free agent signing of ace reliever Bill Campbell coincided with another boost in ticket prices.

The wildness reached its peak when New York came to town and guys from the Bronx (sometimes by way of local colleges) showed up in the bleachers wearing Yankees caps and looking for trouble. They regularly found it, and the Red Sox responded by developing a crowd-control unit known as the "Blue Jackets" to maintain order. Working in conjunction with deputized Boston police officers, these staffers—primarily bulked-up college athletes—patrolled the stands with walkie-talkies and could be seen sprinting to the scene of numerous brawls each game.

Sometimes the fights even extended into the dugout. On Saturday, June 18, 1977, during NBC's nationally televised *Game of the Week* at Fenway, Billy Martin lit in to new Yankees right fielder Reggie Jackson when he felt the high-priced slugger had loafed after a fly ball. The war of words led to shoves in the dugout caught on camera, and Martin humiliated the proud Jackson by pulling him from the game.

The melee came in the midst of a sweltering weekend series at Fenway during which the Red Sox crushed the Yankees with a barrage of home runs like nothing seen before at the ballpark. Boston out-Bombered the Bronx Boys 16 to zero in a three-game sweep, part of a stretch in which the Sox hit 33 long-balls in 10 games. This was the ultimate Fenway club, and by year's end the Sox would have 97 victories (their most since 1949) and a team-record 213 homers—including a league-leading 39 from Rice, 33 from old pal George Scott (back via a trade for Cecil Cooper), and 30 from new third baseman Hobson, who often batted ninth in the powerful Boston lineup. Yaz and Fisk chipped in with 28 and 26, and fans flocked to see the show in record numbers as Fenway drew two million for the first time.

The most significant figures of the year, however, were these: 13, the high in wins by a Red Sox pitcher, recorded by reliever Campbell (never a good sign); and 2½, the number of games the Sox finished behind pitching-rich New York in the AL East. The fact that the '77 AL Cy Young Award went to Yankees closer Sparky Lyle—whom the Red Sox had traded to New York for a washed-up Danny Cater five years before—only made the near-miss that much tougher to take.

Winds of Change

The words *nineteen seventy-eight* do not hold quite the sting they once did for Red Sox fans, made stronger by the blissful events of 2004 and 2007. Still, it's difficult to look back and not wonder just how it all happened. The Sox had added speedy second baseman Jerry Remy atop their vaunted lineup, and they revamped their pitching staff by trading for cocky, young fireballer Dennis Eckersley and signing free agent Mike Torrez, who had won two games for the Yankees in the '77 World Series. Boston rooters salivated at the thought of shutting down the champs with their former ace.

For the first half of the season, things went even better than planned. The Red Sox were 56–25 after 81 games, a .691 pace that gave them a 10-game lead in the AL East over the Yankees and Milwaukee Brewers. New York's season was in turmoil, much of it involving the fiery relationship between the unstable Martin and bombastic owner George Steinbrenner. By July 19, the Yanks had fallen to fourth, 14 games behind, with only the stellar pitching of left-hander Ron Guidry keeping them above water.

With a nine-game lead on second-place Milwaukee to this point, only the most pessimistic fans could have thought Boston would not win the division. But then everything possible went wrong at once. Yaz, Remy, Evans, Fisk, and Hobson all suffered injuries and played hurt much of the second half. Pitchers Torrez and Lee, nearly unbeatable early on, both endured long losing streaks. Slugger Jim Rice—enjoying an MVP season—stayed healthy and hot, but the Sox lost nine of 10 and then scuffled along at a .500 clip. The Yankees, meanwhile,

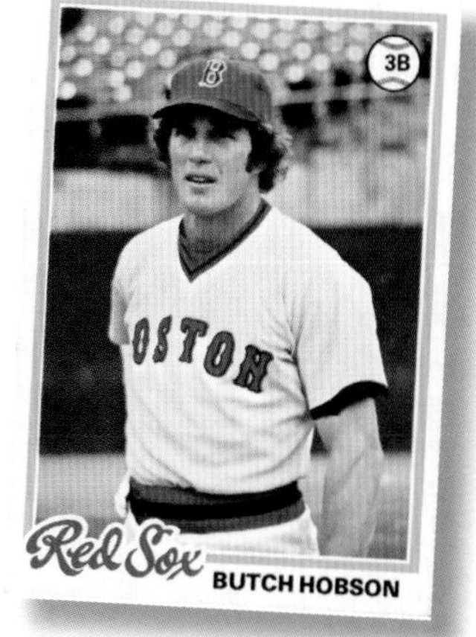

Butch Hobson, featured on this 1978 Topps card, bashed 30 home runs in 1977 and 28 in 1979, but he became infamous for his adventures at third base. In 1978, he erred 43 times for a .899 fielding percentage, the lowest in the majors in 60 years.

Police escort Carlton Fisk and Luis Tiant safely off the field after El Tiante's two-hit shutout over Toronto moved the Sox into position for a one-game playoff against the Yanks in 1978. It was Luis's fifth whitewash of the season.

with Bob Lemon replacing Martin as manager, got hot themselves and vaulted over first Baltimore and then Milwaukee into second place.

In early September, with their division lead down to four, New York came to Boston for four games. What transpired was dubbed the "Boston Massacre," as the Yankees swept the series by scores of 15–3, 13–2, 7–0, and 7–4 to tie the Red Sox atop the AL East. Zimmer, an old-school manager who never saw eye-to-eye with the colorful Lee, had pulled him from the rotation and gave rookie Bobby Sprowl his second major-league start in the finale—even though Lee's lifetime 12–5 record vs. New York was one of the best in history by an opposing pitcher. Sprowl didn't make it out of the first inning.

Demoralized, Boston continued to lose, and the Yankees moved 3½ games in front. Then, to their credit, the Sox bounced back to climb within one game heading into the season's final week. For six days both teams won, until Sunday morning dawned and the Sox needed a miracle—a win at home coupled with a Yankees loss to the lowly Cleveland Indians and 12–15 pitcher Rick Waits—to tie things up and force a one-game playoff. By virtue of a coin toss made already, that game would be at Fenway.

Starting for the Red Sox against the Toronto Blue Jays was old reliable Luis Tiant, one of the best pennant-stretch pitchers in Boston history. Loo-ie, Loo-ie shut out the Jays on a two-hitter as Rice crushed his 46th home run. Fenway fans listened to their transistor radios

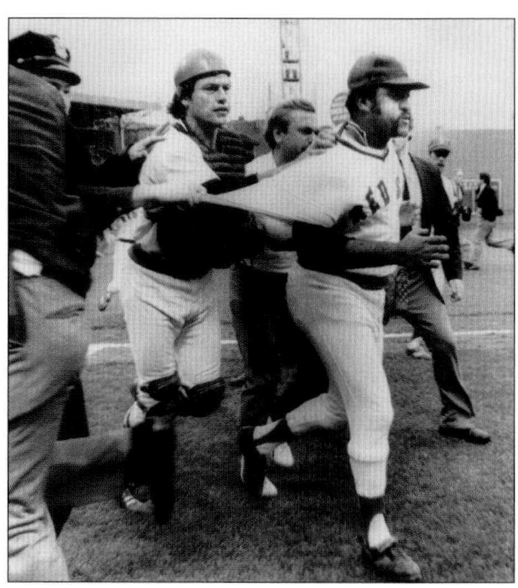

and watched the Green Monster for the score from New York, and when it came in (9–2 Cleveland) cheers went up in the bleachers. For one day, everybody even loved the message board, which read, "Thank you, Rick Waits, Next Home Game Tomorrow."

The second one-game playoff in American League history took place almost 30 years to the day after the first—and at the same venue. On October 4, 1948, it was the Indians who opposed the Red Sox with a World Series berth on the line; on October 2, 1978, it was the Yankees and Sox vying for a ticket to the ALCS. Yankees manager Lemon had a case of déjà vu. As a 20-game winner for the Indians back in '48, he had been warming up most of the game at Fenway in case rookie hurler Gene Bearden faltered against Ted Williams and the Sox. Bearden had won the game, and now Lemon hoped that Ron "Louisiana Lightning" Guidry, 24–3 coming in, could do the same.

"I never saw the ball go into the net. The one thing that I remember as far as running around, was when I touched third base how quiet the ballpark got. What an eerie feeling it was."
—Yankees shortstop Bucky Dent, on his home run in the 1978 American League East playoff

Going for the home team was Mike Torrez, in just the scenario fans had hoped for when Boston picked him up. He was a far less gaudy 16–12, and he had won only one of his last 10 starts, but he knew the Yankees, and the game was at "Friendly Fenway"—where the Red Sox had won at a .725 clip during the season.

Guidry was not at his best, and Yastrzemski put Boston in front 1–0 with a second-inning homer just inside the right-field foul pole. A Rice RBI single made it 2–0 in the sixth, but the Sox lost a chance for more runs when Lynn—who almost always hit the ball to left field—sent a shot to right with two men on that same inning that was tracked down in the corner by an out-of-position Lou Piniella.

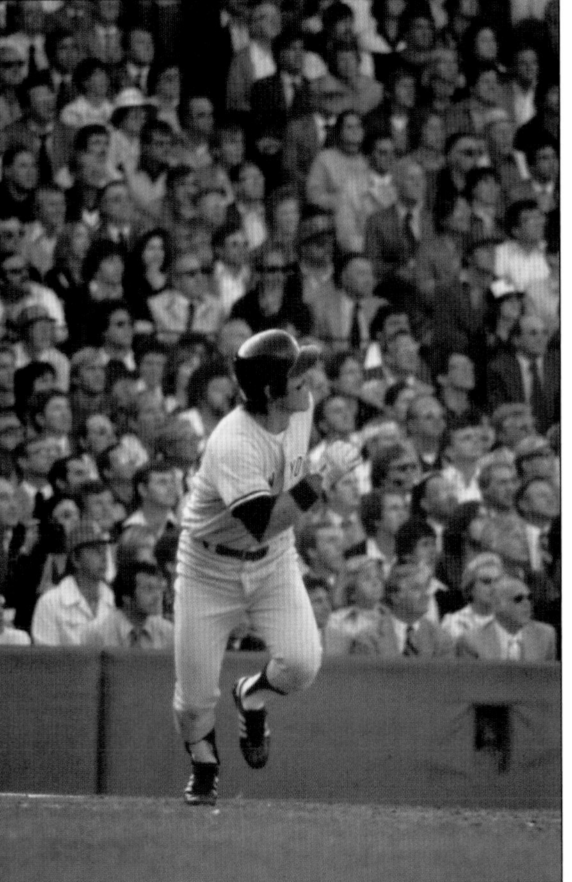

There he is, Bucky "Bleeping" Dent, hitting the homer that ruined the 1978 season for Fenway fans. Dent remembered it so fondly that he built a replica of Fenway at his baseball school, with a manual scoreboard forever set just as it was after his big hit: New York 3, Boston 2.

Torrez entered the seventh with a two-hit shutout. He then gave up a pair of singles, but he got to two strikes on weak-hitting shortstop Bucky Dent when Dent fouled a ball off his foot. He hobbled around in pain, and on-deck batter Mickey Rivers noticed his bat was cracked and gave him one of his own. Torrez chose not to stay loose with some throwing during the delay, and his next pitch to Dent was hit high in the air to left.

From behind the plate, Fisk thought it would be caught. So did Yaz, who backed up to the Wall and pounded his glove. But Lee, an armchair weatherman sitting in the bullpen to which he had been banished, felt otherwise.

"The wind was blowing in over the Wall at the start of the game, but I told them it was going to shift in the fifth or sixth when the land mass warmed up and an on-shore breeze kicked in," recalled Lee. "That's just what happened. Dent hit it into the wind, and I knew it was gone. If they bring me in that inning, I

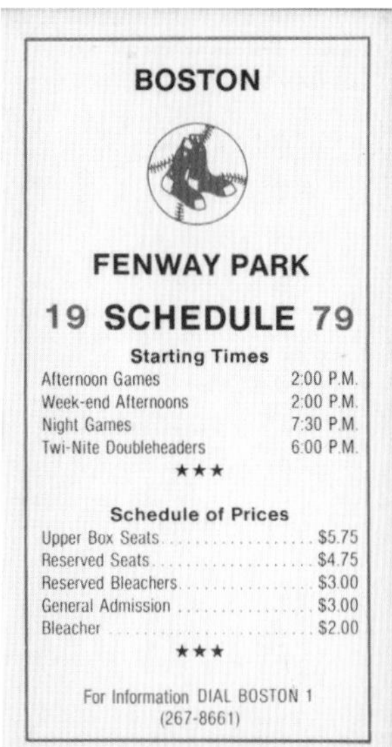

BOSTON

FENWAY PARK

19 SCHEDULE 79

Starting Times

Afternoon Games	2:00 P.M.
Week-end Afternoons	2:00 P.M.
Night Games	7:30 P.M.
Twi-Nite Doubleheaders	6:00 P.M.

★★★

Schedule of Prices

Upper Box Seats	$5.75
Reserved Seats	$4.75
Reserved Bleachers	$3.00
General Admission	$3.00
Bleacher	$2.00

★★★

For Information DIAL BOSTON 1 (267-8661)

Even when you factor in inflation, ticket prices are *way* steeper now than in 1979. Fenway bleacher tickets sold for $28 in 2011 while box seats ranged from $52 to $135.

"Yaz was notorious for extra batting practice after games. After a Saturday or Sunday afternoon game, once the ballpark cleared out, the grounds crew guys would bring the batting cage out and the coaches would bring out a few buckets of balls and Yaz and maybe one or two other guys would start hitting. He was a fanatic."

—Dick Bresciani, Red Sox vice president/Publications and Archives

pitch them away and they hit ground balls and we win. They didn't, and the rest is history."

Yastrzemski slumped at the Wall as the ball settled into the net for a three-run homer. The crowd at Fenway fell silent, although Steinbrenner could be seen clapping from the front row beside the visitor's dugout. Torrez walked the next man, Rivers, and Zimmer pulled him in favor of Bob Stanley. A Maine native who had grown up rooting for the Red Sox and hating the Yankees, Stanley had contributed a 15–2 record and 10 saves to Boston's 99–63 season. But now that season was unraveling, and after Rivers stole second Thurman Munson doubled him home.

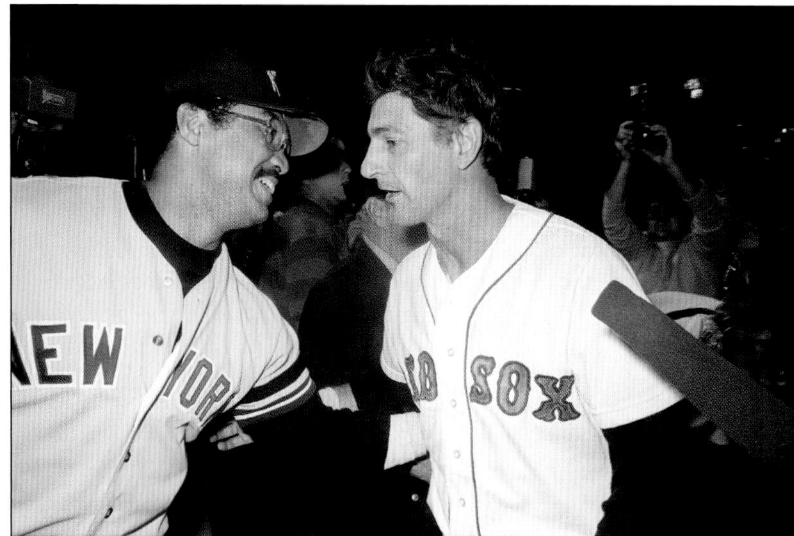

Reggie Jackson, who fielded Yaz's 3,000th hit, offers his congratulations on September 12, 1979. Just two years earlier in the Fenway visitors' dugout, Jackson and manager Billy Martin nearly came to blows.

The Yankees got an extra insurance run in the eighth when Jackson homered off Stanley, but the Red Sox countered with two of their own in the bottom of the inning on RBI singles by Yaz and Lynn off New York closer Goose Gossage. It was now 5–4, and in the ninth the Sox made their final charge. Burleson walked with one out, and then Remy hit a line drive to right that Piniella lost in the late-afternoon sun. Having no idea where the ball was, he put out his glove in a ploy to keep Burleson from scoring—then, amazingly, saw the ball reappear in front of him and one-hop into his mitt. Remy was held to a single, and Burleson had to stop at second. When the next batter (Rice) flew out deep for the second out, Burleson advanced to third and the importance of Piniella's gamble was clear.

Up stepped Yaz, with a chance to tie or win the game with one swing. He had been terrific down the stretch, and had two RBI in this game, but after taking a ball from Gossage he got under a high, inside fastball and popped it up to third. Graig Nettles squeezed it, and the Sox had nothing to show for MLB's second-best record (99–64) except yet another second-place finish. After the game, Bill Lee said goodbye to his friends in the bleachers. He figured he wouldn't be back the next year, and he was right.

On Pearl Harbor Day, as Lee points out today with a laugh, the third-winningest left-hander in Red Sox history was traded to the Montreal Expos for .230-hiting reserve infielder Stan Papi. Echoing what Boston fans everywhere were thinking, a creative spray paint artist inscribed "Who's Stan Papi?" on the back wall of Fenway Park.

Most people still don't know.

Down and Out

After nearly capturing three division championships in four years, and settling for one, the Red Sox began a slide toward mediocrity in 1979. They went a more-than-respectable 91–69, but with the Orioles checking in at 102–57 they were essentially out of the race by early September. Tiant had gotten a low-ball salary offer from management, and when he signed with the Yankees as a free agent, Yastrzemski said the move "ripped out our heart and soul." The fire seemed to be gone from the club.

Much of the excitement in 1979, and for several seasons to come, would thus center on Yaz and his climb up the all-time record lists. In '79, he joined two very exclusive clubs at Fenway. On July 24 he hit his 400th homer off Oakland's Mike Morgan, and on September 12 he drilled hit No. 3,000 onto Yawkey Way off Jim Beattie of the Yankees. This made him just the fourth player (joining Willie Mays, Henry Aaron, and Stan Musial) to attain both milestones—and the first American Leaguer to do so. Reggie Jackson, who fielded the groundball single that just scooted past second baseman Willie Randolph, gained temporary asylum from his Fenway enemies by jogging the ball in and handing it to a relieved Yastrzemski.

By 1980, with the club now struggling along at .500, Zimmer could not even stick his head out of the dugout without being roundly booed by frustrated Fenway patrons. He was mercifully fired near the end of the season, and former Yankees and Tigers manager Ralph Houk was brought in to replace him. Known as "The Major" out of deference to his military rank during World

Rice to the Rescue

During most of his long Hall of Fame career with the Red Sox, Jim Rice was known for having one of the quickest bats in baseball. On August 7, 1982, he used fast reactions of a different sort to help save the life of a young fan at Fenway Park.

Four-year-old Jonathan Keane of Greenland, New Hampshire, was with his family watching the Red Sox and White Sox square off that Sunday afternoon from the second row of seats near the home dugout. In the bottom of the fourth inning, he was hit in the head by a sharp foul ball off the bat of Red Sox first baseman Dave Stapleton, suffering a fractured skull and a laceration over his left eye. While other players and fans recoiled in horror from the blood, Rice ran to the railing of the dugout, took the boy into his arms, and ran with him into the trainer's room, where Red Sox physician Arthur Pappas could examine him.

Pappas said it was the worst case of immediate bleeding he had ever seen at Fenway. He credited Rice's quick reactions for aiding in Keane's survival, as the boy was in an ambulance and on the way to Children's Hospital Boston within two minutes.

Rice, who played the rest of the game with Keane's blood across his uniform, responded to reporters' inquiries afterward by posing his own question: "If it was your kid, what would you do?"

The Red Sox won 83 games and finished 19 games behind the Yankees in 1980. Dennis Eckersley (*pictured*) led the team with 12 victories, giving him 89 wins at the age of 25. He still had 108 wins and 387 saves left in him—most, unfortunately, not in Boston.

War II, Houk at this point in his career resembled a kindly grandfather to ballplayers as many as 40 years his junior. Yaz, now well past 40 himself, played the role of the hard-working dad. He still took extra batting practice in an empty ballpark after every home game.

Although the Red Sox were in the race for division titles in strike-shortened 1981 and in 1982, they were never considered serious contenders. Jaded fans railed at management for trading Burleson and Lynn to the California Angels and allowing Fisk to sign with the White Sox as a free agent, then cheered their former catcher when he returned to Fenway for the first time on Opening Day of 1981 and beat his old mates with a home run.

By the time Yastrzemski played his last home game on October 1, 1983, the Sox were a sixth-place club finishing its first losing season in 17 years. Still, the retiring legend made the end of the year memorable by thanking everybody from bat boys and clubhouse people to "the greatest and most loyal fans." He then took an impromptu jog around the entire ballpark, shaking hands with scores of folks who had watched him for all or part of the previous 23 years. They understood that a passing of the torch was at hand, and they gave Jim Rice—league leader in home runs for a third time that year—a standing ovation when he came up for his last at-bat of the game.

Like Yaz had in midcareer, Rice became a target of boo birds as the Sox struggled through the first two years of the post-Yastrzemski era. His penchant for hitting into double plays at a record clip was one culprit. However, thousands of balls hit off the Green Monster by coach Johnny Pesky over the previous decade had helped Rice develop into a strong defensive player and a worthy successor of the left-field throne previously held by Williams and Yaz. Dwight Evans, meanwhile, became the new favorite of the Fenway Faithful. Using the philosophies of batting coach Walt Hriniak to develop into one of the top hitters in the game, he maintained his status as a Gold Glove right fielder and earned choruses of "Dewwwwwey" for every fly ball he caught.

Like most hitters, Wade Boggs enjoyed batting in the friendly confines of Fenway. His lifetime batting average there was an astounding .369, and he won five batting titles with the Red Sox.

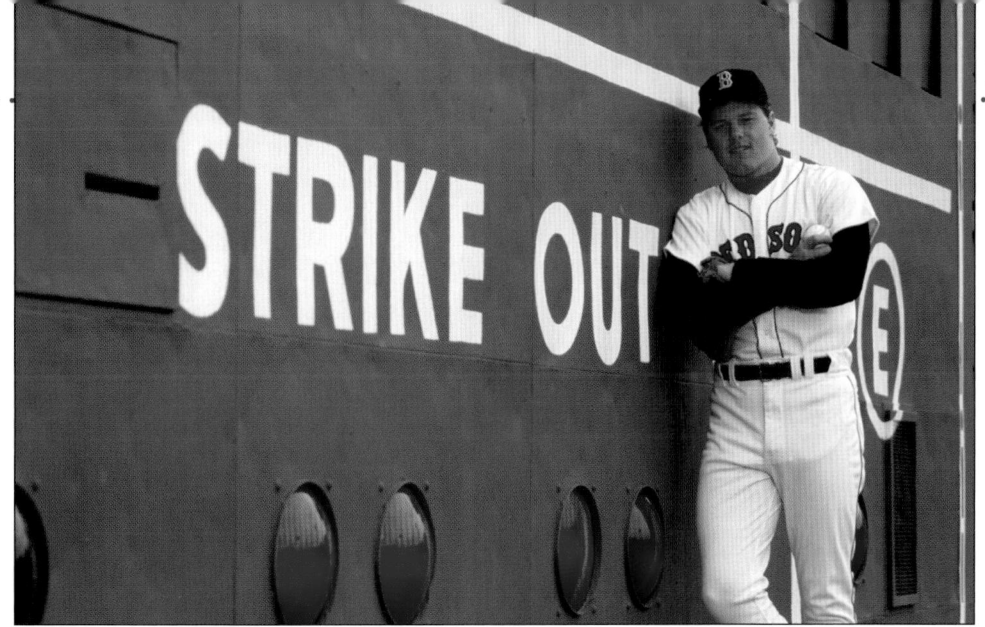

Just one year removed from the University of Texas, Roger Clemens rocketed onto the scene in 1984. He fanned nearly nine batters per nine innings as a rookie and looked like a future Cy Young winner. He would win the award seven times, twice as a Red Sox.

The prototypical Fenway player, however, was new third baseman Wade Boggs. He routinely pounded the Monster with line drives while piling up league-leading batting averages not seen in Boston since the Ted Williams era: .361 in 1983 and .368 two years later. In the latter year, he also obliterated Tris Speaker's 73-year-old team mark by amassing a phenomenal 240 hits, and he set another record of sorts by eating chicken every day of the season. Fans arriving early at Fenway could find the king of superstitions taking exactly 150 grounders and running his wind sprints at exactly the same time, and each at-bat began with Boggs forming the Hebrew letter *Chai* (meaning "life") in the dirt of the batter's box.

Boggs, Evans, Rice, and new first baseman Bill Buckner—brought in from the Cubs for fallen ace pitcher Dennis Eckersley—gave the Red Sox plenty of offense. What they lacked, as was so often the case in Boston, was strong starting pitching to back it up. That started to come in 1984 in three forms: soft-spoken lefty Bruce Hurst; wiry, exuberant Dennis "Oil Can" Boyd; and big Texas fireballer Roger Clemens. The last of this trio was perhaps the most promising, compiling a 15-strikeout, zero-walk game at Fenway during his rookie season that year. New manager John McNamara's first two clubs went a mediocre 86–76 and 81–81, but there was a lot of hope for improvement in 1986.

With Fenway Park nearing its 75th anniversary, fans wanted a big reason to celebrate.

Legendary Red Sox groundskeeper Joe Mooney (*right*) gets the field ready for play. Fenway Park has been called "Mooney's backyard" due to the meticulous way he groomed the dirt and grass.

CHAPTER 8

Tears and Cheers

1986–1999

After stomaching a bitter World Series defeat in 1986, the Red Sox lost in the American League playoffs five times over the rest of the century. Yet there was much to celebrate on Yawkey Way, as stars from Rocket and Pedro to Mo and "Nomah" electrified Fenway Park.

He usually went home around the seventh inning, after his last hot dog was sold, but there was no way Rob Barry was leaving this game early.

It was cold and windy, and there were just 13,414 people in Fenway Park, but he could tell something special was going on. Grabbing his friend Michelle Doherty, who also worked at the ballpark, Barry moved down toward a pair of empty seats about 10 rows behind the Red Sox dugout, where you could hear the thud of Roger Clemens's pitches as they hit Rich Gedman's big mitt.

After the final game of the 1986 regular season, fans waited in line all night at Fenway for ALCS tickets, then picked up pennants like this one across the street at Twins Souvenirs.

This game against the hapless Seattle Mariners was played on an evening when most New England sports fans were focused on the Boston Celtics-Atlanta Hawks match-up in the NBA's Eastern Conference semifinals. Barry, however, had a feeling it was going to be a historic night.

"Hey, Fenway Fraaaaaanks!" a fan yelled as Barry worked his way down the aisle. Even when he didn't have his metal hot dog bin or red peanut sack with him, people often yelled that at Fenway's top vendor. He was as well known walking the stands as any ballplayer, and with good reason. Thanks to his "day job" as a pitcher for Northeastern University, located a mile away on the site of the old Huntington Avenue Grounds, he could toss a four-ounce bag of peanuts across 25 rows of chairs and right into the waiting hands of a smiling six-year-old girl. He also had a deep-throated voice with a Boston accent, a voice big enough to carry through the entire ballpark. And when he wasn't using it himself, others did it for him.

Barry and Doherty settled into their seats just as Clemens struck out Ivan Calderon swinging to start the eighth. A few minutes later, Dave Hen-

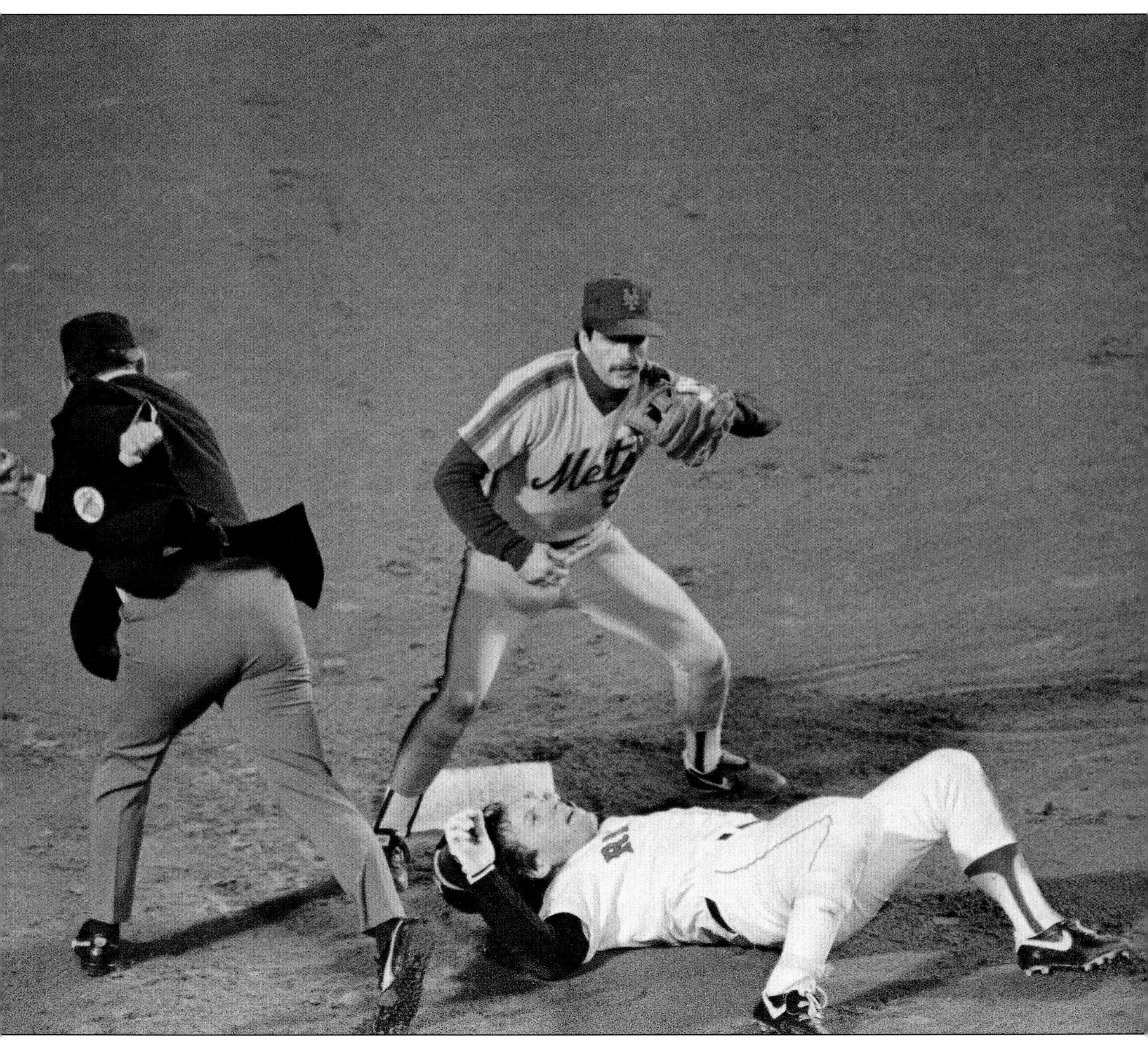

Mets second baseman Wally Backman tags out Red Sox catcher Rich Gedman in the fourth game of the 1986 World Series. Boston won the first two games of the Series on the road, but heartache lay ahead.

derson (remember that name) fanned as well, and Barry gazed at the back of the right-field bleachers. Some kids had been taping pieces of white cardboard with a red *K* on them for each man Clemens whiffed—kind of a human scorebook. Barry counted from left to right. Then he counted again. Could it really be *18* strikeouts? Had anybody ever had more than that in one game?

In the thrill of the moment after Roger Clemens notched his 20th strikeout on April 29, 1986, the ball was not removed from the game. Luckily, the next batter grounded out and the record-setting sphere was secured.

After Seattle shortstop Spike Owen, an old teammate of Clemens from the University of Texas, struck out to start the ninth, the message board noted that Clemens had tied the nine-inning, major-league record of 19 strikeouts (held by Nolan Ryan, Tom Seaver, and Steve Carlton). Not wasting any time, the 6′4″ hurler quickly provided an update by catching Scott Bradley looking for No. 20. Third baseman Wade Boggs came over and shook Clemen's hand, after which Ken Phelps grounded out to end the game.

All told, Clemens threw 138 pitches while allowing three hits, one run (a Gorman Thomas homer in the seventh), and—perhaps most astonishingly—*zero* walks in a 3–1 victory. The glove, cap, and shoes that the 23-year-old hurler wore in the game were sent to Cooperstown the next day, and Red Sox Public Relations Director Dick Bresciani fielded TV, radio, and print media requests from across the country to talk with Clemens.

Fenway was off on a wild and at times excruciating stretch. From 1986 to 1999, the Red Sox reached the postseason six times in 14 seasons—their greatest period of sustained success in 80 years. Each trip, however, would end in disappointment, with Boston failing to win the World Series title that had eluded the franchise since 1918.

It became popular during this period for sportswriters and fans to claim that the Boston franchise was "cursed" because it had sold Babe Ruth to the Yankees a little more than a year after capturing the 1918 championship. Yet as snakebit as the Red Sox seemed, and as much abuse as their fans and players took along the way, one thing remained largely free from cursespeak: Fenway Park. Certainly, many were frustrated by its cramped seats, obstructed views, lack of adequate parking, and narrow concourses, to name just a few complaints. But if you checked your high-maintenance needs at the turnstile, or better yet left them at home, it remained a magical place to see a ballgame.

Still Waiting

From the Rocket's 20-K masterpiece through late October, 1986 was one of the most entertaining and successful seasons in Red Sox history. Boston had its strongest pitching staff in years, led by Cy Young/MVP awardee Clemens (24–4 on the year); excitable, crafty Dennis "Oil Can" Boyd; and left-handed control artist Bruce Hurst. The offensive attack blended veterans such as outfielders Jim Rice and Dwight Evans, first baseman Bill Buckner, and new DH

"There is just something different about being at Fenway. Its history and character make it a special place, and it only takes one visit to feel it."
—Catcher Rick Gedman

Don Baylor (all 90-RBI men) with talented young players such as second baseman Marty Barrett, catcher Gedman, and third baseman Boggs. From 1983 through '89, this hit machine would win five batting titles, average .352, and top 200 hits every year.

Boston went into first place for good in mid-May of '86. Then, after a rough patch in July and August when their lead slipped from 8½ to 2½ games, the Sox won 10 of 11 in early September and pulled away. Crowds swelled at Fenway, and even an exhibition game and home run hitting contest against the New York Mets to benefit the Jimmy Fund drew more than 35,000. Many envisioned it as a World Series preview.

At the center of it all was Clemens. He reached 14–0 before finally losing in early July, and as the season wore on his starts began drawing tremendous "walk-up" ticket interest at Fenway. With tweets and ESPN apps still long in the future, waiting to see the morning box score and how many opponents the Rocket had struck out the previous night became a regular ritual for fans—and would remain so for the next decade.

The staff he led got even stronger when the Red Sox traded for 41-year-old Tom Seaver in July, and rookie Calvin Schiraldi quickly stepped in as a stellar closer after being brought up the same month. Injuries sidelined Seaver for the playoffs, however, and Schiraldi had a critical blown save as the Sox fell behind the Angels three games to one in the best-of-seven ALCS. They looked to be done for the season in Game 5, trailing 5–2 in the ninth inning at Anaheim, but home runs by Baylor and Dave Henderson (acquired along with fellow 20-K victim Spike Owen to add depth) brought the Red Sox back from the dead and into a 6–5 lead. The Angels momentarily tied things up, but a sacrifice fly by Henderson in the 11th inning earned Boston the win and capped his one-day transformation from spare part to folk hero.

The plane ride back to Boston was loose and spirited, and the revitalized

The "K" cards were waving in the Fenway bleachers for Calvin Schiraldi when he struck out the side in the ninth to finish off the Angels in Game 7 of the 1986 ALCS. Roger Clemens earned the win as the Red Sox breezed 8–1.

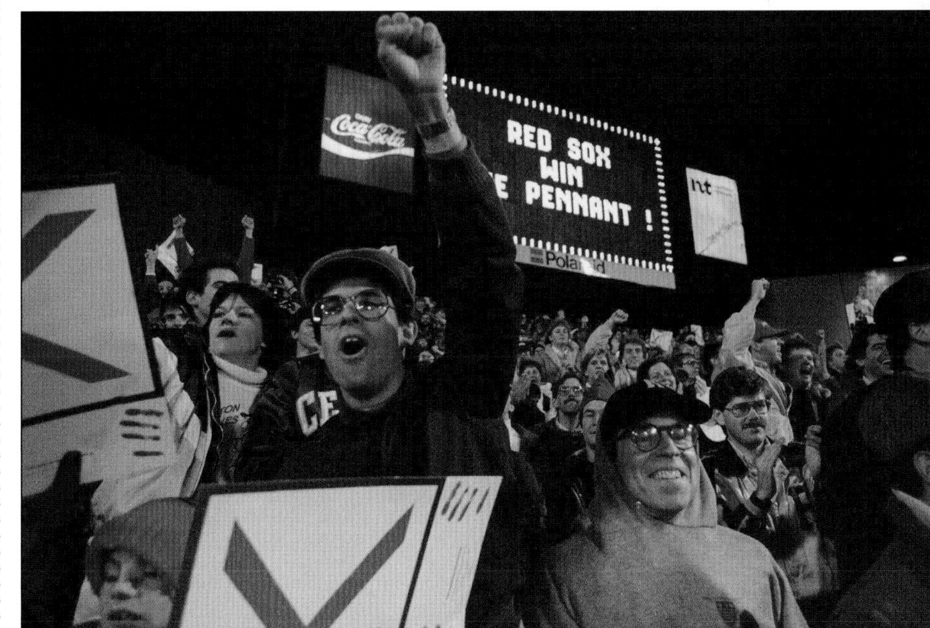

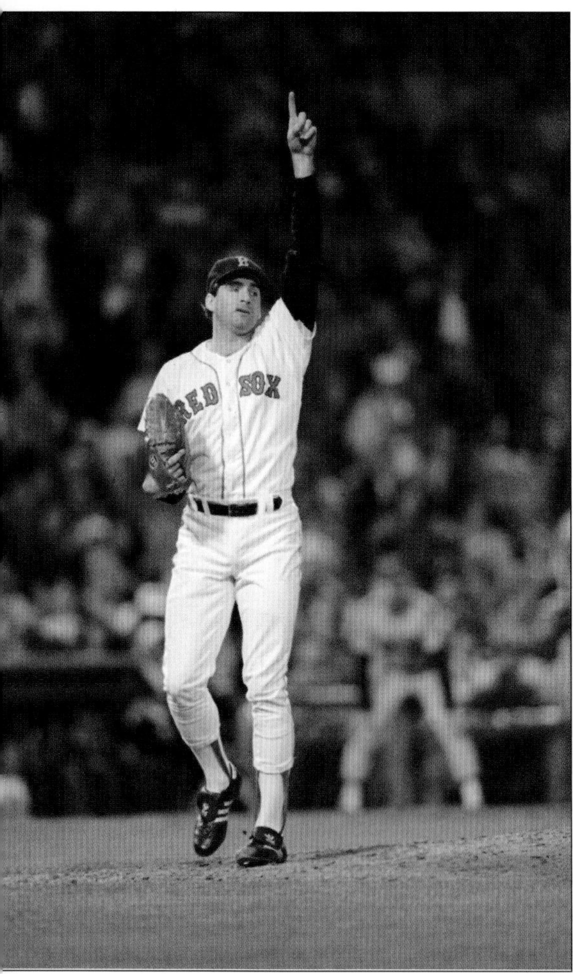

Bruce Hurst celebrates after striking out Lenny Dykstra in Game 5 to notch his second win of the 1986 World Series. Hurst was actually named Series MVP before Boston's 10th-inning meltdown in Game 6, then had the award rescinded.

Sox blew out the Angels in Games 6 and 7 at Fenway. Perhaps intimidated by the mounted police who took a between-innings stroll around the perimeter of the playing field late in the final contest, fans did not storm Joe Mooney's grass as they had for the 1975 pennant-clincher and the final win over Minnesota in '67.

The Sox hit the road for Games 1 and 2 of the World Series against the Mets, who with an intimidating 108–54 record were viewed as a dynasty in the making. Underdog Boston surprisingly won both contests, but the Mets returned the favor by taking two at Fenway to square the Series. Hurst, the winning pitcher in Game 1, authored a complete-game, 4–2 victory in Game 5 to put Boston back up, and a festive home crowd confidently waved their heroes off to Shea Stadium to end 68 years of heartbreak. All they had to do was win one of the last two games in New York.

Game 6 has been well documented. Clemens pitched superbly into the eighth inning, but Boston relievers twice blew the lead—once allowing the Mets to tie the game in the ninth and again after Boston had taken a 5–3 lead in the 10th on a homer by Henderson and an RBI single by Boggs. The agonizing bottom of the 10th, when the Sox were one strike away from a world championship on several occasions before New York completed its improbable comeback, played out on TVs for stunned patrons at Who's On First, Cask N' Flagon, Cornwall's, and dozens of other bars within screaming distance of Fenway. Two Red Sox who had grown up cheering for the team—catcher Rich Gedman of Worcester, Massachusetts, and reliever Bob Stanley, a Maine native—were held largely to blame for the meltdown along with Bill Buckner and manager John McNamara (who left a hobbling Buckner in the game). This seems particularly cruel in retrospect, but at the time nobody was thinking about hometowns. All that mattered were an errant pitch and an elusive groundball.

Rain in New York postponed Game 7 for a day, and as it poured down on Yawkey Way more than one fan parked in front of Fenway hoping to pass on or pick up some good karma. But while Gedman and Evans hit back-to-back homers early in the finale at Shea to help Boston and Hurst to a 3–0 lead, the outcome was the same as in '75. The advantage was erased, the championship eluded. There would be a pennant flying on Fenway's center-field flagpole during its 75th year, but it would signify an American League title rather than the World Series victory that seemed so certain.

"This is the chance you have to take in this business," Henry D'Angelo told Will McDonough of the *Globe* after Game 7, referring to the $100,000 in unusable world champion Red Sox hats,

"I had a fun thing going for years with the bleacher crowd where I would destroy beach balls with a rake. The fans were real tough on me after the [1986] World Series, but on my last day they chanted for me to come out, and had a beach ball waiting for me. One fan even gave me a pot of steamers."
—Pitcher Bob "Steamer" Stanley

pennants, and T-shirts that he and twin brother Arthur were left holding in their now-quiet shop across from Fenway. "We had to have the goods. We had to have the merchandise ready for sale in case they did win it all."

Eternal optimists, the D'Angelos, who still planned to give their big annual gift to the Jimmy Fund of Dana-Farber Cancer Institute, credited the Sox for having a great year and took their own losses in stride. Besides, Red Sox Vice President Haywood Sullivan had helped arrange for Henry to throw out the first pitch before Game 1 of the ALCS—and experiences like that were priceless.

They were also something for Arthur to hold on to during the next summer, when Henry, a Dana-Farber patient, died of cancer at age 60.

House of Magic

The next year and a half was an ugly time at Fenway. On Opening Day, 1987, Stanley, Buckner, and McNamara were roundly booed during the ring ceremony honoring the 1986 championship. A man on Yawkey Way was selling "Hall of Pain" packages, including a "One Strike Away" button and a "68 Years of Anguish" hat. Burdened from the start by demons of the previous season, the '87 Red Sox struggled to a 78–84 record amid a summer-long cascade of jeers that tainted the ballpark's diamond anniversary.

Bad news abounded. Gedman and Clemens were both springtime holdouts. Clemens still managed to win a second straight Cy Young Award, but Gedman got hurt shortly after he returned and would never be the same player. Buckner, a 100-RBI man the previous two years, was vilified unmercifully and then released in July. An infusion of promising rookies—led by outfielders Mike Greenwell and Ellis Burks—offered hope for the future, but bitter fans had a hard time looking ahead. Several players would

The Red Sox wore commemorative patches like this one on their uniforms throughout the 1987 season, but Fenway's diamond anniversary was tarnished by memories of '86.

Bill Buckner, whose 102 RBI in 1986 were forgotten because of his World Series error, cleans out his Fenway locker on July 24, 1987, after being placed on waivers. "I don't know whether it's fair," he said. "It's just human nature."

claim that McNamara was a changed man, and that he had never recovered from the events of October '86.

The 1988 team got off to a similarly lackluster 43–42 start despite the development of Burks and Greenwell into stars and terrific production from Evans, Boggs, and pitchers Clemens and Hurst. There were also embarrassing headlines that threatened to split the team when word of the married Boggs's ongoing affair with Margo Adams was made public. Adams even went on a TV talk show during the All-Star break to discuss the promiscuous behavior of Boggs and his teammates. This didn't sit well with the prim Mrs. Yawkey, nor did McNamara's assertion that "I'm very happy to be one game over .500" at the break.

On July 14, coach Joe Morgan was in the Fenway clubhouse when Sullivan and GM Lou Gorman came in. "Sully went into Mac's office, and Gorman came up to me and said, 'Joe, we're going to make a change, and you're going to be the interim manager until we can find another one,'" Morgan recalled. "I told him, 'Don't try to find one, because you've already got one.'"

This no-nonsense confidence was part of Morgan's DNA, but the truth is that the 58-year-old was thrilled by the opportunity. The first Massachusetts-born manager the Red Sox had employed since Shano Collins in 1931–32, the lifetime resident of working-class Walpole had grown up attending Fenway doubleheaders with his dad and later starred in baseball and hockey at Boston College. Signed by the Braves after graduation, Morgan played just 88 major-league games but could proudly recall hitting a triple off the Green Monster in his only Fenway at-bat (with Cleveland) in 1959. As a well-respected manager in the Red Sox system for nearly a decade, he had nurtured many future major-leaguers and earned the nickname "Tollway Joe" for his off-season job working as a snowplow driver on the Massachusetts Turnpike.

Rain wiped out Morgan's first game at Boston's helm, but what came next was worth the wait. Starting with a doubleheader sweep on July 15, the Red Sox

Sounds of Fenway

If you grew up going to Red Sox games in the 1970s and '80s, you knew the sounds as well as you knew the tune to "Happy Birthday."

Organist John Kiley and public address announcer Sherm Feller, both Boston area natives, were beloved parts of the Fenway Park experience. When you heard Feller's familiar drawn-out basso—"Ladies and gentlemen, boys and girls, welcome to Fenway Park"—it made you feel you were home. He held the job from the magical summer of 1967 until his death in 1994. Feller was also a disc jockey and a talented composer who penned the pop hit "Summertime, Summertime" and pieces performed by the Boston Pops. Today, his Fenway greeting is still available as a computer wav file, and older fans appreciate that current PA man Carl Beane could be the winner of a Sherm Feller sound-a-like contest.

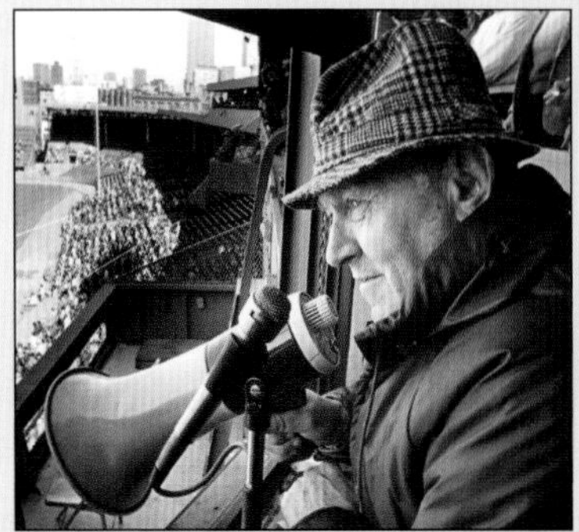

Sherm Feller

Kiley is the answer to every Boston sports fan's favorite trivia question: *Who is the only man to play for the Celtics, Bruins, and Red Sox?* He actually played—played the organ, that is—for the Braves as well, performing for the city's National League club before they skipped town in 1953 and Tom Yawkey hired him. He stayed at the Fenway keyboard until 1989. He will forever be remembered for breaking into the "Hallelujah Chorus" after Carlton Fisk's Game 6 home run—and for making "Hava Nagila" sound cool.

Despite losing all eight of his playoff games as Red Sox manager, getting swept by Oakland in the 1988 and 1990 ALCS, "Walpole Joe" Morgan always gets a hero's welcome at Fenway. Fans have not forgotten the "Morgan Magic" summer of 1988.

won their first 12 games and 19 of their first 20 under their new manager to rise from fourth place to first. Hardened by his long apprenticeship, Morgan was not afraid to speak his mind or stand up to veterans, and he got into a brief tussle with Rice in the runway that led to the Red Sox clubhouse when he pinch-hit for the fading superstar late in a game. "I'm the manager of this nine!" Morgan barked as he came back to the bench, and Mrs. Yawkey agreed—removing the interim tag from his title.

Media dubbed the streak "Morgan Magic," a phrase that still conjures up memories of the sweltering summer of '88 and some of the most exciting days in Fenway history. The Sox established an American League record with 24 consecutive home victories from June 25 to August 13 (the first five under McNamara), and they drew 30,000 or more fans to their last 56 home contests. While they cooled off a bit in late August, they won when they needed to in September to pull out the AL East title.

Unfortunately, they ran right into a juggernaut. The Oakland A's of 1988–90 were one of the more talented clubs of the past half century. Led by "Bash Brothers" Jose Canseco and Mark McGwire, old friend Dave Henderson, and pitchers Dave Stewart, Bob Welch, and Dennis Eckersley, they won three straight AL pennants and swept the Red Sox in a four-game '88 ALCS, although the series was closer than it sounds. The first two games were decided by one run, and Boston had a 5–0 lead early in the third contest before Oakland poured on the power. Eckersley, the former Red Sox starter turned lights-out closer, saved all four wins.

After a second-place finish in 1989 that ended with the unceremonious departure of the team's all-time leader in games pitched (Stanley) and third-leading home run hitter (Rice), Morgan worked a little more magic the next

In this December 1988 photo, construction of the "600 Club" is well underway at Fenway Park. The premium seating and dining area was later renamed the "406 Club" to honor Ted Williams, who batted .406 in 1941.

year. The Red Sox led the Blue Jays by one game in the AL East, and they could clinch the 1990 division title on the final day of the regular season with a win against the White Sox at Fenway. Boston was up 3–1 going into the ninth, thanks to excellent work from starter Mike Boddicker, but with two outs Chicago put two men on against closer Jeff Reardon. Ozzie Guillen, representing the tying run, drilled a line drive toward the right-field corner just beyond the foul pole—an area that juts away from the rest of the park and is hidden from view to almost all but the few rows of fans seated around it.

Boston right fielder Tom Brunansky was playing Guillen to pull. As he went into a dive/slide for the ball, Brunansky's momentum carried him into the corner and out of the sight of 33,000 fans. Chicago runners, also unable to see the play, sped around the bases, chased by revelers who had prematurely stormed the field. Brunansky made the catch just before he hit the low half-wall, and as fans grabbed at his hat he leaped up and ran toward umpire Tim McClelland to show him the ball and seal the victory.

It was a fantastic way to finish the regular season, but unfortunately the defending World Series champion A's were once again waiting in the wings—and now they also had Rickey Henderson. In a replay of the 1988 ALCS, Oakland swept the Red Sox in four straight.

Poor Choices

As the Red Sox failed to return to the World Series, the team's racial makeup again became a topic of controversy. The progress of the late 1960s and '70s seemed to be moving backward. Burks was the only African-American on the club to start the 1991 season, and this lack of diversity extended to the Fenway stands—where *Boston Globe* reporters once counted just 71 black fans in a crowd of 34,000. The team's past woes with regards to race were well docu-

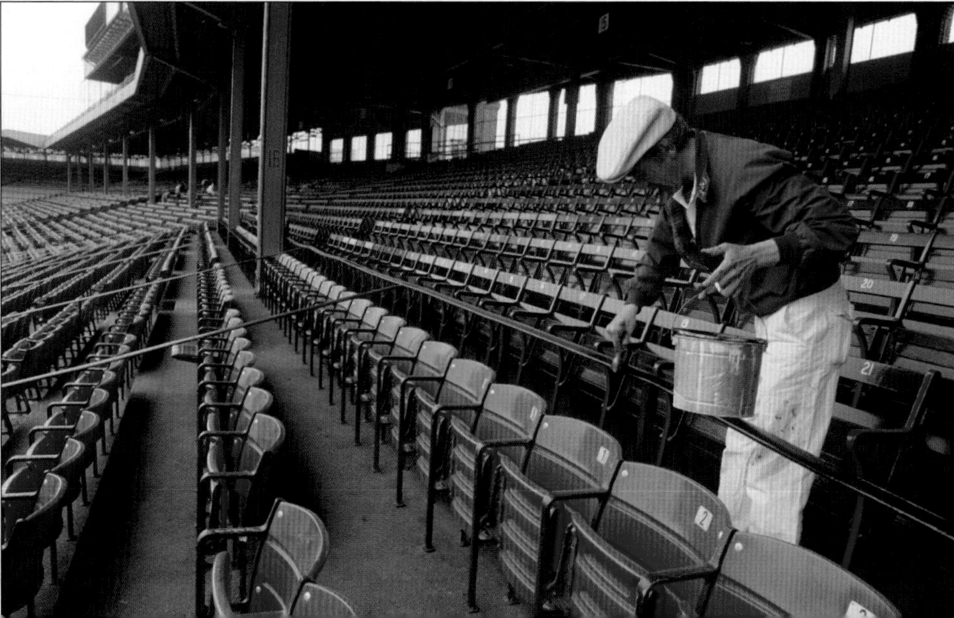

Three days after Rick Duncanson touched up the Fenway stands, Jack Morris and Roger Clemens painted the corners for a combined 20 strikeouts in Boston's 1988 home opener. Detroit won 5–3.

mented, and Boston was looked at warily by African-American players who were free agents or had the ability to block trades to certain clubs. Kirby Puckett, Bernie Williams, and other top black stars sought by the Red Sox continually chose to go or stay elsewhere.

Left to select from the second tier of free agents, the Red Sox spent poorly on underachieving pitchers Danny Dawrin and Matt Young and fading slugger Jack Clark while allowing their own dependable No. 2 man (Boddiker) to depart for Kansas City. Throw in a disastrous trade that sent future Rookie of the Year and NL MVP Jeff Bagwell to Houston for middle reliever Larry Andersen, and the result was a long summer at Fenway in 1991. The highlight was actually a blast from the past—a return by Ted Williams to his old stomping grounds to celebrate the renaming of Lansdowne Street in his honor. Ted finally tipped his hat to the Fenway fans, but he couldn't do anything to save Joe Morgan. After guiding his flawed club to a respectable third-place finish, the most popular Red Sox manager since Dick Williams was fired.

Taking his place was former Boston third baseman Butch Hobson, who had been respected as a hard-nosed player. As a manager, however, he never seemed comfortable with the pressure of the job or with Fenway's loyal but demanding fans. His three years at the helm produced three straight losing seasons, including the team's first last-place finish since 1966. Home attendance sagged from its Morgan Magic heights, and a baseball strike that began on August 11, 1994, and wiped out the remainder of that season alienated fans and decimated Fenway-area businesses.

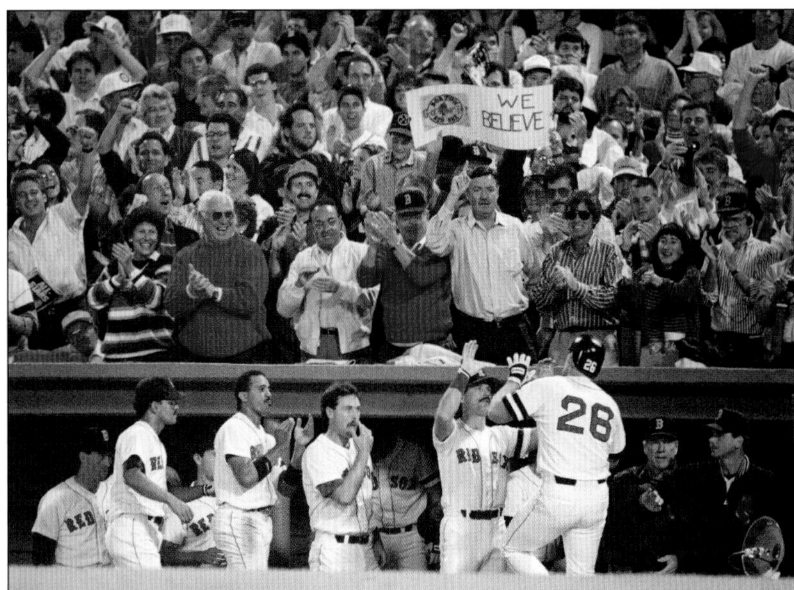

Boston fans certainly believed in the Red Sox in the fourth inning of Game 1 of the 1990 ALCS, when Wade Boggs (26) homered to put Boston up 1–0. But the Oakland A's scored seven in the ninth to secure a 9–1 win, and they swept the Sox in four games.

It was a time of mostly unpopular change at the old ballpark. The team had added private suites atop Fenway's left- and right-field stands in the 1980s, but they often sat empty as businesses had a tough time getting clients excited for a night at the park. A section of 606 stadium club seats called the "600 Club," built behind home plate in 1988–89 and completely enclosed by thick, soundproof glass, made fans feel like they were watching the game from inside a fishbowl—with the sounds of the park piped in through speakers rather than open air. The media griped that the refurbished press box, moved up above the 600 Club, was now too high to follow the nuances of the game, and some even blamed the team's dissipating power—Brunansky led the '92 Sox with 15 homers and the team had just 84—on wind currents changed by the new construction.

Changes at the top of the team were also the subject of scrutiny. When Jean Yawkey suffered a stroke and died in 1993, she left control of the team to the Jean R. Yawkey Trust, which was managed by businessman John Harrington—who with no prior experience in the game now had two votes on all baseball decisions to Haywood Sullivan's one. The two clashed tremendously, and Sullivan was eventually bought out for $33 million. An aging Gorman was made an executive vice president and succeeded as general manager by 35-year-old Dan Duquette. A Massachusetts native and lifelong Red Sox fan, Duquette had a strong baseball acumen but struggled with the public relations role of his position. The relatively unknown Kevin Kennedy was brought on as manager to replace Hobson. Fans (and Duquette) had hoped for an acclaimed leader such as Oakland's Tony LaRussa, but Boston was no longer a desirable destination for top managerial candidates.

Mike Greenwell celebrates the 1995 AL East title at Fenway with the help of a police horse. A fan favorite, "The Gator" hit .312 at home over 12 Red Sox seasons.

Exit Rocket, Enter Pedro

Initially in 1995, everything worked out. Some of Duquette's early signings—old A's nemesis Jose Canseco, discarded knuckleballer Tim Wakefield, outfielder Troy O'Leary—performed above expectations. Canseco combined with homegrown first baseman Mo Vaughn (39 homers and 126 RBI in an MVP season) to give the team its best 1–2 power punch since Lynn and Rice, and O'Leary and shortstop John Valentin added additional offensive support. The most surprising story of all, however, was Wakefield, who a year after going 5–15 in the minor leagues went 14–1 with a 1.65 ERA in his first three months with the Red Sox—paving the way to an AL East title. Clemens also rebounded following two subpar years, but Boston once again drew an unlucky postseason draw. The Cleveland Indians entered with a 100–44 mark that dwarfed Boston's fine 86–58 slate, and Cleveland swept their best-of-five series.

By the time the Red Sox made it back to the postseason in 1998, the makeup of the team had changed considerably. The oft-injured Canseco had been traded back to Oakland, the media-hungry Kennedy had been replaced as manager by folksy, down-to-earth Jimy Williams, and Boston had two new franchise players.

After Duquette locked horns with free agent Clemens on a four-year contract extension—the GM thought the Rocket, a deceiving 10–13 in 1996, was in the "twilight of his career" at age 34—the proud Texan signed with Toronto and won two straight Cy Young Awards. Duquette took the heat from fans, especially after Clemens struck out 16 in his first game back at Fenway the next summer and glared up at the ownership box. The GM redeemed himself in the winter of 1997–98, however, by trading two prospects to Montreal for the National League's best young pitcher: Pedro Martinez.

Beginning with his first game at Fenway—a 12-strikeout shutout of Seattle—Martinez lit up Yawkey Way with more energy than any pitcher since Luis Tiant and more pure dominance than any hurler since the heyday of Smoky Joe Wood. Starts by the diminutive (5′10″, 170 pounds) right-hander with the devastating fastball, curve, and slider lent a festive air to the ballpark. Fans waved *K* cards with "Pedro Power!" inscribed on them, and they stood, rhythmically clapping, each time he reached two strikes on a batter. Boston's large Dominican population started coming out in full force to games, brandishing flags from their homeland in their compatriot's honor and giving the Fenway stands a more diverse feel than ever before.

On offense, Martinez had two big weapons backing him up. Vaughn, a gregarious team leader and the most popular African-American player in team history, was in the midst of a dominant four-year stretch in which he averaged .320 with 40 homers and 120 RBI per season. The big-boned "Hit Dog" was especially potent at Fenway, where in 1997 he was joined in the everyday lineup by rookie shortstop Nomar Garciaparra—a wiry five-tool player who combined acrobatic defensive skills with a powerful, disciplined bat. Garciaparra quickly became a fan favorite who was greeted with yells of "Nomaaah!" each time he stepped to the plate. In 1997, he led the league with 209 hits and 11 triples while setting a major-league record with 98 RBI from the leadoff spot. Named Rookie of the Year, he was runner-up for MVP the next season when he more often hit third or fourth and raised his power totals to 35 homers and 122 RBI.

These sluggers had a new Fenway target to aim at starting in 1997, when several 25-foot-high Coca-Cola bottles

By mid-1999, Nomar Garciaparra was being heralded as the best pure Red Sox hitter since Ted Williams. The day before signing for these Fenway fans, he belted two grand slams and tallied 10 RBI.

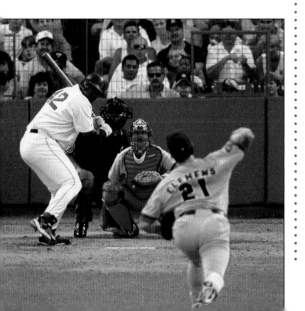

In his return to Fenway, Roger Clemens struck out Mo Vaughn three times on July 12, 1997—and earned a standing ovation for his eight stellar innings of work. Vaughn was in the midst of a four-year tear, averaging 40 home runs and 120 RBI for Boston.

"You're so close to the fans. You walk in there and it's almost like you're sitting on the field. It's so pretty, and the Wall magnifies the whole field."
—Manager Joe Morgan

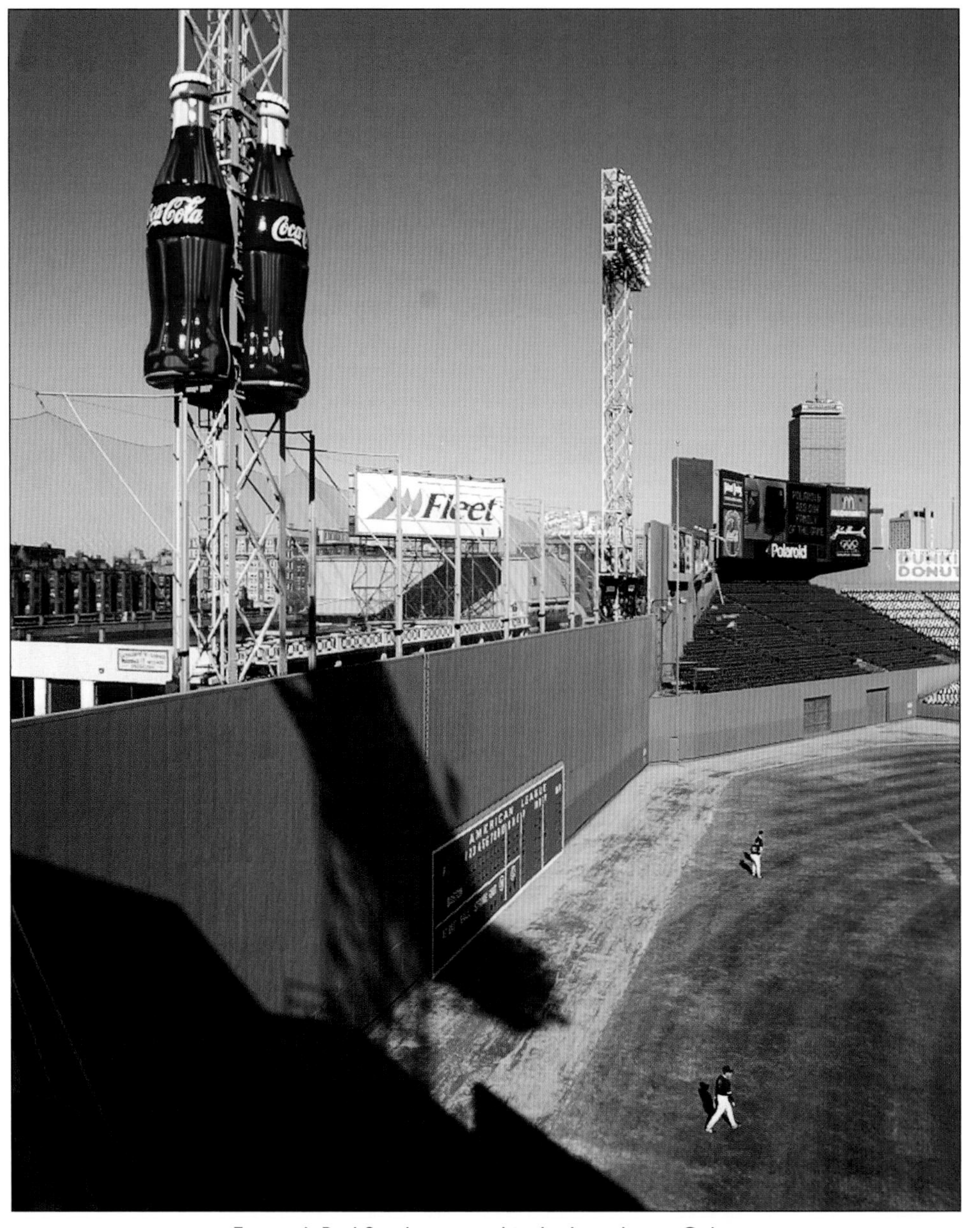

For each Red Sox homer to hit the brand-new Coke bottles atop the Green Monster in 1997, the soft drink company gave $1,000 to the Jimmy Fund.

debuted in the light towers above the Green Monster. Fans loved seeing the occasional moon shot bounce off the bottles, and overall the '98 Sox hit 205 homers—which when combined with one of the league's best pitching staffs resulted in a second-place AL East finish.

Thanks to baseball's new three-division alignment, in which three first-place teams and a "wildcard" club with the next best record would all qualify for the postseason, being second best to the Yanks was not as frustrating. Confidence was high when Boston crushed '95 nemesis Cleveland 11–3 in the AL Division Series opener, breaking a 0–13 stretch for the Red Sox in postseason play. However, the Indians came from behind to take each of the next three contests, including a pair of one-run victories at Fenway, to capture the series.

The off-season of 1998–99 was a public relations disaster for the Red Sox. Free agent Vaughn ended bitter contract negotiations by departing for greener pastures in Anaheim. Moreover, team management tried to have street vendors booted off Yawkey Way, stating that area residents had complained about the traffic and congestion. Boston Mayor Thomas Menino intervened with a Christmas Eve save, in which he declared that the pushcarts would remain and that Fenway would now be closed to auto traffic on game days. "Fenway Park without peanut and sausage vendors is like Christmas without snow," the mayor said at a press conference held outside the ballpark's main gate. "This Christmas we have snow. And this spring we'll have vendors."

Vendors had plenty to hawk in 1999, as the Red Sox finished second in the AL East to New York and secured another wildcard berth behind stellar seasons from Garciaparra (a league-leading .357 average) and Cy Young winner Martinez (an AL-best 23–4 record, 2.07 ERA, and 313 strikeouts). Facing Cleveland yet again in an American League Division Series, the Sox dropped the first two games but then broke through with three

Wally's World

Wally the Green Monster is such a beloved part of the Fenway Park landscape, it's hard to imagine there was ever a time when he wasn't popular. When he made his first appearance, however, he might as well have been wearing a Yankees uniform.

On April 13, 1997, just before a game between the Red Sox and visiting Seattle Mariners, Wally emerged from the door in Fenway's left-field wall. Initially, the 30,300 fans didn't know quite what to make of him. But when he came back out to lead the crowd in singing "Take Me Out to the Ballgame," he was roundly booed. "In a place like this, where you have so much history and tradition, it's too much," said Red Sox first baseman Mike Stanley of Wally's inauspicious debut. "We have the old-school kind of fans here."

But like rock 'n' roll on the Fenway loud speakers, Wally grew on fans. Kids loved the furry Elmo-like character, and parents found that he was a great distraction to divert youngsters away from food vendors. Besides, you had to admire a guy who was always smiling no matter how bad the Red Sox did.

Once broadcaster Jerry Remy started bonding with a Beanie Baby-sized Wally on his broadcasts, giving him his own beach chair in the TV booth, the mascot's popularity was assured. Wally was soon in demand for birthday parties and corporate functions, and today he has his own autograph sessions when not roaming the Fenway stands.

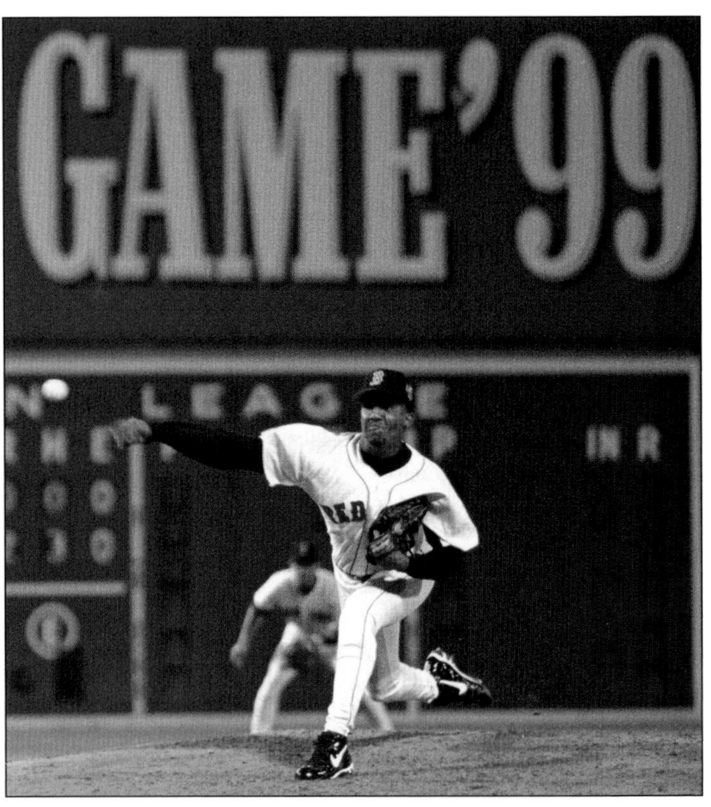

Above: Although a hand injury limited him to beer duty here, 30-year vendor veteran Rob Barry can normally throw peanuts for distance and accuracy that would make Dwight Evans proud. *Right:* After an emotional first pitch by Ted Williams, Pedro Martinez struck out the side in the first inning of the 1999 All-Star Game at Fenway. Martinez was 23–4 in 1999, and his career record at Fenway was 58–19.

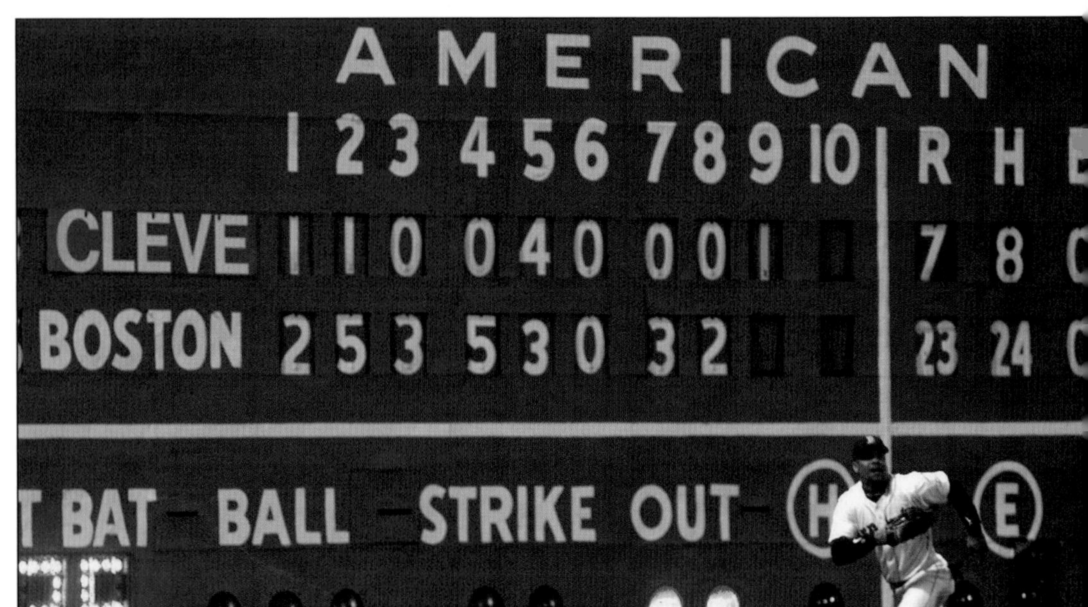

The scoreboard tells the story in the ninth inning of Game 4 of the 1999 ALDS. The 23 runs by the Red Sox set a postseason record. Boston won 12–8 the next day to win their first playoff series since 1986.

straight wins to capture the set. Included was a 23–7 Game 4 blowout at Fenway in which John Valentin had seven RBI and a thrilling Game 5 clincher on the road in which Martinez rebounded from a bad back suffered in the first game to pitch six hitless innings of relief in a 12–8 come-from-behind win.

The victory set up a wildcard-created dream scenario, a seven-game ALCS match-up with the dreaded Yankees, the reigning world champions. The old rivals split a pair of one-run games in New York and then came to Fenway for one of the most hotly anticipated contests in the park's history. Facing Martinez would be none other than Roger Clemens, who had signed with New York as a free agent that winter. Like the Joe Wood-Walter Johnson match-up at Fenway in 1912, this was billed as a heavyweight bout—Cy Young vs. Cy Old—and one fan paid $1,200 for four tickets.

In the end, it wasn't much of a battle at all. Boston racked Clemens for six runs and five hits over just two innings and Pedro notched 12 strikeouts over seven in a 13–1 laugher. One group of fans started chanting, "Where is Ro-ger?"; another group yelled back, "In the show-er!" The good times, however, didn't last. Regrouping for the next two games at Fenway, the Yankees blew them both open in the late innings to capture the AL flag.

It wasn't the end-of-the-century finish that Boston rooters were hoping for, but it did bode well for the future. If the 20th century belonged to the Yankees, maybe Fenway and the Red Sox could rule the 21st.

Mid-Summer Classic

Initially seen as a chance to highlight Fenway Park a last time before it went under the wrecking ball, the 1999 All-Star Game may have helped save the doomed venue that hosted it.

Red Sox ownership was already touting designs for a new Fenway when more than 110,000 fans descended on Boston to enjoy All-Star week activities that started with the John Hancock FanFest—a mix of baseball-themed events including clinics with big-leaguers, Hall of Famer autograph sessions, and make-your-own baseball cards. The Home Run Derby drew wall-to-wall human traffic on Lansdowne Street as people battled to catch moon shots hit over the Green Monster by the likes of Mark McGwire, Sammy Sosa, and Ken Griffey, Jr.

When the big night of July 13 came, the evening started with a Field of Dreams moment as living members of MLB's "All-Century Team"—Musial, Mays, Aaron, and the rest—took the Fenway diamond alongside their modern-day counterparts. One legend was missing from the group, and then fans saw him: Ted Williams, waving as he was driven around the field. Frail but beaming, the 80-year-old icon stepped to the mound and delivered a first-pitch strike to fellow Red Sox legend Carlton Fisk before being greeted and hugged by stars young and old. Players and fans were in tears.

It seemed the game would have a hard time living up to this level, but American League starter (and game MVP) Pedro Martinez came close—striking out the first three batters and five of the first six to start the AL on its way to a 4–1 victory. It was an event that left a powerful impression on all who saw it live or on TV, and it made it hard to imagine a world without Fenway.

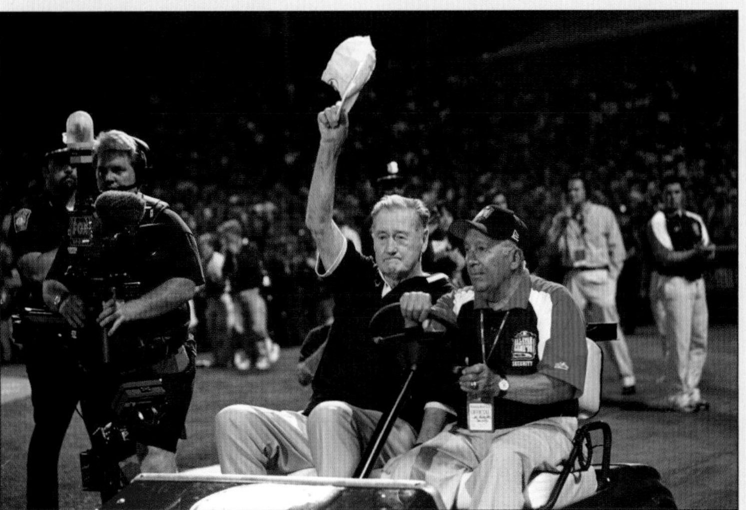

Ted Williams at the 1999 All-Star Game

CHAPTER 9

Home of Champions

2000–TODAY

At the turn of the millennium, Red Sox CEO John Harrington wanted to tear down Fenway, saying the team couldn't stay competitive in the small, antiquated ballpark. But new ownership kept Fenway Park, refurbished it, and celebrated the team's first world championship in 86 years.

When Boston broke Cleveland's MLB record with its 456th consecutive home sellout, Red Sox players said thanks by handing out special laminated souvenir tickets like this one to fans as they entered Fenway. The streak continued into 2011.

The applause was calm and reserved, more suited for the opera house than a sporting event. As Pedro Martinez walked from the center-field bullpen toward the Red Sox dugout, and the late-afternoon sun splashed down on his face, he smiled at the fans standing and clapping along the first-base side of Fenway Park.

It was October 18, 2004. At approximately 1:22 a.m. that morning, the Red Sox had won one of the most thrilling games in their history, a 6–4 victory over the Yankees capped by a David Ortiz home run in the 12th inning. Boston still trailed the best-of-seven American League Championship Series three games to one, but with Pedro starting on this day, the home crowd hoped the Sox could squeeze out another victory and keep their rivals from celebrating a pennant on the Fenway grass.

Martinez struck out New York superstar Derek Jeter swinging to start the game. This time, the cheers were unmistakably of the ballpark variety, loud and frenzied. In Section 39, Row 31, at the top of the center-field bleachers, a group of fans with red-painted faces calling themselves the "K-Men" would hold up white and red *K* cards for this and all six strikeouts that Pedro recorded on the night. In doing so, they continued a K-Men tradition that had gone on uninterrupted since Martinez's first days with the Red Sox seven seasons before.

Clearly playing off the adrenaline of the previous game, Boston jumped on Yankees starter Mike Mussina for two runs in the bottom of the first and led 2–1 through the middle innings. Martinez was not at his best, however, and when New York loaded the bases in the sixth on two singles and a hit batsmen, a cry of "67!" could be heard. Reaching into his "K-Bag" for

Who's down three games to one? As they awaited for David Ortiz after his game-winning homer in Game 4 of the 2004 ALCS, Red Sox players seemed to sense that greater things lay ahead. It was Ortiz's fourth walk-off hit of the year—and not his last.

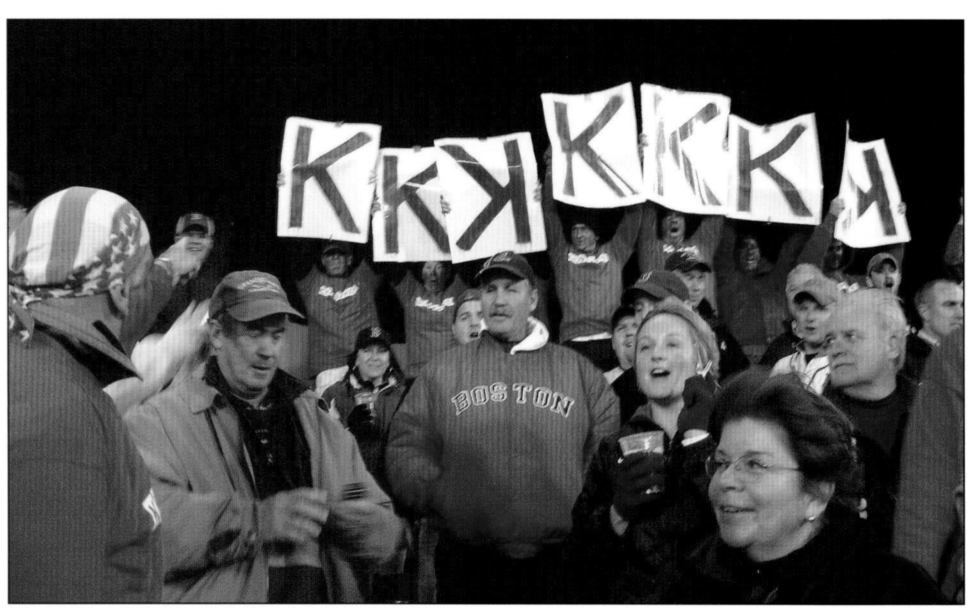

Kevin McCarthy (*in USA bandana at left*) snuck into Fenway late on the night of October 11, 1967, hoping to see Game 7 of the World Series the next day, but he was ejected after sunrise. Today, he and the "K-Men" have their own special cheering section in the Green Monster seats.

the red jacket he had worn to the 1967 World Series, "K-Men" leader Kevin McCarthy began passing it around to the other members of his crew—which included his son Ryan. A second good-luck charm, a red-painted baseball, was given to a young child in the stands to rub as Jeter stepped to the plate.

The talismans didn't work. Jeter hit a line shot to right for a three-run double, and the capacity crowd of 35,120 seemed to exhale all at once. Boston needed to score quickly, before Yankees closer Mariano Rivera got into the game, and did so in the seventh thanks to a leadoff homer from Ortiz off Tom Gordon. After a walk and a single, New York manager Joe Torre had seen enough; he brought Rivera in, far earlier than usual, and Red Sox catcher Jason Varitek came through with a game-tying sacrifice fly.

Here the score stayed, all the way to the 14th inning. Both teams had chances to break the deadlock, and the K-Men turned to their lucky ball and jacket several more times for assistance. Hearts skipped several beats as three of Tim Wakefield's knuckleballs bounded past Varitek in the 13th, but the captain stopped them when he needed to with runners in scoring position.

By the bottom of the 14th, incredibly, the game had already surpassed the previous contest as the longest in postseason history. Despite the early 5:10 P.M. start, it was already nearing 11 P.M. when Ortiz came up with two on and two out. Big Papi battled Esteban Loaiza for nine pitches, fouling several off, before fisting the 10th on a short flare into right field. It landed just inside the foul line, and after Johnny Damon sprinted home from second, the entire Red Sox team mobbed him at home plate.

Fans screamed, high-fived, and hugged each other as if the pennant had been

"We have two brands here—the Red Sox and Fenway Park. The commitment to preserve and protect Fenway for generations to come clearly was the right decision."
—Sam Kennedy, Red Sox chief operating officer

won. The Sox still trailed the series three games to two as the teams headed back to New York, and no club in big-league history had ever even forced a Game 7 after being down three-nil in a playoff series, let alone win one. But after nearly 11 exhilarating, exhausting hours of baseball in a 24-hour span, Boston had come back from the brink twice and given their long-suffering patrons reason to celebrate—and hope. The cheers of "19–18!" that Yankees fans had shouted incessantly during the series—a not-so-subtle reminder of the last time the Red Sox had won a World Series—would start anew in the Bronx two days hence. But for now the only sound rising above the raucous crowd was the hard-pounding lyrics of "Dirty Water," the classic Boston-themed rock song that had become Fenway's victory anthem.

Saving Fenway

Given the opponent, the circumstances, and what transpired next, Games 4 and 5 of the '04 ALCS might have been the most important in Fenway Park's long history. Yet if John Harrington and the powers that be had had their way a few years before, they never would have taken place in this venue.

When the then-Red Sox CEO marked his 63rd birthday on the eve of the 1999 All-Star Game in Boston, his cake was carved to resemble the "New Fenway Park" he had proposed the team build across the street from the original 1912 structure. There was no way for the Red Sox to stay competitive, Harrington claimed, with a 35,000-seat antiquated ballpark, nor was there a feasible way to enlarge the old facility. Over the next year, Harrington and his staff would put out an all-media blitz to gain support for his $550 million, publicly funded plan, which included replicating a Green Monster and quirky outfield dimensions in the new 45,000-seat stadium and leaving portions of the old Fenway standing as a museum,

Like a kid with a new toy, Red Sox CEO John Harrington (*left*) shows MLB Commissioner Bud Selig a model of the proposed new Fenway Park during a May 26, 1999, press conference.

Harrington's proposal called for the Red Sox to take over land for the new ballpark by eminent domain, and it faced a very vocal opposition. Sure, the naysayers admitted, many of Fenway's grandstand seats were still the originals designed for 5′6″ men from the early 20th century. Yes, not every seat in the house had a perfect view. But if popular new ballparks such as Camden Yards in Baltimore and Jacobs Field in Cleveland were built in a retro style that honored the beauty and uniqueness of parks such as Fenway, then why do away with the real thing?

In the summer of 1998, amidst the vendors on Lansdowne Street, a group

As the debate over whether to build a new, larger Fenway intensified from 1998 to 2000, the nonprofit "Save Fenway Park!" group produced stickers, pins, and pennants to rally support against the proposed stadium.

calling itself "Save Fenway Park!" set up its first booth in response to early rumors of the ballpark's demise. A year later, after Harrington went public with his plan, the Save Fenway folks began handing out leaflets disparaging the CEO's proposal and offering an alternative: renovating the existing park.

"We have a ballpark; we don't want a mallpark!" they shouted to passersby. "Improve it—don't remove it!" According to models designed by Boston architect Charles Hagenah, the fliers explained, Fenway could be expanded to include: an upper deck, increasing capacity to 43,500; 73 luxury suites (more than Camden Yards); wider seats with more legroom; additional restaurants, concession areas, and restrooms; a family picnic area and autograph hut; and no obstructed views. The current playing field, including the Green Monster, would be untouched, and no taxpayer subsidy would be necessary to finance a renovation.

Green and white "Save Fenway Park!" buttons, T-shirts, and bumper stickers started popping up around Boston early in the 2000 season. The Red Sox issued a press release in which Harrington stated that the team was prepared to privately finance all costs related to a new ballpark up to $350 million, although they would still count on the city to acquire the land and prepare the site. Harrington said architects and other building experts had told him that renovating the existing Fenway would be dangerous because of crumbling pillars, antiquated plumbing, and other challenges. "It would be easier to straighten the Leaning Tower of Pisa," he said.

As debate over the fate of their ballpark continued, the Red Sox started the 2000 season as *Sports Illustrated*'s favorite to win the World Series. They wound up short of the playoffs, but they had some outstanding individual performances. Nomar Garciaparra won his second straight batting title with a .372 mark, and Martinez's 1.74 ERA—nearly two full runs better than the AL's second-best finisher, Roger Clemens (3.70)—buoyed his status as the game's best pitcher. Closer Derek Lowe chipped in with an AL-high 42 saves.

Injuries derailed the Sox in 2001. The club signed free agent outfielder Manny Ramirez, one of the game's best hitters, to an eight-year, $160 million contract, but Boston lost the second half of its projected 1–2 punch for all but 27 games when Garciaparra had wrist surgery during spring training. Varitek and Martinez also spent significant time on the disabled list, and when GM Dan Duquette sought to spark the club by firing manager Jimy Williams and replacing him with pitching coach Joe Kerrigan, the move was a disaster. Kerrigan was woeful at the helm, and Boston barely finished over .500. Ramirez's 41 homers and 125 RBI were wasted.

A New Regime

The off-season of 2001–02 was one of the most significant in team history, as a new ownership group took the helm of the Red Sox. It was considered all along that Harrington would sell to one of several locally based bidding teams, but in the end it was the tandem of former Padres owner and TV producer Tom Werner and former Marlins owner and investment genius John Henry that got the nod. For a total of more than $720 million—$420 million from Werner and Henry, plus $300 million from a group of minority owners—69 years of Yawkey ownership officially came to an end on February 27, 2002. Under the new arrangement, Henry would be principal owner and Werner chairman.

The move was initially chastised in Boston as a set-up by Commissioner Bud Selig and Major League Baseball to put two of "their guys" at the helm rather than native New Englanders. But the new bosses quickly won over local fans with their candor and commitment to change. Bringing aboard former Orioles and Padres executive Larry Lucchino as president and CEO, they fired Kerrigan and Duquette—the latter of whom deserved a better fate after vastly improving the team's image and bringing many key players into the fold. Popular former bench coach Grady Little took over as manager, and Mike Port became interim general manager.

Although it was not entirely ruled out, talk of a new ballpark quieted down. Janet Marie Smith, the architect who had worked with Lucchino on con-

Man in the Monster

Christian Elias got the world's coolest part-time job strictly by accident. He tried to get a spot on the Fenway grounds crew when he was 18, but there were no openings. They did, however, need somebody to work the Wall. "I had been to plenty of games at Fenway," he recalled, "but I never thought about what went on back there."

He soon learned, developing a system that has changed little in the 21 years since. Before each game, he and his two assistants get out all the plates for the American and National League teams playing that day, along with numbers denoting the pitching match-ups, and hang them on the front of the scoreboard. During games, they have only about 90 seconds between innings to go outside with their ladder and make any necessary changes, so they constantly watch MLB.com on their laptop for scores. Two guys handle the outside games, while the other works the line score for the Red Sox game from inside.

The room in which they work is cramped and dingy—too hot in summer and too cold in spring and fall. Still, it's got a great view and plenty of character. Ballplayers have autographed its concrete walls over the decades, and there is even a log of all of Ted Williams's 1951 homers. There is also the chance to befriend ballplayers and celebrities who step inside for a peek. "Manny [Ramirez] used to come in all the time to talk," said Elias, who once turned down a $5,000 offer for a *21* plate from a Roger Clemens fan. "We always like company."

What they don't like is extra innings. There is no toilet inside the Monster.

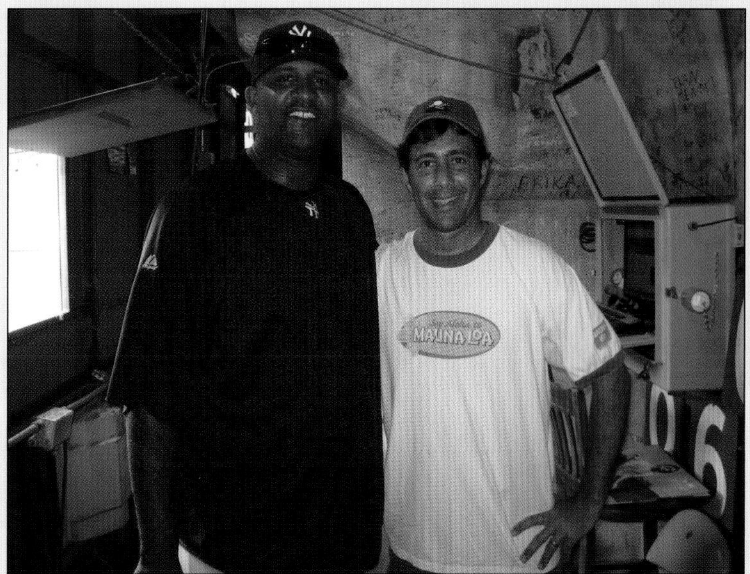

CC Sabathia with Christian Elias in the latter's Fenway "office"

struction in Baltimore of Oriole Park at Camden Yards—the most acclaimed of the retro parks—was now given the challenge of revitalizing 90-year-old Fenway. Improvements began immediately; by the 2002 home opener, 400 seats had been added at various levels, along with new food and drink kiosks and two glass broadcast booths where fans could watch pregame and postgame radio interviews.

Nicknamed the "Pesky Pole" since the 1950s, Fenway's right-field foul pole was "officially" named for Red Sox legend Johnny Pesky on his 87th birthday in 2006. This spot, which is only about 295 feet from home plate, is a favorite destination for such fans as Trevor and Mary (in from Las Vegas).

These were the kinds of moves that had been missing in the Yawkey regime, where tradition had too often stood in the way of innovation. They were also fiscally sensible; the changes projected out to $3.5 million in additional revenue, with new dugout seats (located on former foul territory, inches from the dugouts) going for $200 apiece. Although there was some grumbling about rising costs—baseball's smallest park would now have its highest ticket prices—it was clear that New Englanders would be willing to pay more to watch a competitive team.

This was certainly the case in 2002, when the Red Sox finished with a terrific 93-69 record. Highlights included 33 homers and a batting title (at .349) from Ramirez, 56 doubles and 120 RBI from Garciaparra, and stellar pitching performances from Martinez (20–4), converted starter Lowe (21–8), and new closer Ugeth Urbina (40 saves). Boston again failed to reach the postseason, but Lowe provided playoff-type excitement in pitching a 10–0 no-hitter at Fenway on April 27—the first at the ballpark since Dave Morehead's gem in 1965.

The new stewards of Fenway earned additional respect for the classy way they handled the July 5 death of Red Sox icon Ted Williams at age 83. More than 25,000 fans attended a day-night celebration of the Kid's life at Fenway later that month, and every last detail was given careful thought. As a *9* glowed in the "At Bat" column of the manual scoreboard, Boston players past and present added flowers to a beautiful arrangement formed in the shape of Ted's famous number. Friends such as Williams's teammate Dom DiMaggio and his Marine "wingman" John Glenn shared reflections. While Curt Gowdy's 1960 broadcast of Ted's legendary last at-bat was played over the loudspeakers, a spotlight shone on the pitcher's mound and Jack Fisher, the Orioles right-hander whose fastball Williams had slammed into the home bullpen at Fenway on that damp September day.

At the same time that the past was honored, new traditions began at Fenway. Families were invited to play catch on the grass each Father's Day, and kids got to stand at home plate and shout "Play Ball!" to start each home contest. For one inning each Sunday, kids got to grab the microphone as "Little Stars" and call out Red Sox batters as they stepped to the plate. And before each bottom of the eighth, the crowd joined in singing the old Neil Diamond hit "Sweet Caroline."

It was if the old ballpark had gone from black and white to Technicolor overnight, and in September 2002 it got

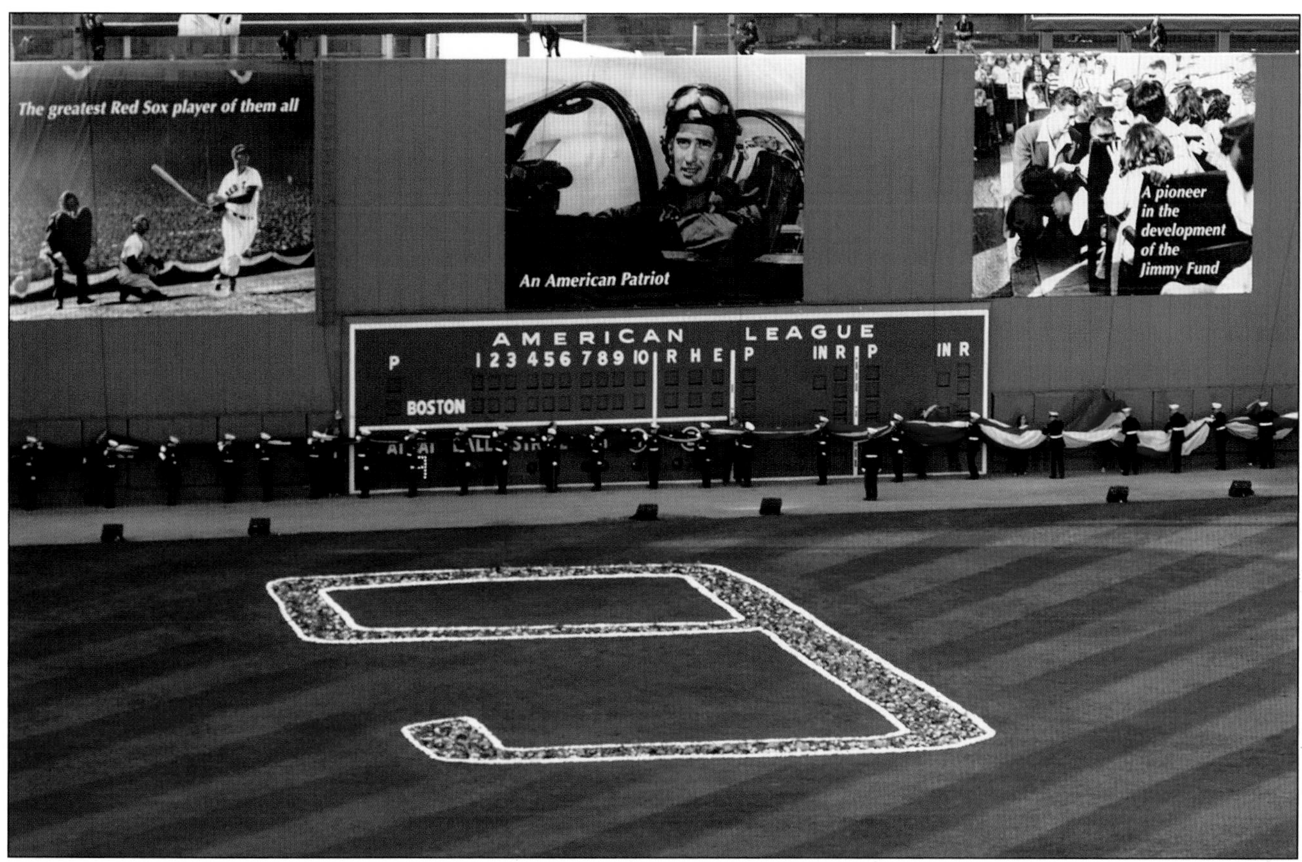
The greatest Red Sox player of them all
An American Patriot
A pioneer in the development of the Jimmy Fund
AMERICAN LEAGUE
BOSTON

Marines from Fort Devens in Ayer, Massachusetts, carry off a large flag that was unfurled during the tribute to Red Sox legend (and fellow Marine) Ted Williams at Fenway Park on July 22, 2002.

even brighter. Yawkey Way, the street fronting Fenway's main entrance, was turned into an open-air concourse accessible throughout games, offering food, live music, and a carnival-type atmosphere. More than 60 years after he was routinely chased out of the ballpark for selling pennants and other items, Arthur D'Angelo and his sons now had a store that was *part of the ballpark.*

Henry, Werner, and Lucchino were quickly developing a strong reputation as guys who understood the psyche and needs of Boston baseball fans, and they took another huge step in the right direction with their next hire: Theo Epstein as general manager. A lifelong Red Sox diehard who had grown up a mile from Fenway, he knew the team's rich history—the good and the bad—and was determined to help write a new chapter. And although he was just 28 years old, the youngest GM in big-league annals would not be outworked.

Excitement at Fenway reached new heights in more ways than one in 2003, as the net atop the Green Monster was replaced with 269 seats that drew rave reviews and quickly became Boston's most sought-after tickets. Plenty of balls made their way into the hands of folks atop the Wall that summer, as two newcomers brought in by "Theo and the Trio"—DH David Ortiz and first baseman Kevin Millar—were among six Red Sox players with 25 or more home runs. The team set a new franchise record with 238 homers altogether, and although the pitching was a bit shaky after Martinez, the offensive fireworks got manager Grady Little's club back to the playoffs as a wildcard entry.

The 2003 postseason brought dramatic highs and lows. Trot Nixon's 11th-inning walk-off homer against Oakland at Fenway helped Boston avoid a three-game sweep in the ALDS. In fact, it spurred the Red Sox to three straight wins and the series triumph. This set up another ALCS date with the Yankees, and a classic seven-game showdown ensued.

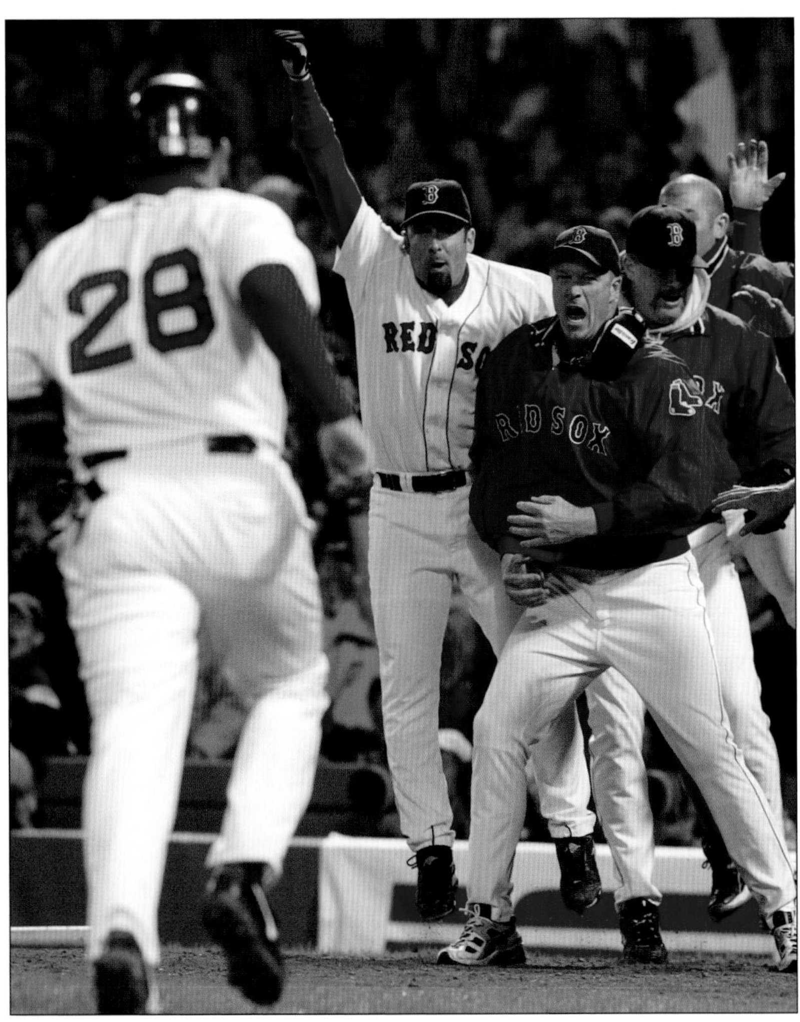

Doug Mirabelli scores the winning run ahead of Trot Nixon, whose pinch-hit homer turned the 2003 ALDS around.

Knuckleballer Tim Wakefield shined for the Sox with two wins, but Boston was still faced with the unenviable task of having to win the last two games at Yankee Stadium. They took the first step in a 9–6 shootout in Game 6, and they held a 5–2 lead after seven strong innings from Pedro in the finale. But then logic went out the door. Little left a visibly tiring Martinez in too long, and the Yanks rallied to tie the game. Then, in the bottom of the 11th, New York's Aaron Boone crushed Wakefield's first pitch for a pennant-clinching home run.

Champions at Last

Little, on whom bitter Boston fans placed total blame for the loss, was fired as expected a few days later and replaced with former Phillies manager Terry Francona. The pitching staff got a big upgrade in starter Curt Schilling and closer Keith Foulke, both of whom shined in 2004. Schilling led the staff with a 21–6 record, and Foulke contributed 32 saves. There was plenty of offense as usual, as both Ramirez and Ortiz reached 40 homers and 130 RBI, but Garciappara missed the first 57 games with an Achilles injury and was (understandably) unhappy after learning—along with everyone else—that the Sox had tried to acquire Texas slugger Alex "A-Rod" Rodriguez to take his spot at shortstop. A brooding Nomar was becoming a distraction, and the entire team was in a funk defensively.

Then at the end of July came two incidents that jump-started Boston's season. On July 24, the Yankees—who had wound up trading for Rodriguez—were at Fenway for a match-up of the AL East leaders. In the third inning, A-Rod claimed he was hit by a pitch from Boston's Bronson Arroyo and started walking toward the mound. Varitek intercepted him, the two got into a shouting match, and eventually things turned physical when Varitek shoved his glove in Rodriguez's face. The fight ignited the crowd, and the Red Sox came back for a thrilling 12–11 win against the usually infallible Rivera.

A week later, at the trading deadline, Epstein made the gutsiest move of his Boston tenure. He traded Garciaparra—one of the most popular players in team history—to the Cubs in a three-way deal that brought Boston two strong defensive performers in shortstop Orlando Cabrera (who took Nomar's spot) and first baseman Doug Mientkiewicz. The logic was that Nomar, due to be a free agent, probably wouldn't re-sign with Boston after the A-Rod incident. Since the Sox were scuffling along at just a bit over .500 with him anyway, why not shake things up and try to win with more defense?

The move proved brilliant. Cabrera and Mientkiewicz both shined down the stretch, and others picked up the offensive slack. Boston went 42–18 after the trade, secured the wildcard, and beat Anaheim three straight in the ALDS—winning the finale on a walk-off homer at Fenway by Ortiz. Waiting in the next round was—who else?—the Yankees.

When catcher Jason Varitek quieted a jawing Alex Rodriguez with his glove on July 24, 2004, prompting a bench-clearing brawl at Fenway, it ignited the Red Sox to an 11–10 victory over the Yankees. They would go 46–20 the rest of the way.

Early on, nothing went right for Boston. Schilling, who had been battling an ankle injury late in the season, struggled mightily in a 10–7 loss at New York in the opener, and Martinez was edged in Game 2 by Jon Lieber. Boston fans hoped some home-cooking would help, but Game 3 at Fenway was a total disaster as the Yankees crushed Arroyo and five relievers for 22 hits in a 19–8 laughter. Boston fans were booing their own team by the fifth inning and were leaving a chilly, morgue-like Fenway by the seventh. The odds against a comeback were now astronomical—it had never been done in 25 previous three-games-to-none situations—but the Red Sox still wanted to win once to salvage some respect.

Game 4 started off miserably when A-Rod hit a two-run homer in the second, but starter Derek Lowe settled down and kept things close. The Red Sox scored three times in the fifth to go ahead, but New York bounced right back an inning later to chase Lowe and regain a 4–3 advantage. By the ninth inning, with the greatest closer of all-time coming on in Rivera, things looked bleak.

Then it happened. Kevin Millar drew a walk, and Dave Roberts—a speedy late-season pickup by Epstein—came in to pinch run. Everybody in the ballpark knew he was going to try and steal second, and that's what he did—getting his outstretched arm to the base just ahead of Jeter's smooth, sweeping tag. It was the most important millisecond in Red Sox history, as Bill Mueller followed with a single to bring Roberts home with the tying run and set the stage for Papi's two nights of heroics.

After his steal for the ages, pinch runner Dave Roberts scores on Bill Mueller's single to tie Game 4 of the 2004 ALCS in the bottom of the ninth. Roberts would pinch run and score the tying tally in Game 5 as well.

The celebration after Game 5 was of the pennant-winning variety, so perhaps the Fenway fans on hand—including Jack Fabiano, Bill Nowlin, Arthur D'Angelo, and many more who had waited decades for a happy ending—anticipated what was to come. The two teams went back to the Bronx for Game 6, where Curt Schilling redefined guts under fire by pitching seven innings of four-hit ball with blood seeping out of his sock from a surgically repaired ankle. Boston got the 4–2 win, setting up a winner-take-all finale that was over almost before it began. The Red Sox scored twice in the first (on an Ortiz homer), four times in the second (on a Johnny Damon grand slam), and twice more in the fourth (on another Damon homer). Lowe pitched six one-hit innings, and the 10–3 final capped what many immediately called the greatest comeback in sports history. Back in Kenmore Square, thousands of fans began partying around Fenway Park, at one point setting fire to a car unlucky enough to have New York license plates.

It's hard to imagine a World Series being anticlimactic for either team involved, but that was definitely the case with the 100th fall classic. Beating the Yankees in the way that they did helped the Red Sox exorcise decades' worth of demons, and by the time they met up with the NL champion St. Louis Cardinals they were loose and confident. They nearly blew a huge lead in Game 1 at Fenway before hanging on for an 11–9 win, but none of the other contests were that close. The Sox never trailed in the four-game sweep, and they outhit St. Louis .283 to .190. Manny Ramirez, the

"The fans are behind us. As soon you walk in there, you definitely feel you want to kick somebody's ass."
—Slugger David Ortiz, on Fenway Park

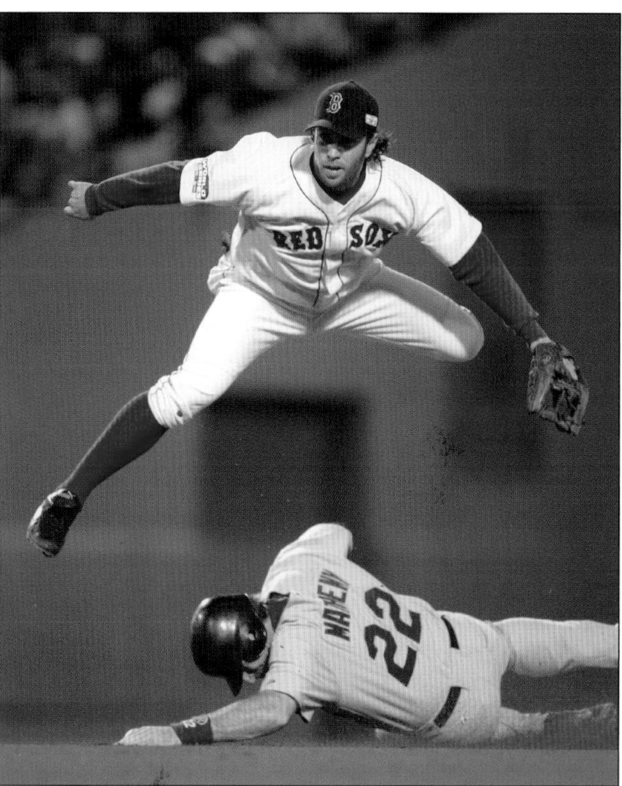

Red Sox second baseman Mark Bellhorn completes a double play in Game 2 of the 2004 World Series. Bellhorn had been the Game 1 hero with a tie-breaking, eighth-inning homer in Boston's 11–9 win, and he cracked a key two-run double in this contest as well.

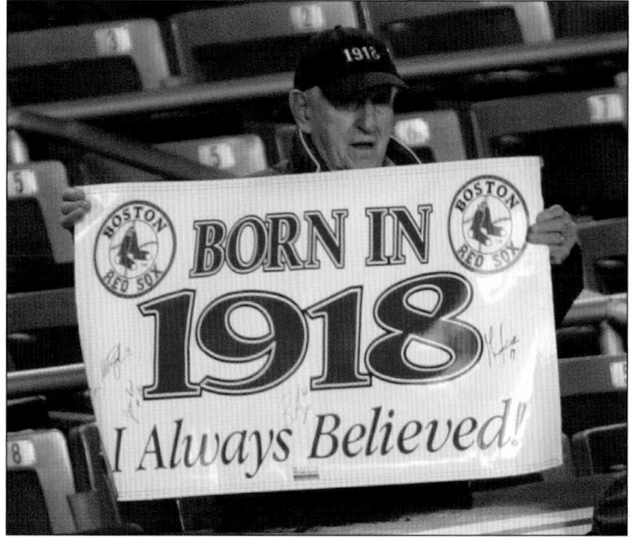

Above: David Ortiz celebrates his third postseason walk-off hit in 10 days at Fenway Park, a game-winning single in Game 5 of the 2004 ALCS. The 14-inning contest featured 35 players, 14 of them pitchers. *Right:* An old-timer displays his Red Sox pride at Yankee Stadium on Opening Day, 2005. This octogenarian and many others were still basking in the glow of Boston's 2004 World Series victory—its first since he was in diapers.

"It's pretty impressive how much energy and adrenaline flows through this stadium. It's always been that way and always will be for me. Sitting in the same dugout as Ted Williams really makes you reflect and have an appreciation for the game."
—Infielder Kevin Youkilis

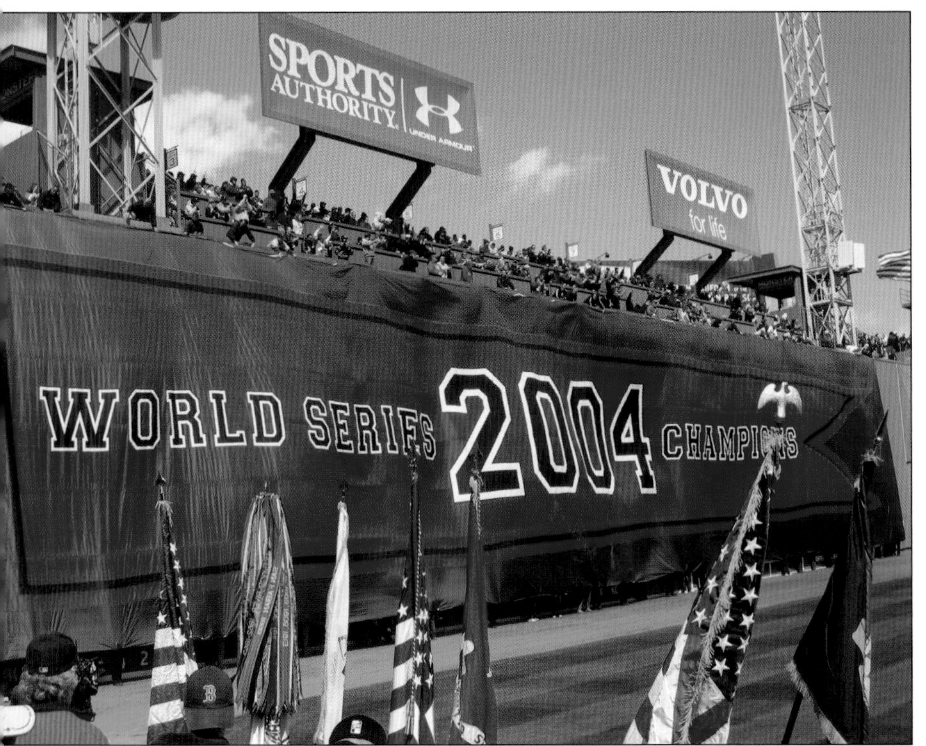

After fans seated atop the Green Monster helped unfurl long, narrow pennants depicting the Red Sox' World Series titles of 1903, 1912, 1915, 1916, and 1918, they sent the Opening Day, 2005, crowd into a frenzy when they covered all five with this massive wall-long salute to the 2004 champs.

other half of the club's dynamic power duo, was named MVP.

Early in the morning after Game 4, John Henry addressed hundreds of fans who had waited all night in the cold to greet the Red Sox buses when they arrived at Fenway Park from Logan Airport. "We've brought this home for them," Henry said. "They've waited their entire lives for this, always saying with hope, 'This is the year.' Well, this *is* the year." One banner read "Our (Late) Parents and G-Parents Thank You," and the message could have been as much for the park as the team.

Two days later, the victorious players, owners, and other Red Sox personnel began a three-mile parade through the streets of Boston. It seemed only appropriate that Fenway should be the starting point for the biggest gathering (3.2 million people) the city had ever seen, because it was there that the dream—and so many more before it—had started.

End of the Edge

Fans who felt cheated because the Red Sox had clinched the World Series on the road got their payback on April 11, 2005, in a stirring Opening Day ceremony. The hour-long extravaganza included the arrival of the championship rings, which were walked across the field to the Red Sox dugout by U.S. military personnel who had served in Iraq and Afghanistan. Fans were also treated to the unfurling of a Green Monster-sized "World Series Champions" banner across the entire left-field wall, and they witnessed the raising of the more traditionally sized championship banner on the center-field flag pole by Johnny Pesky and Carl Yastrzemski. The loudest ovation of the day came when Pesky received his ring after 64 years with the Red Sox organization.

It was the team's 146th consecutive sellout, a streak that dated back to May 15, 2003 (and was still going strong after an MLB-record 600-plus games heading into 2011). The Opening Day opponents, meanwhile, were none other than the New York Yankees, who were good sports about the whole thing (especially Rivera). Although the rest of the Bombers were booed when introduced, Rivera received an ovation as a "thank you" for his two blown saves the previous fall. He smiled and waved, earning another cheer.

The edge was now off for Red Sox fans. They still loved their team and hated the Yankees, but now it was a kinder, gentler hatred. No longer would Boston fans need to listen to chants of "19–18!" in their own ballpark, and no longer would they be haunted by memories of Bucky Dent, Joe Morgan, and others who had done them in there.

The years since 2004 have been exciting ones at Fenway. The '05 Red Sox rode the coattails of Ortiz (.300, 47, 148) and Ramirez (.292, 45, 144) to their first AL East title since 1995, but their pitching was hurt by the losses of Martinez and Lowe to free agency and ace Schilling to injury. The Chicago White Sox humbled Boston in a three-game ALDS sweep, but it was still a successful season at Fenway because of an announcement made in late March: the Red Sox were officially abandoning any plans to build a new ballpark.

Although Boston finished a disappointing third in 2006, its first time below second place in nine years, it was still an exciting summer thanks to David Ortiz. Big Papi set an all-time Red Sox record with 54 home runs, a league-leading total that surpassed Jimmie Foxx's old team mark of 50 set in 1938. The record-breaking 51st came off Twins ace Johan Santana at Fenway on September 21, and it so delighted Ortiz that he hit another one for good measure later in the game.

Fans who wondered if they would have to wait another 86 years for a Red Sox championship got their answer in 2007, as Boston got huge seasons from third

Singing Star

The Red Sox have had everyone from Steven Tyler to Ray Charles sing before games at Fenway Park, but it's hard to imagine a more powerful performer than Jordan Leandre.

On August 27, 2004, Leandre was a four-year-old bone cancer patient at Dana-Farber Cancer Institute's Jimmy Fund Clinic when he became Fenway's youngest anthem singer. His moving rendition, before which he limped to home plate in a full-body cast necessitated by treatment, drew a huge ovation and led to additional pregame gigs—including before Boston's thrilling Game 5 victory over the Yankees in the '04 ALCS.

Jordan Leandre at Game 2 of the 2007 ALCS at Fenway

Jordan was back to sing again in 2005, this time from a wheelchair, but by August 2007 he was able to walk independently to the microphone. Again the crowd roared, and the cheers grew louder when Leandre punctuated his performance with a run around the bases—the first time he had run anywhere in several years. Waiting to mob him at home plate were Jimmy Fund Chairman Mike Andrews and his teammates from the '67 "Impossible Dream" Red Sox.

"My feelings for Fenway are large, and I don't want anything bad to happen to it because it's my second home," said Leandre, who by 2010 was a cancer-free Little League pitcher. "Every time you go back there is always another experience waiting for you to inhale, because it is just so beautiful."

After homering in Game 7 of the 2007 ALCS vs. Cleveland, Red Sox rookie Dustin Pedroia leads off Game 1 of the World Series with a home run against Colorado at Fenway. Boston romped 13–1 and swept the Series. Two years later, Pedroia won the AL MVP Award.

baseman Mike Lowell and pitcher Josh Beckett—plus the usual great production from Ortiz and Ramirez—to capture its second World Series title in four years. They made quick work of Anaheim in the divisional playoffs but had to rally from a 3–1 deficit in the ALCS against Cleveland with three straight wins. The final two came at Fenway, including the pennant clincher on October 21 behind the pitching of rookie Daisuke Matsuzaka, who had electrified the home crowd often during the regular season as Japanese *K* cards, rally head scarves, and a huge Asian media contingent all showed up on Yawkey Way. An emerging superstar, first baseman Kevin Youkilis led the offense throughout the series with three homers and a .500 average (14-for-28).

The World Series against the Colorado Rockies was not anticlimactic this time, but it was just as easy as in 2004. Another four-game sweep, another clincher won on the road—this one made all the sweeter by big performances from a recovering cancer patient (Game 4 winner Jon Lester) and a pair of rookies (second baseman Dustin Pedroia and centerfielder Jacoby Ellsbury). All three broke out in a big way in 2008. Pedroia earned Rookie of the Year honors in his first full season, Ellsbury hit .280 with a league-high 50 stolen bases, and Lester went 16–6. However, visions of back-to-back titles were squashed by the suddenly grown-up Tampa Bay Rays. The former laughingstocks of the East toppled both the Sox and Yanks in the regular season. They then edged past Boston in a seven-game ALCS by winning the final game at Fenway in a great pitcher's duel between Lester and Matt Garza.

The sellouts at Fenway continued through 2009 and '10, as the ever-expanding park drew three million fans for the first two times in its history. There would be no postseason success in either season, however, as the Angels swept Boston in the '09 Division Series and the Red Sox of 2010 finished out of the playoffs for just the second time in eight years. By the end of '10, the only regulars left from the 2004 champions were Ortiz, Varitek, and Wakefield, but a new, younger nucleus had formed around Youkilis, pitchers Lester and Clay Buccholz, and '09 MVP Pedroia, A pair of blue-chip newcomers in fleet outfielder Carl Crawford and slugging first baseman Adrian Gonzalez, both acquired in the 2010–11 off-season, had fans hop-

These young fans will never forget the thrills of the 2007 championship season. Someday, perhaps, they will take their children, or even their grandkids, to America's oldest ballpark.

ing that more October glory was in the team's near future.

The last stages of the new ownership's 10-year, $285 million improvement project at Fenway took place in the winter of 2011, highlighted by the construction of three high-definition LED message boards in the outfield. Other changes to the park in recent years included conversion of the old glassed-in 600 Club to two open-air facilities—the EMC Club and State Street Pavilion; the development of two ballpark restaurants—the Bleacher Bar underneath the center-field seats and Game On! at the corner of Brookline Avenue and Lansdowne Street; the opening of the Budweiser Right Field Roof Deck; and numerous concourse, restroom, and concession stand improvements. Modifications assured that the park would remain structurally sound for another 40 to 50 years.

Meanwhile, on a cold, snowy day in February 2011, a smiling young woman in a wool hat, gloves, and a Red Sox jacket fit for skiing gathered a group in the sprawling souvenir store that the D'Angelo twins had made famous. Green Monster clocks, Wally dolls, and authentic Fenway seat backs and dirt lined the shelves and cases around them. A red plastic seatback cost $200; the dirt was a steal at $20.

"Welcome to Fenway Park, America's oldest and most beloved ballpark," the tour guide said, and then asked the folks where they were from. A few were from California, one from Florida, one from Illinois. Yesterday, she told them, she had a couple visiting from Japan. "Imagine that," she said, as she led the group out the door and across Yawkey Way.

The funny thing is, none of them seemed surprised at all.

Index

BOST